Mastering
Team Leadership

Palgrave Master Series

Accounting	Global Information Systems
Accounting Skills	Human Resource Management
Advanced English Language	Information Technology
Advanced English Literature	International Trade
Advanced Pure Mathematics	Internet
Arabic	Italian
Basic Management	Java
Biology	Management Skills
British Politics	Marketing Management
Business Communication	Mathematics
Business Environment	Microsoft Office
C Programming	Microsoft Windows, Novell NetWare
C++ Programming	and UNIX
Chemistry	Modern British History
COBOL Programming	Modern European History
Communication	Modern United States History
Computing	Modern World History
Counselling Skills	Networks
Counselling Theory	Novels of Jane Austen
Customer Relations	Organisational Behaviour
Database Design	Pascal and Delphi Programming
Delphi Programming	Philosophy
Desktop Publishing	Physics
Economic and Social History	Practical Criticism
Economics	Psychology
Electrical Engineering	Shakespeare
Electronics	Social Welfare
Employee Development	Sociology
English Grammar	Spanish
English Language	Statistics
English Literature	Strategic Management
Fashion Buying and Merchandising	Systems Analysis and Design
Management	Team Leadership
Fashion Styling	Theology
French	Twentieth-Century Russian History
Geography	Visual Basic
German	World Religions

www.palgravemasterseries.com

Palgrave Master Series
Series Standing Order ISBN 0–333–69343–4
(outside North America only)

You can receive future titles in this series as they are published by placing a standing order.
Please contact your bookseller or, in case of difficulty, write to us at the address below with
your name and address, the title of the series and the ISBN quoted above.

Customer Services Department, Macmillan Distribution Ltd
Houndmills, Basingstoke, Hampshire RG21 6XS, England

Mastering
Team Leadership

Roger Cartwright

Business Series Editor
Richard Pettinger

palgrave
macmillan

First published 2002 by
PALGRAVE MACMILLAN
Houndmills, Basingstoke, Hampshire RG21 6XS and
175 Fifth Avenue, New York, N.Y. 10010
Companies and representatives throughout the world

PALGRAVE MACMILLAN is the global academic imprint of the Palgrave
Macmillan division of St. Martin's Press, LLC and of Palgrave Macmillan Ltd.
Macmillan® is a registered trademark in the United States, United Kingdom
and other countries. Palgrave is a registered trademark in the European
Union and other countries.

ISBN 0–333–99298–9

This book is printed on paper suitable for recycling and
made from fully managed and sustained forest sources.

A catalogue record for this book is available from the British Library.

Library of Congress Cataloging-in-Publication Data
Cartwright, Roger.
    Mastering team leadership / Roger Cartwright.
        p. cm. – (Palgrave master series)
    Includes bibliogaphical references and index.
    ISBN 0–333–99298–9 (paper)
        1. Teams in the workplace. 2. Leadership. 3. Supervision of employees.
        I. Title. II. Series.

HD66 .C374 2002
658.4'092–dc21   2002073543

10   9   8   7   6   5   4   3   2   1
11   10   09   08   07   06   05   04   03   02

Printed and bound in Great Britain by
Creative Print & Design (Wales), Ebbw Vale

◼ ⩔ Contents

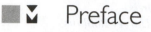 Preface

It is difficult to find a qualification in supervisory studies, business studies and management that does not require the student to carry out studies involving the leadership role of supervisors and managers and the importance of team work and group dynamics. It is also noticeable that more and more advertisements for jobs stress the importance of the applicant understanding the importance of team work and the need for the applicant to work as part of a team. Indeed, the subject is of such importance that the UK Institute of Management (IM), as the professional association for managers, launched a stand-alone qualification entitled 'Foundation Certificate in Team Leadership' in 2001.

Many supervisors' and managers' first step on the managerial ladder was an appointment as a team leader. Leading a team requires a distinct set of skills and knowledge, hence the IM's decision to certify these skills as a separate entity. These skills are not innate, they need to be learnt and applied together with a good understanding of the conceptual framework that underlies successful leadership, team work and team building. Teams, while formed of individuals behave differently to those individuals, in effect developing their own behavioural patterns.

This book seeks to explore the nature of leadership, team work and team building to equip both those in work and those studying supervision and management with the necessary knowledge to understand and to harness the factors in operation in this most important aspect of organisational life.

In addition to the book there is also a web site that you can access at ⟨**www.palgrave.com/studyskills/masterseries/cartwright2**⟩

The web site contains links to other material on the web and also includes extra material to aid you in your study of teams and leadership. If you wish to contact the author about any of the material in this book, full details can be found at: ⟨www.rogercartwright.net⟩.

The book is arranged in such a way as to consider the *individual* and his or her motivation first, then the *behaviour of teams* followed by a consideration of *leadership*. Each of Chapters 1–10 begins with a list of the Learning Outcomes that are covered within it.

Roger Cartwright

Foreword

The word 'team' is used so indiscriminately these days as to risk losing all meaning. Everybody appears to be part of a team. Even the most autocratic managers will proudly point to their suppressed underlings as members of their 'team'. A danger always exists that when an important word in the English language becomes diluted in meaning, people forget about the real thing.

Management has been wedded to command and control and only recently discovered the vital importance of team work. The lessons came through from sport, especially football. Whether teams succeed or fail has been found to depend as much on the manager as on the players. As all football fans know, a change of manager can work wonders. People may well ask why this should be. Here Roger Cartwright sets out to provide some answers. He does so by examining some major issues, providing a digest on what leading writers have said about them and offering an overview. Combining a wide perspective on the subject with a selective grasp of detail is never easy, yet the author faces up to this dilemma with admirable balance. In doing so, he ensures that the reader does not become overloaded, but is drawn out and stimulated by thought-provoking questions posed at regular intervals.

Here is a book on a much discussed field that should broaden the horizons of readers. And for those readers whose horizons are already broad, there is sure to be something new to discover or rediscover. Just as we need to change the players in a team from time to time, so also can we gain by varying our perceptions of a familiar subject.

MEREDITH BELBIN

◼ ⊻ Acknowledgements

Behind every author there are those who provide support, encouragement and ideas. As with all authors of non-fiction texts the role of those mentioned in the bibliography must be acknowledged.

The author and publisher would also like to thank Belbin Associates for figures 6.12 and 6.13.

Special thanks are also due to Suzannah Burywood at Palgrave Macmillan, Richard Pettinger (the series editor and also a close friend and my one-time tutor) and to my wife June who not only provided the illustrations for Figures 3.1 and 6.2–6.11, but really is 'the wind beneath my wings'.

ROGER CARTWRIGHT

Crieff

Every effort has been made to contact all copyright-holders of material used in this book, but if any have been inadvertently omitted the publishers will be pleased to make the necessary arrangement at the earliest opportunity.

 **Introduction**

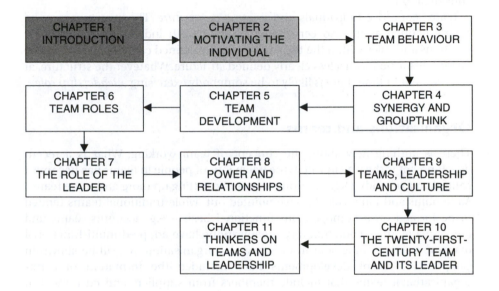

CHAPTER 1 INTRODUCTION	→	CHAPTER 2 MOTIVATING THE INDIVIDUAL	→	CHAPTER 3 TEAM BEHAVIOUR

CHAPTER 6 TEAM ROLES	←	CHAPTER 5 TEAM DEVELOPMENT	←	CHAPTER 4 SYNERGY AND GROUPTHINK

CHAPTER 7 THE ROLE OF THE LEADER	→	CHAPTER 8 POWER AND RELATIONSHIPS	→	CHAPTER 9 TEAMS, LEADERSHIP AND CULTURE

CHAPTER 11 THINKERS ON TEAMS AND LEADERSHIP	←	CHAPTER 10 THE TWENTY-FIRST-CENTURY TEAM AND ITS LEADER

Learning outcomes – Teams – The importance of leadership – The organisation of work – Organisations – Why study teams and leaders? – The Institute of Management Certificate in Team Leading – SMART and C-SMART criteria – Summary – Questions – Recommended further reading

---

LEARNING OUTCOMES

By the end of this chapter you should understand:

- The *aims* of this book
- How to define *groups* and *teams*
- The importance of *leadership*
- How *human characteristics* are similar to those of other primates
- Different ideas about *work*
- What *organisations* are
- Why it is important to study *teams* and *leaders*
- The need to put *customers* at the centre of all team activities.

Teams

'. . . must be a team player.' It seems as though nearly every time one looks at a job advertisement, team work appears as part of the job requirements.

This book is about teams and leaders. The ability to work as an effective member of a team is very important in the modern world of work. However organisations also require people who know their own mind and are able to act on personal initiative. As will become apparent through the pages of this text, it is the balance between the *team* and the *individual* that is the important consideration.

Teams comprise individuals and possess a *structure*. The structure may be clearly defined as in a soccer or netball team, with individuals having clear positions and roles within the team and a clearly defined captain/leader, or may be loosely formed with a less clearly defined structure. Whatever the structure, at any moment in time there is likely to be somebody exercising a *leadership role*.

Organisations and teams

There is nothing new about the concept of team working. What is a recent development is the way in which the behaviour of people in teams has become a fruitful area of study. Organisations seem to be setting up more and more teams. As Robbins and Finley (2000) have pointed out, while traditional teams tended to be formed on a homogeneous functional basis – e.g. accounts teams and personnel teams – contemporary organisations have adopted multi-functional teams drawing membership from across the organisation. As will be shown in Chapter 10, recent developments have included the formation of extra-organisational teams that include members from suppliers and customers in addition to staff from the organisation.

Definition

This book centres on a concept known as *group dynamics*. Chapter 3 considers the derivation of definitions for groups and teams. The definitions that are used in this book and that are expanded in Chapter 3 are:

● Group

'A group, in the context of occupation or profession, is a collection of individuals operating within the constraints of mutually accepted norms (rules) and values who perceive that, as regards their occupation or profession they are clearly distinct from other collections of individuals even if they belong to the same organisation.' (Cartwright *et al.*, 1993)

● Team

'A team is a small group engaged upon a specific task for which group members have a clearly defined role and in which each member has a vested interest in success.'

Group and team behaviour has its origins in our early history. Human beings have always formed discrete groups and from those groups teams have been formed for *specific tasks* – the hunting band being a well-known example.

During the 1980s and 1990s team work was being hailed as the panacea for all organisational ills. There is no doubt that properly constructed teams can add considerable value to organisational activities. The concept of *synergy* that will be introduced in Chapter 3 allows a well-constructed team of six, to perform as though there were seven members. Unfortunately in life there is always an opposite, and a badly constructed team of six can perform as if it had only five members. Organisations like the positive aspects of synergy – pay six people and 'get one free'. Organisations are less happy about paying for six and receiving the output of only five.

Teams are composed of *people*. People have egos and needs. They need to be nurtured, protected and developed. It is not possible to just set up a team and then fail to look after it. There is a responsibility on those in strategic control of organisations to ensure that their teams are able to grow and means giving them space and allowing them to make mistakes.

The importance of leadership

Human beings belong to an animal group known as primates. Primates, a group that contains many of the most advanced land mammals, have certain key characteristics, many of which are related to eating brightly coloured fruits and an arboreal life swinging through trees – the environment in which primates first evolved. These characteristics include:

- Rotating the two bones of the lower arm, the radius and the ulna over each other and also touching (opposing) the thumb with all the other fingers on the hand. This makes for a very complex joint ideal for grasping branches and twisting rather than pulling fruit off trees. In the case of human beings (and to a lesser extent chimpanzees, gorillas and other great apes and monkeys) the complex movement allows for the use of increasing complex *tools* – many of which require such a high degree of dexterity (just look at the wrist and arm movements made when using a screwdriver)
- *Stereoscopic and colour vision* – important for gauging distance and distinguishing colour – useful if you eat brightly coloured fruits and for using tools as this requires hand–eye coordination and accuracy
- Living in fairly large social groups and thus possessing effective means of *communication* between group members is necessary for co-operation and maintaining group bonds
- High *intelligence*
- Highly structured and hierarchical *social groupings*. Leadership is a fundamental survival requirement for such groups.

Humans have over 90 per cent of their genetic material in common with other higher primates. It is no surprise that the behaviour of chimpanzees and gorillas intrigues so much, as we can often see reflections of our own actions in it. Desmond Morris, the anthropologist, broadcaster, writer and ex-curator of the London Zoo, has shown how the leadership qualities and communication techniques of humans are mirrored by other primate societies. In his book *The Human Zoo* (1969), he compared the 10 most important rules of leadership and dominance in primate societies and argued that they applied equally to all leaders from baboons to modern presidents and prime ministers – work that is covered in detail in Chapter 7.

Whether we like it or not, it would appear that much of our behaviour has its roots in our shared primate ancestry, a point made by Nigel Nicholson in *Managing the Human Animal* (2000), where he points out that despite our technological evolution, behaviourally we have not changed very much in the last few thousand years. One of the reasons we are so intrigued by the way other primates behave is that when watching them we have, perhaps, a greater understanding of what they feel than with any other type of animal, as their expressions and gestures are so like our own.

Leadership is a key function in any social grouping. It does not have to be the same leader all the time, leadership can switch between individuals according to circumstances, as will be explored later in this book. However, direction is important for work activities and leaders are very much concerned with providing direction.

It is not possible to study teams without a consideration of the individuals who make them up and the role of the leader. This book begins with a consideration of the individual and his or her motivations and why it is advantageous for people to give up part of their individuality to be part of a team (Chapter 2).

Chapters 3 to 6 look at teams in respect of their formation, behaviour and development. This is followed by a consideration of leadership, especially leadership in the contemporary, global business environment (Chapter 7). Chapter 8 looks at power, what it is and how it is used.

Finally the book explores the relationship between teams, leaders and national/organisational culture and the skills that leaders in the twenty-first century are likely to need (Chapters 9–10).

Chapter 11 looks at the key thinkers on leadership, and what they have contributed to the debate.

The organisation of work

To comprehend how teams and leadership relate to the world of work, it is necessary to consider how work is *organised*.

The earliest ideas of management were rooted in small, often family-run, businesses. They had to be small as the infrastructure for people to live more than walking distance from their places of work was not in place. Once railways and tramways began to be developed for public use from the 1830s onwards, people were able to live further from work and organisations were able to expand: there is a finite limit to expansion if everybody needs to live near the workplace. In the nineteenth century, industries were labour-intensive and so the bigger the enterprise, the more workers were required, generating a need for accessible and affordable housing.

Prior to the industrial revolution, few people had travelled much beyond their birthplace. Organisations were small and the workforce tended to be homogeneous, with similar backgrounds and a similar culture. The railroads and steamships allowed for large-scale population movements, making labour plentiful but more diverse. F. W. Taylor, the originator of the concept of 'scientific management', was appointed as a management consultant at the Bethlehem Steel Corporation in the USA in 1898. He proceeded to conduct a series of management experiments on a workforce that was very diverse and contained not only those born in the USA but those who had arrived from nearly every western and eastern European country, each with their own culture and their own language. The results of these experiments led to the ideas of scientific management, piecework and a very structured work pattern based solely on pay as a motivator. Taylor, sometimes called the 'Father of Work Study', believed that jobs should be broken down into small tasks and that a time and performance standard could be calculated for an average worker for each job. The harder people worked, the more they were paid. This type of 'piece-work' (workers were paid for each *piece* manufactured) is still seen today in many low-skill manufacturing and assembly tasks.

The idea that money was the prime motivator and thus the prime management factor held sway well into the twentieth century. Classical management ideas stated that the role of managers was to recruit suitable workers and then calculate work patterns so that the rate for the job equated to the scientifically calculated amount of work that should be achieved. Those who failed to meet their targets received less pay and eventually faced dismissal. Those who overachieved would receive more. If everybody overachieved then the targets were too low, and would be raised. All workers received the same treatment. This 'Scientific Management', as it came to be called, suited simple manufacturing tasks requiring more brawn than brains.

As the twentieth century progressed, jobs became more technologically complicated and the workforce better educated, as universal education for all became the norm throughout much of the industrialised world. The research by Elton Mayo at the Hawthorne Plant of the General Electric Company in Chicago, Illinois, between 1927 and 1932 began to cast doubts on the universal applicability of Scientific Management. Mayo found that work conditions, social factors and group dynamics were important factors in worker behaviour – a movement towards a more 'Theory Y' approach (see chapter 2). The Hawthorne studies showed the complexity of *motivation and management*, a subject that is also considered in depth in Chapter 2.

In terms of an overall management concept, the *contingency approach*, in which the methods and tools of management are not fixed but are contingent upon the situation, provides a firm foundation. What works well in one company may fail in another. What is applicable to one group of workers may cause resentments in a different group. The modern manager needs to realise that not all employees will react the same way to similar situations. Modern management theories are based on the idea of a *bank of skills* that the manager can draw upon according to the circumstances.

Think/discussion point

- How have different organisations or people dealt with similar problems?
- Is there just one way of approaching a management problem, or should the solution be contingent upon a variety of factors?

Organisations

People work for organisations, either large or small. 'Organisation' is a word that will be encountered frequently in this book. Organisation as a term is one that is freely used in general conversation and yet one that is not easy to define in clear terms.

Argyris (1960) defined organisations as:

'intricate human strategies designed to achieve certain objectives.'

A later writer, Pugh (1971), considered that:

'Organisations are systems of inter-dependent human beings.'

Being all-embracing, Pugh's definition covers everything from the UK government, Virgin Group (Sir Richard Branson has been involved with record sales, an airline, financial services and even soft drinks), Tesco (the UK supermarket organisation), a corner shop, large and small manufacturers and even a family, all of which depend for their success on people working with and depending on each other. Details of the web sites for companies and organisations mentioned in this text can be found on the web site associated with this material.

With a little imagination, even Argyris' definition could encompass the family as an organisation, as the family has developed biologically and socially as an excellent method of ensuring the survival of children to maturity – the covert biological objective. It should be noted that this is not a way of saying that the Western concept of the nuclear family is the only acceptable form, as there are many variations of family structure in the world, each suited to a particular culture and way of life and each of equal importance.

Business can be described as the *exchange relationship between organisations.* All business relationships involve some form of trade or exchange – goods for money, services for money, goods for services. Money, that apparently all-important factor in our lives, is nothing more than a convenient common denominator that allows a trade to take place.

Why study teams and leaders?

One of the points that will be made when considering the phenomenon of groupthink in Chapter 4 is that people in a group or team can behave very differently than they do as individuals. Some of the most disturbing acts of the past 75 years have been carried out by groups. A massacre carried out by an individual can be put down to a single aberrant personality but when carried out by a group must raise the question of how a number of people could behave in that way: Did they all agree? Were they all psychopaths or were they ordinary people caught up in mass hysteria? If the latter, then could it happen to you and me?

It is the fact that group behaviour can be so different to that of the individual that requires it to be studied. It will also be shown that the nature and style of leadership is an important determinate of group behaviour, even more so than the behaviour of an individual. Given that we live in groups, work and teams and are subject to a number of leader's wishes, a study of the subject is useful for anybody. For those wishing to be supervisors and managers however, an understanding of teams and leadership is crucial.

Despite what we might desire, humans are still very much tribal animals. We may call the tribes by new terms such as 'countries', 'regions' or even 'companies', but we still behave very much as our ancestors did. We can be recognised from members of other tribes by such things as language, dress (even corporate uniforms are a form of tribal behaviour), entertainment preferences and the foods we eat. If anybody doubts that tribalism is present even in the most sophisticated of the world's societies they have only to look at the dress and behaviour of sports' supporters. The tribal behaviour of soccer fans has become a problem in many areas of the world.

The Institute of Management Certificate in Team Leading

At the start of the twenty-first century, the Institute of Management (the professional association for managers) in the UK introduced a Certificate in Team Leading as part of their Professional Development Programmes and Qualifications for Managers. The key topics considered by the Institute as important for team leaders are:

- Organising and developing yourself
- Organising and communicating information
- Organising and improving your team's work
- Organising your team's performance
- Maintaining and developing effective working relationships
- Helping your team members to develop their performance
- Resolving customer service issues.

The Institute's topics are indicative of how management, supervision and team leading have changed. Gone are words such as 'controlling' and 'direction,' to be replaced with 'organising', 'developing' and 'helping' – facilitory rather than police-type roles.

Smart and C-smart criteria

Of especial importance is the last of the Institute's topics – customer service. For many years organisational behaviour studies were inward-looking and paid too little regard to that most important person to any organisation, the one who ultimately pays the wages – the customer. That approach is now changing, as organisations become much more customer-centred and focused. Traditionally, teaching of decision-making and objective-setting techniques stressed the importance of setting SMART criteria for objectives, the acronym standing for:

- Specific
- Measurable
- Agreed
- Realistic
- Timely (i.e. with deadlines and timescales attached).

In *Mastering Customer Relations* (2000), a companion volume to this text, the author suggested that SMART should be amended to C-SMART with the all-important CUSTOMER DRIVEN being the most important element in contemporary business. Unless the customer is put at the centre of an organisation's activities success can only be at best partial. Hence it is gratifying to see the Institute of Management including customer service as part of a qualification in team leading, as all work-based teams exist to satisfy the needs of an internal or external customer.

Chapter 2 will examine the individual and his or her motivation. This is an important topic as the basic unit of any team is the individual members.

SUMMARY

- *Leadership and team/group behaviour* are important parts of most primate societies
- Many *human characteristics* are similar to those of other primates
- There have been different ideas about the *relationship between people and work*
- Earlier ideas about people and work centred on *money* being the prime motivator
- Modern ideas about people and work suggest that there are *social aspects* to work that are important motivators
- Modern managers, supervisors and team leaders need a *bank of skills* so that they can deal with individuals contingent upon the situation
- Modern management is less about control and more about *facilitation*
- *Organisations* are the structures humans have devised to carry out tasks involving a number of individuals

- It is important to study teams and leaders because people may behave very differently when they are *members of a team* than they do as individuals
- Despite increasing technological sophistication, much human behaviour is *tribal* in character
- There is a need to put *customers* at the centre of all team activities.

QUESTIONS

1   Why is it important for those involved in managing or supervising people to have a knowledge and understanding of teams and leadership?
2   What examples can you find in daily life over the past few weeks of tribal behaviour, either in those around you or those you have read about?
3   Why should customer service be important in a study of teams?

Recommended further reading

Nigel Nicolson, *Managing the Human Animal* (2000), provides useful further information on the topics covered in this chapter.

◼ ⊻ **2** Motivating the individual

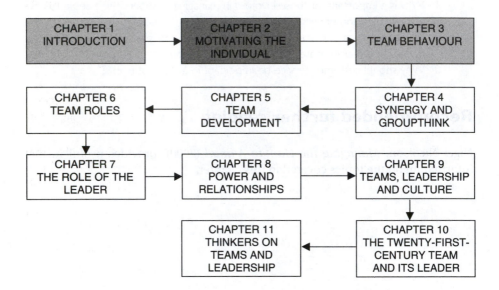

| CHAPTER 1 INTRODUCTION | → | CHAPTER 2 MOTIVATING THE INDIVIDUAL | → | CHAPTER 3 TEAM BEHAVIOUR |

Learning outcomes– What is motivation? – Needs and wants – Maslow's hierarchy – Types of need – Herzberg's motivators and hygiene factors – Facilitory needs – The role of money – Spending patterns and the spending life cycle – Assumptions about people and work – Theory X and Theory Y – The importance of achievement – Catching in or catching out? – Schein's typologies – McClelland's needs concept – Ardrey and the territorial Imperative – Vroom, Expectancy and the Motivational Calculus – Psychological contracts – Theory Z – Summary – Questions – Recommended further reading

---

LEARNING OUTCOMES

By the end of this chapter you should understand:

- The basic models of *motivation*
- The difference between *needs* and *wants*
- The *assumptions* that are made about people at work
- The role of *money*

- The *social context* of motivation
- How people's motivation *changes over time*
- *Team/group membership* as a motivational factor
- The importance of *success*.

What is motivation?

Motivation is the study of *what drives people*. It is concerned with the satisfying of needs and the preferred way of such satisfaction – a person's wants.

Needs and wants

It is necessary to consider the differences between *needs* and *wants*, two concepts that are frequently confused and sometimes treated as synonymous, which they are not.

A need is something that somebody *cannot do without*; a want is the method by which they would like the need to be *satisfied*, in many ways a want can be described as a need with added value. For instance, a person's need may be for nourishment; however, what they would like is steak and French fries. The hunger needs to be satisfied but it may be that a much simpler meal would achieve that just as effectively, in a physiological sense, as the more elaborate want.

Maslow's hierarchy

Abraham Maslow (1970) suggested that needs were *hierarchical* in nature and that a need can only be truly satisfied when the ones below it have been dealt with. Any activity that a person undertakes will have its derivation within that person's physiological, psychological or emotional needs.

Maslow proposed that human beings have five levels of needs (Figure 2.1).

Maslow's concept was that humans (and other animals) would put *physiological* needs such as food and water before *safety*, which comes before *belonging*. *Esteem* needs are met only when the needs up to and including belonging have been met and *self-actualisation* becomes a motivator only when all other needs have been fulfilled. The Maslow model has some fairly major inconsistencies in that it fails to explain how an artist or poet can starve whilst working on their masterpiece – a not unusual occurrence – since the model postulates that such self-actualisation should not take precedent over physiological needs. It does however, explain the risks that animals will take to obtain food and water even in the face of apparent danger. A human equivalent is that of sailors who have been shipwrecked and have taken to the lifeboats, drinking seawater, which can be fatal because the need for water (physiological) overrides that for safety.

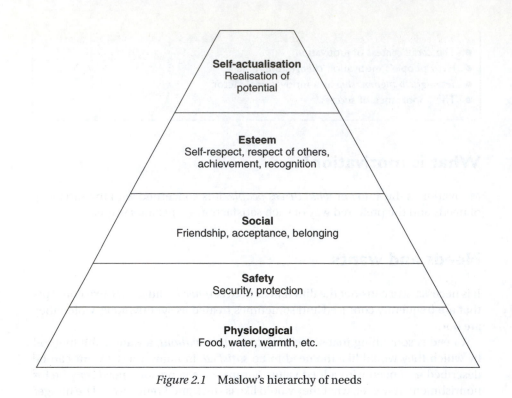

Figure 2.1 Maslow's hierarchy of needs

Types of need

Maslow's hierarchy is useful in that it allows us to distinguish between levels of needs. In respect of human beings, physiological and safety can be described as *lower-level* or *basic* needs. These are needs that we share with all living creatures. Belonging is a *middle-level* need shared with other social animals, whilst esteem and self-actualisation are *higher-level* needs. Self-actualisation is probably unique to humans, but there is evidence that self-esteem may be present to a degree in other advanced primates.

Thus a baker, in selling bread, is satisfying the lowest or most basic need. While bread may seem a mundane, everyday product, it receives many mentions in religious texts testifying to its importance as not only a food but also as a symbol of basic human needs. Bread has achieved political significance when its price has risen and rioting has broken out! The satisfaction of hunger is a *primary* need.

There is also a need to be able to purchase the bread in safety and convenience – this can be described as a *secondary* need and relates to a slightly higher position on the Maslow hierarchy.

Given that humans are social animals, there is also a *tertiary* need of some belonging and recognition. Psychologists are beginning to recognise that there is a social as well as a commercial aspect to something as mundane as shopping. 'Shopping therapy' may have started as a gag from comedians but it is possible that there is a serious side to the concept. The plateau at the top of Figure 2.1 is a

MOTIVATORS, presence of which lead to satisfaction	HYGIENE FACTORS, absence of which lead to dissatisfaction
ACHIEVEMENT	POLICY AND ADMINISTRATION
RECOGNITION	SUPERVISION
WORK ISSUES	RELATIONSHIPS
RESPONSIBILITY	WORK ENVIRONMENT
ADVANCEMENT	SALARY
GROWTH	PERSONAL LIFE
	STATUS
	SECURITY

Figure 2.2   Summary of Herzberg's findings

refinement of the Maslow model by the author as he believes that self-actualisation (or fulfilling one's potential) is almost infinite.

Herzberg's motivators and hygiene factors

Frederick Herzberg (1966) writing in the context of work, concluded that there were factors which led to satisfaction and thus motivated people (he termed these *motivators*) and those which did not motivate but led to dissatisfaction and thus demotivation (which he named *hygiene factors*). His results are summarised in Figure 2.2.

Herzberg's research showed that recognition and achievement are important motivators. The role of money is less defined in his findings. A lack of a suitable salary is a demotivator, but is money in itself a motivator? This point is addressed later in this chapter.

Needs are very basic and it is *wants* that grow in importance once basic needs are satisfied. If a person is starving, a meal, any meal will suffice to satisfy their basic physiological need for food. Once the means (usually money) exist to choose how the need is satisfied, then it is wants that are important. 'I need lunch, I want a steak and French fries!'

Facilitory needs

In modern society basic needs are satisfied using money and money has to be earned, giving rise to what may be termed a *facilitory* need (a new term first introduced in the author's *Mastering Customer Relations* (2000).

In order to earn money, large numbers of people *need* to travel to work (they have little or no choice) and thus transportation is a facilitory need in order to fulfil basic needs. Their preference for transportation forms their wants; they may want a motorcar, or for environmental or cost reasons prefer to travel on public transport. Put succinctly, they do not need a motor car but they do need transportation in order to gain the money to fulfil their basic needs such as food and shelter.

- How well do you distinguish between needs and wants?
- Do you say that you need something when you really mean that you want it?

The role of money

Money is an important part of people's lives, but is it a motivator? Herzberg's work suggests that a lack of money is a demotivator but his work was carried out among a managerial population where basic needs were likely to be well taken care of. It cannot be denied that money has a motivational role, but the degree of motivation may well depend on the particular *stage of life* a person is at and how much they make a connection between money and achievement/recognition.

One of the issues in modern society is that everything seems to be given a cash value. Some things however, have values that cannot be directly equated with a cash equivalence. The British honours system of awards bestowed (in theory by the monarch but in practice by the government) is a means of rewarding people without paying a cash sum. While cynical critics may say that this is being somewhat mean, recipients of MBEs (Member of the British Empire) and other awards seem genuinely pleased at the non-cash nature of the awards. Indeed, there has been considerable public concern at rumours that some awards may have actually been purchased. Tom Peters and Bob Waterman (1982) in the video that was made to accompany *In Search of Excellence* showed how the presentation of a small cash gift for excellent work could have a motivational multiplier effect if it was done in such a way as to raise the status of the recipient by, for example, having a special ceremony. The actual amount was unimportant, it was the fact that management were making the presentation in a public forum that acted as the motivator. The term 'motivational multiplier' is a new one first introduced in this book and is derived from the military concept of a force multiplier (see Chapter 8) – i.e. anything that allows a military force to act in a manner that multiplies its effect. Radar and the system of controlling aircraft was a force multiplier for the Royal Air Force (RAF) during the Battle of Britain in 1940, as are modern satellites that provide exact dispositions of enemy forces, allowing the commander of a smaller force to target attacks more effectively. A *motivational multiplier* is an act that provides far more of a motivational impulse than might be expected. Being able to use such a multiplier requires managers to have a good knowledge of what is likely to motivate individuals and also of the assumptions they make about people and work.

Money has, perhaps unfortunately, become the yardstick by which achievement is measured. In this respect the things that money can buy – cars, clothes, televisions, holidays, to name but a few – are not necessarily actual needs but wants that confer some form of status upon the owner in the eyes of those he or she wishes to impress.

Spending patterns and the spending life cycle

One method of assessing the motivational effect of money is to consider what might be termed the *spending life cycle* of the individual.

Taking the example of a young person starting out on their job, it may well be that they either live at home or in cheap rented accommodation and while they will be expected to contribute to household expenses, much of their disposable income will be spent on personal needs and wants, including food, fashion items, transportation and entertainment. There will be little disposable income left over for saving. The more they earn, the more they are likely to spend. This can be termed **Earn and spend**. Money is likely to be a good motivator but not if earning it requires a considerable sacrifice of leisure time.

If, after a few years they are in a long-term relationship and are considering settling down and perhaps buying a home, the pattern may change to **Earn and save**. It may well be that all their spare cash goes into a savings account. At this stage, money may be an excellent motivator, as the individual may be willing to sacrifice present leisure time for future savings income.

As time, and hopefully salary increases, there will be more disposable income. If there are no children involved the couple are likely to be DINKYs (Double income, no kids yet) and may well revert to **Earn and spend**. If they have children there will be a need to revert to saving for college, university, retirement and maybe even weddings but the pattern is likely to be **Earn – save some – spend some**. Time with the family will be sacrificed unwillingly and employers will have to provide compensation not just in monetary but also time terms.

Upon the children setting up on their own the individual can now **Spend and desave** – i.e. use their savings to improve the quality of life. The so-called 'grey' dollar, pound, euro, yen, etc. has become very important in recent years. The motivation to work may be no longer financial. Many retired people who have financial security still undertake either paid or voluntary work where the motivational impetus is social or achievement-driven. The money received is just by the by.

The modern approach to management is a contingency approach in which the methods and tools of management are not fixed but are contingent upon the situation. What works well in one company may fail in another. What is applicable to one group of workers may cause resentments in a different group. In the spending life cycle covered above, extra money earned through overtime may well motivate a person saving for their first home but be less attractive to the older worker who wishes to spend quality leisure time with the family. For them, recognition may be much more of a motivator. Managers and team leaders need to understand what is motivating each individual they have responsibility for. As the individuals will be at different points in the spending life cycle, they will each be motivated by different factors – or, more likely, a different balance of factors of which money is only one.

As workforces have become more diverse, managers need to realise that employees inhabit a *series of worlds*. There is the world of work, there is the country of which they are a citizen and there is their cultural world. These worlds may have very different values, and these values may be in conflict. Good employers and managers should be aware of this and take account of such values wherever possible in the workplace. As organisations become more and more global, the onus is on the organisation and its managers to ensure that where it is operating in another culture it does so in a manner that is tune with that culture.

Think/discussion point

- Where are you in your spending life cycle?
- How does this influence your motivation?

Assumptions about people and work

The early writers on management and supervision of the late nineteenth and early twentieth centuries including Taylor (1911) and Fayol (1916) were considering the situation in organisations where there was not just a distinction between workers and management in terms of tasks but also of education and social position. They believed in the necessity for detailed operational instructions and strong supervision, as they considered that the uneducated workforce required tasks broken down into simple components. Workers were there to *do* and *be controlled* and not to *think* and *be empowered*. Fayol (who was a French mining engineer working in the Belgian Congo during the First World War) praised the idea of initiative, but only when shown by management. (It must be remembered that there were at this time clear class distinctions in Europe and to a lesser degree in the USA.) Managers and workers did not talk, save to give orders and report back. Social intercourse between these groups was virtually unknown. As educational standards rose throughout the twentieth century, it became possible to loosen the span of control by allowing for initiative. This brought about a new component to organisational structure, that of the *technicians*. Technicians began to bring about their own empowerment through their technical expertise and were often motivated by the achievement of a technical advance. In many ways they were the manufacturing equivalents of artists, where developing a more efficient product could be, for them, almost an end in itself. *Expert power*, which is what technicians possessed, is discussed in Chapter 8. This group of workers came to the fore as steam engines developed – they were the only people who could build and work these new inventions. Managers were forced, sometimes unwillingly, to seek their advice if the organisation was to make the best use of the potential of new technologies. Technicians also brought forth a whole new training system, that of technical education. While the older universities of the world including Oxford, Cambridge, St Andrew's, Harvard, Yale, the Sorbonne and Heidelberg have their roots in classical education for the ruling classes, the Massachusetts Institute of Technology (MIT), CALTECH, the University of Manchester Institute of Science and Technology (UMIST) are products of the rise of the technician and the need for specialised technical education.

Theory X and theory Y

Douglas McGregor, a US researcher considered that there were two positions that managers could adopt when considering their workforce. – Theory X and Theory Y.

The first position, which he named *Theory X*, held that:

- The average human being dislikes work and avoids working if at all possible
- This dislike of work means that employees need to be controlled, directed and even threatened if necessary if the organisation is to fulfil its objectives
- People require direction but do not want responsibility.

In contrast, *Theory Y* held that:

- Work is a natural human function
- People relish responsibility
- The rewards people seek are not only monetary
- The intellectual and creative potential of most employees is underutilised.

McGregor's point was that if a manager is an adherent of Theory X he or she will probably be a controlling, directing type of manager whilst a manager who holds that Theory Y is nearer to reality is likely to adopt a more facilitating, empowering approach.

Theories X and Y were not put forward as examples of what is, but more as illustrations of the two poles of views held by managers in respect of their workers. As educational opportunities have increased it appears that Theory Y is closer to reality than Theory X. There are lazy individuals in any society but in the main, work is a fruitful experience, providing social interaction, achievement and recognition, in addition to monetary reward. St Augustine made the distinction between work and toil, referring to work as the natural state of man before the species became corrupted (in St Augustine's culture this was in the Garden of Eden) when work became toil. In a modern sense, toil is work that provides little reward for the person carrying it out.

The importance of achievement

Two of the most important writers on motivation, Abraham Maslow and Frederick Herzberg, have stressed the importance of achievement and recognition and what Maslow termed self-actualisation – i.e. fulfilling one's own potential – as motivational factors (as discussed earlier in this chapter). All of these are Theory Y traits and are not particularly amenable to management by control. Thus a Theory X approach is unlikely to assist in achieving the higher levels of motivation.

Catching in or catching out?

While the concept of management having some form of policing function still exists within some organisations, it has become clear that strict control motivates people not to worker harder but to devote effort into not being caught out. Many managers have found that life is actually better if instead of going around trying to catch people out, they try to catch them in instead. Most workers are doing things correctly for most of the time but in the old system it would be the few occasions when they did something wrong that brought them to the attention of management. Such an approach leads workers to try to cover up errors and thus organisational learning is stunted, as it is often the case that more is learned from things that go wrong than things that go right. The idea that managers should move from a policing, controlling function to that of being a facilitator and coach has been a key feature of the work of the US 'management guru' Tom Peters.

Schein's typologies

E. H. Schein (1980), working in the USA, developed a set of typologies to describe human motivation. He described four types of 'man', using the word to represent the human species. While this may be politically incorrect in today's society, Schein's terms have been retained to avoid confusion with other texts that also use the original terms.

Schein's four typologies are:

● Rational–economic man
● Social man
● Self-actualising man
● Complex man.

As will be seen when considering complex man, we are all a combination of these typologies, which just like personality and the concept of team roles to be discussed in Chapter 6, is in a different balance for each of us.

Rational–economic man

Rational–economic man is the person Taylor and Fayol (see earlier) were thinking about when they produced their ideas about management. Rational–economic man is sand to be motivated entirely by *economic needs*. This is, of course, far from the truth but may represent certain of the stages in the spending life cycle discussed earlier. There are, as was shown, times when economic necessity is the overriding motivational factor, but they do not last for the whole of a lifetime. Even in the poorest of financial situations, people still have to find time for leisure and family.

Social man

The content of this book derives from the fact that humans are social animals. Belonging, as was shown earlier, is a middle-level need. Recognition also requires the individual to belong to a group – else who will recognise his or her achievements? The early management writers did not pay much regard to belonging. Between 1927 and 1932, a team led by Professor Elton Mayo were asked to look at productivity within the giant Hawthorne Plant of the General Electric Company in Chicago, Illinois. The results of this study showed a new facet to motivation.

During a set of studies on the level of lighting on productivity, the team came up with a remarkable finding. They were not surprised that, when the lighting for a test group of workers was increased, productivity rose: this could be put down to working in a better environment. However, when after a number of increases in light level had produced increasingly higher levels of output, they reduced the lighting to below its original level, productivity still increased. The advice of Mayo and his team was sought.

Mayo carried out further experiments by altering various working conditions (e.g. meal breaks) both positively and negatively, and discussing these changes with the subjects before implementation. The result: increases in productivity.

After a series of tests, Mayo concluded that the key factor was the *involvement* of the employees. There needed to be a modification of the classical ideas. Workers were not just units to be programmed to work; how they did depended on how they were treated as human beings. Mayo believed that the results of the earlier experiment could be explained by the fact that the subjects felt themselves special by virtue of being singled out as the test group.

The findings of the Mayo study as regards the study of groups and teams can be summarised as follows:

- Groups serve the needs of both the *organisation* and the *individual*
- Most groups have both *formal* and *informal* functions
- One of the important facts about groups in the organisational context rests on the ability of their members to *unite against management* and frustrate their policies. (This rather negative aspect of group dynamics was a direct finding of the study, and needs to be borne in mind as one of the downsides of working with groups)
- The informal functions and norms (rules) may go *counter* to the formal functions and norms (rules)
- The satisfaction that an individual gains from group membership may constitute a *more potent reward* than management can offer
- Individuals may thus be subjected to *conflicting motivational forces*

- *Group unity and solidarity* is also a means to force management to improve a group's rewards.

Mayo concluded that there is a *social* aspect to both work and motivation, and that employers should take this into consideration. One of the reasons people go to work in addition to earning money is social interaction. This explains why those who are retired and financially secure may well seek out activities, including work, that provide such interaction.

Self-actualising man

If rational–economic man is predominantly a Theory X equivalent, self-actualising man could be said to represent Theory Y. Just as self-actualisation is the ultimate in the Maslow hierarchy of needs, so Schein's self-actualising man is self-motivated. Theory X might be described as working to live whereas Theory Y is the opposite and self-actualising man lives to work! As Handy (1976) states, such a person integrates his or her goals with those of the organisation they work for.

One of the key points about self-actualisation is that it requires a knowledge of the past, an appreciation of the future, a complex language to express ideas and self-awareness, and it may be that it is only humans that possess all four at these.

Complex man

Schein's conclusion was, not unsurprisingly, that individuals are a different mixture of all the above factors at different times in their lives, depending on circumstances. Humans are variable and thus those responsible for motivating people need to analyse the particular *dominant motivational factors* operating at any one time within the complex individual.

McClelland's needs concept

Building on the ideas above and looking purely at human motivation, D. C. McClelland (1960) suggested that human motivation was based on a balance between three needs, once basic physiological needs such as food, water and shelter had been met. The three needs are:

- *The need for power (n-Pow)* – discussed in more detail in Chapter 8. Certainly a motivator for those seeking supervisory and managerial positions, power can be a considerable driver.
- *The need for affiliation (n-Aff)* – this can be equated to Maslow's belonging needs, Herzberg's recognition and Mayo's work on the social implications of groups. While there are some who shun the company of others, most people wish to belong.
- *The need for achievement (n-Ach)* – a need discussed in some detail earlier. It appeared to McClelland that n-Ach was the key human motivator. One of the

problems that this can cause is in relationships with others. Too high an n-Ach at the expense of n-Aff can lead to a very task-centred person who is more concerned with achievement than getting on with others. While this may motivate the individual it can actually act as a demotivator to others. G. A. Cole, the UK management writer, believes that while high n-Ach may be useful for the individual entrepreneur, a person with high n-Ach working in a traditional organisation may find that their progress is frustrated by organisational constraints. It is not only low achievers that managers find difficult to manage, high achievers can also present problems, especially when part of a team – an issue that is considered in Chapter 6.

Ardrey and the territorial imperative

One of the early texts that influenced the author was Robert Ardrey's, *The Territorial Imperative* (1967). Working primarily with animals other than humans, Ardrey recognised three basic needs:

- Security
- Identity
- Stimulation.

These can be loosely equated with Maslow's physiological/safety, belonging/esteem and self-actualisation needs.

The importance of stimulation has become recognised in zoos throughout the world as methods of ensuring both the physiological and psychological needs of captive species have become better understood and implemented.

The main thrust of Ardrey's work however, was the motivational aspect of *space*. Territory is an imperative and thus a need for a great many species including humans. We now recognise the stress that overcrowding causes and the discomfort that an invasion of our personal space creates. When this happens the individual is motivated to change the situation whenever possible.

Vroom, Expectancy and the Motivational Calculus

The Expectancy Theory of Motivation

V. H. Vroom (1964) was the originator of what has become known as the Expectancy Theory of Motivation (Figure 2.3). Vroom's concept was that the perception that effort will lead to effective performance, and then that an effective performance will lead to rewards and that such awards are available to the individual, produces a motivational effort for the individual, the effort leads to performance and the performance to some form of reward. Achieving the award starts a *feedback loop* in that it reinforces the original perceptions. The mechanism becomes *self-feeding*, broken only when the anticipated reward does not appear despite the required performance. This is why breaking promises can have such a damaging motivation effect as the perception becomes that effort

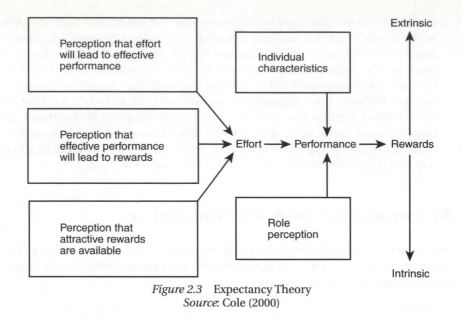

Figure 2.3 Expectancy Theory
Source: Cole (2000)

leads to no reward and thus no effort need be put in. Self-actualisation and achieving one's potential – the satisfaction of a job well done – are *intrinsic* rewards. Pay and promotion are *extrinsic* rewards.

Performance will also be affected by the individual's perception of their role within the organisation and by their individual characteristics, including their personality and the skills they possess. One of the 'spin-offs' of expectancy may be that the individual becomes motivated to acquire new skills in order to improve performance and thus gain greater rewards.

The motivational calculus

Handy (1976) talks about a *motivational calculus* that allows an individual to decide how much effort to put in to a task based on needs and rewards.

Each need has a strength and each reward can be quantified in how instrumental it is in reducing that need. The effort required will depend on both these factors. This explains, in theoretical terms, why persistent failure produces a lowering of goals. If the need is high and considerable effort is expended but with little reward, it may be better to lower the need if possible and be sure of obtaining at least something. Consider a hungry person. They hear that there is a bowl of rice round the corner and a full meal 5 miles away. Which should they go for? Walking 5 miles will expend considerable energy and the meal may have gone, as somebody else may have arrived first. If it is still there the reward is high (provided that the energy in the meal is more than expended getting to it). Less energy will lead to more chance of the rice reward – that may be the better option. Decision-making, a behaviour with close links to motivation, depends on weighing up such situations based on need and reward.

Psychological contracts

Under the law of many countries there is a formal contract between employer and employee, just as exists between supplier and customer. In relationships between humans there are also informal, but no less important *psychological contracts*. A development from the USA in recent years has been that of the 'pre-nuptial' agreement between two people prior to their marriage. Such an agreement, binding in law, states what is to happen to their possessions if they divorce. Psychological contracts, although informal and unwritten, are very important in the management of relationships.

In terms of work motivation, in addition to a contract of employment there will be certain things expected of the employee and he or she will expect certain things from the organisation, including respect (although in the UK this forms part of the implied terms of a formal contract of employment). It is possible to treat somebody purely in accordance with the law, and yet for them still to feel unsatisfied. Within teams it is unlikely that there will be a formal contract expressing who does what and how, but there will certainly be expectations from team members. These form part of the psychological contract that is signed up to (metaphorically) during the Forming and Norming stages of team development (covered in Chapter 5).

Written contracts, because they are transparent, are easier to peruse to see if there has been a breach by one or more of the parties. It is less easy to see whether, first, all the parties see the psychological contract in the same way and secondly, if there has been a breach. Communication is all important. Tom Peters (1987) coined the phrase, 'Management By Wandering About' (MBWA). It is by going around and speaking to both subordinates and colleagues that an idea of their perception of the psychological contract can be determined.

Handy (1976) has divided psychological contracts into three types:

- Coercive
- Calculative
- Co-operative.

Coercive contracts tend to be illegal in commercial dealings. A coercive contract is one where one of the parties possesses overwhelming power over any other parties to that contract. In the UK, the Unfair Contract Terms Act of 1977 provides protection against such behaviour. In psychological contracts it is obvious that the contract between, say, a prisoner and prison staff is coercive in that the prisoner probably does not want to be in prison. There have been cases, however, of the homeless or those who have become institutionalised through a long prison sentence and then being released, actually committing minor crimes in order to have a warm bed or to re-enter the system. Such events are rare however. The prison services need a coercive contract initially, although sensitive treatment of prisoners may make the contract less coercive and more co-operative. The psychological contract between a prisoner and those providing education can become co-operative if the prisoner realises the personal benefit that education will bring.

A coercive psychological contract may produce compliance if the circumstances are such that the coerced individual needs the job, but as soon as circumstances change, he or she may seek alternative employment. Coercion never acts as a true motivator but only as what might be termed as a 'pseudo-motivator', in that what appears to be genuine motivation is fear. Fear can be a motivator, but all animals tend to act so as to reduce fear and for an employee this may mean removing themselves from the situation as soon as possible. This type of motivation is likely to produce the bare minimum required to avoid getting into trouble.

Most work psychological contracts tend to be *calculative*. Both sides have something to gain although both may have to make compromises. A request for overtime offers the employee extra wages but may cost time that could be spent doing other things – an opportunity cost. The employer gains extra output but has to pay for it. Provided the reward is commensurate with the effort such contracts work well. If the balance tilts too much to one side or the other, they become coercive. The rewards in both coercive and calculative contracts tend to be extrinsic.

The ideal psychological contract is one that is *co-operative*, i.e. the parties receive an intrinsic reward. This occurs when their goals and objectives coinside. Co-operative contracts are most likely to occur when employees are given maximum empowerment and are able to exercise high levels of responsibility – an important motivator according to Herzberg (quoted earlier).

Theory Z

The incredible rebirth and success of Japanese organisations since the Second World War led those studying management to consider the motivation and work ethic of Japanese workers. A 1981 study by Pascale and Athos that compared major US and Japanese organisations, came out in the same year that W. Ouchi produced his Theory Z concept (to add to Theory X and Theory Y covered earlier).

Theory Z was based on the employment conditions in many Japanese organisations at the time. Theory Z, unlike McGregor's ideas was based on the *organisation* and not people. Theory Z organisations were characterised by offering life time employment (thus ensuring a considerable degree of financial security), providing social activities for employees (including shops, schools and medical care), involving permanent staff in shared decision-making and had subordinate–manager relationships based on *mutual respect*.

In the 1980s this was a very different picture to that in many Western organisations, where worker–management relationships often appeared to be based on *mutual distrust*. The idea of organisations providing schools and medical care was not new, as it had been introduced in the UK during the industrial revolution through the efforts of Robert Owen in New Lanark and the Lever organisation at Port Sunlight. What was new to Western ideas was the close identification of the workforce with the organisation. Theory Z organisations, it was believed, were better at motivating their employees than traditional ones.

What was not noticed at the time was the incredible stress executives were put under, stress that undermined their social and family relationships and the use of temporary female labour that did not enjoy the privileges of the permanent staff and the dependence on a growing economy.

In the late 1990s, the downturn in Asian business growth hit Japan hard and organisations found that they could no longer guarantee lifetime security. The psychological contract however had been, 'if you are loyal and work exceptionally hard, we will look after you'. Once that contract was broken, Theory Z began to look flawed. Perhaps, as the author believes, it was not a different phenomenon, only Herzberg and Maslow in operation in a culture where respect is the norm. Different cultures motivate people differently. In the Japanese case the sense of community is very strong and the culture encourages a more social rather than individual approach to life.

Motivation is key to understanding teams and leadership. Teams are made up of individuals each with his or her personal motivation. Chapter 3 considers the behaviour of people in teams. Bear the importance of belonging as a motivational factor in mind when reading Chapters 4–6 on team behaviour, as it is the need to belong that underlies much of the behaviour of individuals within a team situation.

SUMMARY

- Motivation is the study of *what drives people*. It is concerned with the satisfying of needs and the preferred way of such satisfaction – a person's wants
- Needs and wants are often *confused*
- Maslow believed that needs were arranged in a *hierarchy*
- Needs can be described as *primary, secondary, tertiary* and *facilitory*
- Herzberg differentiated those things that led to satisfaction (*motivators*) and those that caused dissatisfaction if not present (*hygiene factors*)
- *Achievement* and *recognition* are important motivators
- Money is not always a motivator but it does act as a *facilitator* for other things and is often the means by which achievement is measured
- The importance of money in a motivational sense depends upon the individual's position on their *spending life cycle*
- Theory X has a very *negative* view about people's attitudes to work while Theory Y is much more *positive*
- It is better to try to catch people *in* than *out*
- Motivation (and people) is highly complex with a *balance of factors* at work
- Managers should try to understand the *balance of motivational factors* at work within each individual
- People make *psychological* contracts with each other that may be coercive, calculative or co-operative
- *Theory Z* was an attempt to describe motivation within Japanese organisations.

1 Why is it important for those involved in managing or supervising people to have a knowledge and understanding of how individuals are motivated?

2 What is the 'spending life cycle', and how does it help explain the differences in money as a motivational factor for different individuals at any one time or for the same individual over time?

3 How would a believer in Theory Y differ in their approach to motivation from one who believes that Theory X represents a truer view of the world?

4 Why do you consider belonging, achievement and recognition are so important in motivation? Illustrate your response with reference to motivational concepts and thinkers

Recommended further reading

John Adair, *Effective Motivation* (1996), is an excellent and highly readable source of material for those studying motivation.

◪ **3** Team behaviour

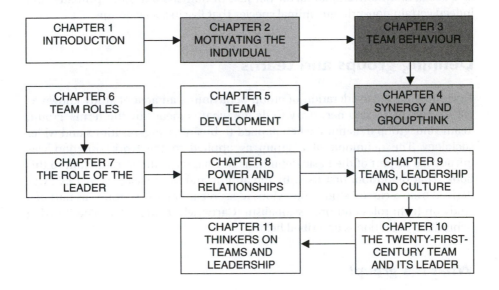

Learning outcomes – Defining groups and teams – Psychological awareness – Perceptions of membership – Teams – Size and span of control – Types of teams – Membership: core and ancillary – Families as groups and teams – Multiple membership – Summary – Questions – Recommended further reading

---

LEARNING OUTCOMES

By the end of this chapter you should understand:

- How to define *groups* and *teams*
- The meaning of *psychological awareness*
- The importance of a *perception of membership*
- The concept of the *span of control*
- Team *typologies*
- How people may be *core* or *ancillary* team members
- The functioning of *families* as a team
- The issues of *multiple team membership*.

Chapter 2 concentrated on the individual. Chapters 3–6 are concerned with the group/team within which the individual operates. This is important in the later discussion of leadership, as leaders are not just leaders of individuals but of groups of individuals.

Chapter 1 stressed the importance of understanding the way humans behave in groups and how that behaviour might, under certain circumstances be radically different to the behaviour that might be expected of the individuals making up that group if they were acting singly. The point was made both in Chapter 1 and also in Chapter 2 when considering the importance of belonging as a social and motivational factor not just in humans but other primates and indeed certain non-primate animal species that live in social groups.

Defining groups and teams

To commence a consideration of group behaviour – an area of study known as *group dynamics* – it is necessary to define what is meant by the terms 'group', 'team' and 'group dynamics' when applied to business, organisations and wider sociology. The definition of a group as applied to the work situation was introduced as part of the basic definitions in Chapter 1, the introduction to this book. That definition, first used by the author and his colleagues in 1993, was derived from a careful study of previous ideas regarding work groups as part of a study on team roles and professionalism (Cartwright *et al.*, 1993). The thinking behind the definition is described below.

What is a group?

In simple linguistic terms a group is a *gathering of individuals*. By even the simplest definition, the implication is that there must be more than one individual.

Consider the queue for a London bus or the line awaiting entry to a Broadway show: can these people be considered a group in the way an organisation might define the word, based on what has been stated about individuals and leaders earlier in this book? Physically they are a collection of people and they are all in the same place apparently for the same or similar primary reason, but the key issue to address is the relationship, if any, between them.

Various writers have wrestled with a definition of groups that will be useful to students of group dynamics. Group dynamics may be defined as:

'The behaviour patterns of individuals acting as a group or team.'

Definitions of a group often use the concept of common, shared goals and interdependency. Homans (1950) defined a group as a number of people who communicate with each other over a period of time and where the number of members is small enough for the communication to be face to face:

'We mean by a group, a number of persons who communicate with one another, often over a span of time, and who are few enough so that each person is able to communicate with all the others, not at second hand through others, but face to face.'

This definition is rather restrictive and does not take into account modern information and communications technology (ICT) that has increased the methods by which humans can communicate at a distance while retaining a personal element in the relationship. Later in this book the behaviour of large professional groups will be considered; the members of these bodies most definitely believe that they are members of a group, while Homans would exclude them on the grounds of size. The Homans' definition would exclude our queues of people above, as they are (hopefully) not going to be waiting for so long as to encompass his time-span requirement.

Fiedler (1967) considered that a group was defined by the sharing of a common fate and interdependency, in the sense that what affects one will affect the other members:

'By this term [group] we generally mean a set of individuals who share a common fate, that is, who are interdependent in the sense that an event that affects one member is likely to affect all others.'

The members of the queues in both scenarios quoted earlier all share a common fate but an individual in the queue may well not care about the effects of the bus not arriving or there being any show tickets available to anybody but himself and those in the queue (if any) he or she has a relationship with other than the coincidence of being in that particular queue.

The psychological group

In 1949, Deutsch produced a definition that considered that a psychological group is one in which the members perceive themselves as pursuing interdependent goals:

'A psychological group exists [has unity] to the extent that the individuals composing it perceive themselves as pursuing promotively interdependent goals.'

The concept of a *psychological group* is very germane to our discussion as it separates those groups that have formed almost randomly and where the only connection between the members is a goal that each could pursue on their own and groups where the members actually need each other.

To illustrate this point, Figure 3.1 is an illustration of the composition of the bus queue under consideration.

Each of the figures in Figure 3.1 has been allocated a letter to aid identification. B is the daughter of A and D is the son of C; A and C are best friends. E is on his way to work as is I. F and G are boy and girl friend and with them is her friend H (i.e. a couple) while J and K are going shopping but have never met before.

With this information it can be discerned that there are in fact two discrete groups – (A + B + C + D) – Group 1 and (F + G + H) – Group 2 – and four distinct

Figure 3.1 The composition of the bus queue

individuals, E, I, J & K. I is scratching his head in puzzlement – have J and K pushed in ahead of him?

Consider the order that they are in and then the following scenarios:

- *The bus arrives and they all find room on board*

    In this scenario there is no need for any interaction between the groups and the separate individuals. What happens to J and K and where they go will have no impact on the other individuals or the members of Groups 1 or 2.

- *The bus arrives but there are only two spare places on board*

    The decisions that will need to be made in this case are more complex. The first people with priority to board are the members of Group 1 – i.e. A + C and the two children. The children cannot board on their own, so does the group split up and A + C or B + D volunteer to be left behind? Probably not. Experience shows that rather than split the group up they will offer the places to the next in line. Group 2, consisting of three members would face a similar problem if they were offered only two places. Whether F and G as a couple would be prepared to leave H at the bus stop would depend on the relative strengths of the relationship – and, of course, the urgency of the journey.

- *The bus does not arrive*

    In this scenario the queue might well become a psychological group as they would all face the same problems and might feel that a complaint as a group would carry stronger weight with the bus company than that by individuals. Indeed experience shows that this is often the case. Any problem with the journey, whether it is a delay or an accident, could provide an opportunity for all of the passengers to begin to behave as a group as described by the various writers above.

Shared values or norms

Cattell (1951) saw a group as a collection of organisms in which the existence of all in a specified relationship is required for the satisfaction of the individual:

'The definition which seems most essential is that a group is a collection of organisms in which the existence of all in their given relationships is necessary to the satisfaction of certain individual needs in each.'

Given the importance of belonging as a human need as described in Chapter 2, the importance of Cattell's thinking becomes evident. A social species cannot exist without others of the same species in close proximity. While Cattell's definition is somewhat wide-ranging and could apply to a crowd or mob it does stress the interrelationship between group members.

Sherif and Sherif (1956) stressed the holding of shared values and norms defining a group as:

'a social unit which consists of a number of individuals who stand in (more or less) definite status and role relationships to one another and which possesses a set of values and norms of its own regulating the behaviour of individual members, at least in matters of consequence to the group.'

This is a definition that takes the concept of a group in the terms of this book to a different stage. What characterises this type of group is the *adherence to prescribed rules* and an understanding of the relationship between members. Interestingly in some but not all cultures the bus and theatre queues do follow strict rules. Pushing in is a major social blunder in many societies (the UK and USA included). In these cultures waiting one's turn has become, like 'women and children first', one of the rules by which members subscribe to their society.

The penultimate definition to be introduced is that of Shaw (1976). Shaw stressed the importance of mutual influence, defining a group as:

'two or more persons who are interacting with each other in such a manner that each person influences and is influenced by each other person.'

Group loyalties and implications of membership

Running through the work of all the above is the concept of *perceptions of membership*, whereby if the members do not perceive themselves to be a group, then they will be less likely to behave as a group.

Finally, Smith (1945) states:

'We may define a [social] group as a unit consisting of a number of separate organisms or agents who have a collective perception of their unity and who have the ability to act and/or are acting in a unitary manner towards their environment.'

In considering work groups and teams this led the author (Cartwright *et al.*, 1993) to the following definition as quoted in Chapter 1:

'A group in the context of occupation or profession, is a collection of individuals operating within the constraints of mutually accepted norms (rules) and values who perceive that, as regards their occupation or profession they are clearly distinct from other collections of individuals even if they belong to the same organisation.'

A group at work may have both *organisational* and *professional* loyalties and the above definition allows both of these to be addressed by recognising the wider implications of membership of the professional group that may cross geographic and organisational boundaries – e.g. a person may be a member of the personnel department at work, their work group, but a member of the Chartered Institute of Personnel and Development (CIPD), with its own code of professional conduct.

The above definition allows individuals to belong to a *whole series of groups*, adopting the norms and values prevalent with the group they are identifying with at the moment in question. This is a similar concept to the 'Language Registers' proposed by Bernstein (1961) and discussed in Chapter 4 when the ability of groups to use language to reinforce membership and even to exclude others is considered.

Two other important characteristics of a group in respect of this book are the concepts of psychological awareness and perception of membership.

Psychological awareness

The members of a mob will be aware, in a physical sense, of there being others around them. There may also be a spillover of emotion from one member to another – mob hysteria being a much-quoted example.

The members of a work or social group as being considered in this book are likely to have developed a much deeper, psychological awareness of each other. The longer the group exists, the more the members know what their colleagues are actually thinking and how they are likely to behave in any given situation. It may well be, as will be considered later in this chapter, that the group is developing an *entity of its own*.

Perceptions of membership

Put simply, a person is a member of a group if they perceive that they are a member. The negative may be a truer statement. If a person believes that they are not a member of a group then they are almost certainly right. It is possible to believe that one is a group member when the rest of the group does not share that belief. However, the person is normally put right in their views fairly quickly. Somebody who perceives that they are not a group member will not tend to conform to group norms or adopt group identity and will thus stand out as a non-member.

Having defined a work group it is also necessary to consider collections of individuals that do not fit into the definition – for example, crowd, mob and queue. What distinguishes these is the lack of relationships and adherence to rules even when pursuing a common goal. A mob may present many of the attributes of a group as defined above but it is unlikely that the fate of an individual will bother the other individuals in the mob. The question of group size will be considered later but experience suggests that even the most focused mob will consist of a number of distinct groups.

Other words that have applicability within group dynamics are: 'team', 'population', and 'squad', and these are considered below:

Think/discussion point

Consider those groups that you perceive yourself to be a member of.

- What common characteristics do the members have?
- How does the group define itself to differentiate it from members from those of other, perhaps similar, groups?

Teams

What is a team, and how does it differ from a group?

The *Concise Oxford Dictionary* defines a team as either a set of players forming one side in a game or secondly as two or more people working together. They also add animals to the second definition, as in a team of oxen. This inclusion of animals is in fact derived, according to Adair (1985) from the Anglo-Saxon concept of a team, a definition that originally applied to the use of oxen for ploughing.

It is the second definition that is of most use in a book on this subject. The oxen are a team when they are pulling a cart but not when they are grazing. The word 'team' is more or less synonymous with a *task* or a *set of tasks*.

The first definition is of less use outwith (a most useful Scottish word) the area of sports, and yet can go some way to differentiating between work teams and work groups.

Consider a football club. The outward manifestation of the club is often the eleven players who are on the field at any one time (for this analogy, it assumed that they are all well behaved and that nobody has been sent off). The club however, as an organisation, will be made up of a series of groups: players, coaches, managerial staff, administrators, medical personnel and cleaners. A series of such groups owing allegiance to a single entity make up an organisation.

There are usually more than eleven players. A major club is likely to have a number of teams, 1st team, 2nd team, youth team reserves. Together these form the club's squad of players. It is from this squad that the manager will choose a particular team to take the field against the current opponents. Typically he will choose 15 or 16 players to allow for substitutions.

Each member of this team will have a specified role (or maybe two) – goalkeeper, striker, defender or midfield player. While football players may have two or even three positions they can perform successfully in, it is rare that strikers are also accomplished defenders and visa versa. In cricket, the all-rounder is a much valued player as most of the top players in the world are either better as bowlers/fielders or batters – i.e. they have a *specialism*.

The concept of *personality roles* adopted within teams as proposed by Meredith Belbin (1981, 1993) forms the central part of Chapter 6

We can define a team as a small group engaged upon a specific task, for which group members have a clearly defined role and in which each member has a vested interest in success. In the early years of the twenty-first century, the British Broadcasting Corporation (BBC) developed a very successful quiz show 'The Weakest Link' hosted by the celebrity Ann Robinson that eventually went on to further success in the USA. The idea of the quiz was that a group of eight or nine contestants (the number depended upon the format, there being slightly different formats for daytime and evening shows) built up winnings by answering questions in succession. However at the end of each round the group had to vote off the member deemed the weakest link. Each player had a vote and the person who gained the most votes was eliminated. In the event of a tied vote the person who was the strongest link statistically had a casting vote. At the end of the quiz only two players were left and they then competed head to head, the eventual winner taking home all of the money won throughout the quiz – every other player left with nothing. The group was referred to throughout the programme as a team but that is, in fact, the last thing that they were. Although they were able to discuss strategy between rounds and certainly had a common objective, the fact that they voted members off (sometimes it was the strongest link who received the most votes as a result of individual tactics to remove opposition) is not the behaviour of a team. The group in this case might be described as a 'pseudo-team' in that it exhibited some of the features of a team but was in fact driven by individual agendas that coincided for brief periods during the programme.

The terms 'group' and 'team' are often used to cover the same type of collections of individuals, and in many cases this is legitimate. The concept of *groupthink*, to be considered at length later in this chapter, could have been called 'teamthink'. However the phenomenon is one that occurs both in focused teams and in the groups from which they are formed. Team development, as covered in Chapter 4, however, is a concept that occurs within teams but is far less marked in the looser groups from which the teams are formed – hence the term 'team' is the correct one to use.

In this book, the use of the term 'group' will include teams but where a team is referred to, it is deemed to apply more in the team than the group situation as defined in the definitions that began the chapter. Unfortunately the boundaries between a focused team and the more general group are not clearly defined in practice and the reader will have to use their experience and an analysis of the composition of the group or team and its situation to decide which word applies.

Size and span of control

Belbin (cited earlier) believes that even a team of nine is unwieldy. It is rare to find a sports team with more than 12–15 players engaged at any one time. The issue of *size* is closely linked to *communication* and its effectiveness (see Chapter 4) and what is termed 'the span of control'.

In 1933, a French management consultant, V. A. Graicunas (as quoted by Cole, 1993) developed a formula to indicate the growth in the number of possible relationships as the number of subordinates increased. If there is one boss A and two subordinates B and C, there are actually six different combinations of relationship. (Remember that the relationship boss A has with subordinate B – i.e. AB – is actually different to subordinate B's relationship with A – i.e. BA). The possible relationships are AB, BA, AC, CA, and BC, CB. By the time there are six subordinates there are 222 possible relationship combinations!

Urwick (1947), one of the earlier UK writers on management, believed that the maximum number of subordinates one person could supervise directly was no more than six. He stressed that this number could be increased where the work was not that of a team. A supervisor could control many more staff, provided that each was engaged upon a discrete task.

While the leadership of a team may not be a fixed position (as will be discussed in Chapter 8), teams do require leaders, and thus this helps fix the effective size of a team. Major projects may, of course involve hundreds or even thousands of people and organisational structures to encompass the use of large numbers have been developed, often as hierarchies. By dividing the task up between a series of teams, each with its own team leader, the problems of the span of control can be alleviated as shown by the structure in Figure 3.2, a structure used by many organisations.

If each team comprises a leader plus six people then it can be seen that the effective span of control for the manager is now 21. It should also be noted that there are likely to be inter-team relationships that are semi-independent of the manager or even the team leader. The *task culture concept* introduced by Handy (1976) and further expanded by him in 1978, an organisational culture much aspired to in the later years of the twentieth century, is based on a matrix

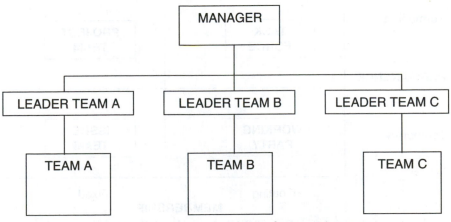

Figure 3.2   Organisational structures for managing teams

where the previously established rigid hierarchy was broken down by improved communications between departments and teams at a sub-senior managerial level.

Think/discussion point

- Using an organisation with which you are familiar, how does it reflect the need to accommodate the concept of span of control?
- Is it possible to demonstrate the span of control on the organisation's structure chart?

Types of teams

While the word 'team' is often used generically to indicate any small, focused work group, there are in fact four basic team typologies based on the permanence of the team and its composition (Figure 3.3).

All of the above terms are relative; nothing in life is truly permanent. The use of the terms in Figure 3.3 should be taken as indicative of a trend. A permanent team will probably have a life of months or even years while a temporary one will often deal with a single issue over a short period of time, probably measured in no more than days or weeks. Similarly in a fixed team the membership will be stable with people leaving only owing to illness, promotion or a change in domestic circumstances, whereas a floating team will have a constant flux in its membership.

Working party

There can be few people in management today who have not represented their section, department or even organisation on a working party. In the strictest

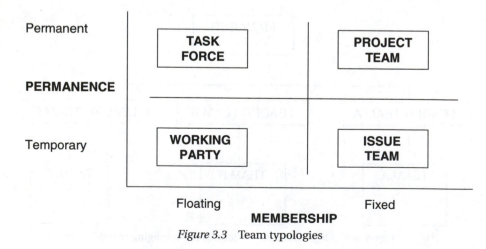

Figure 3.3   Team typologies

sense of the term working parties are set up to bring together people from a variety of areas and disciplines to examine an issue and normally have a fixed date by which they should report. While there will nearly always be a representative of each department or section, the individual may change and thus working parties can be described as temporary teams with a floating membership.

Task force

Working parties that achieve a degree of permanence often retain the working part title when they have become, in fact, a task force. Membership still floats – i.e. new members come and go and there is considerable deputisation – but the time span is now much longer. These task forces can achieve a life of their own in that they continue long after their original function has been achieved. This will be considered in Chapter 4 when considering the disbandment of teams as part of the team life cycle.

Membership of both working parties and task forces may be part-time owing to the floating nature of membership.

Project team

A project team has the same permanence as a task force but the membership is of a more fixed and quite possibly full-time nature. It is likely that the team will be small but this is not necessarily the case. Such a team will be hard to break up as will be shown in Chapter 4. In fact the organisation may well move the whole team to a new project rather than break it up.

Issue team

Issue teams could also be called 'crisis teams'. They are formed with a permanent membership but on a temporary basis to deal with a particular issue and may require the full-time attention of the members.

Membership: core and ancillary

In most teams there are likely to be those who are permanent members of the team – *the core* – and others who are drafted in to provide ancillary and expert assistance – *ancillary* members. Hastings *et al.* (1994), in their work on Super-teams, stress the importance of the 'invisible team' – i.e. those members of the ancillary team who perform vital tasks but at first sight might not even be considered team members. How many team leaders remember to thank the cleaners and caterers after a team presentation? These are people whose contribution is often forgotten and yet who can make a great deal of difference to team effectiveness. The membership and role of this 'invisible team' needs to be kept in mind when communicating objectives and passing on praise.

The work of Bernstein (1961) on language registers and the implication for groups and teams is discussed in Chapter 4, but basically he argued that people use different language in different situations. Groups and teams, as will be shown in Chapter 4, can use a *group language*, or 'groupspeak' as it will be referred to, as a means of not only strengthening group identity but also to excluding outsiders. It is important that members of the ancillary part of the team do not feel excluded by those in the core if the latter wish to see the skills of ancillary members used to their maximum effectiveness.

Think/discussion point

- Identify the core and ancillary members of teams to which you belong.
- What means are used to ensure that ancillary members feel part of the team for the period they are working with it?

Families as groups and teams

The work of Morris (1969) on leadership, to be covered in Chapter 7, involved the study of primate groups that were, to a large extent based on extended family groups. The family is also the first of the permanent small groups listed by Stott (1958). Stott states that the family is characterised as a small, permanent group, with a variety of interests and considerable face-to-face contact. In addition the family has genetic ties that bind the members together, it being said that 'blood is thicker than water'. Interestingly, the saying is in fact rather inadequate as blood can be freely given to non-genetically related individuals provided that the limitations of blood grouping are kept in mind. There is no doubt that Stott is correct when he stresses the strength of kinship ties, any form of family break-up being considered a great tragedy. One of the common objectives of the family group (albeit sometimes a subconscious one) is the passing on of genetic material to ensure the continuance of the family. Much of the behaviour of all forms of life centres on the successful production of successive generations carrying the genes that make up identity.

Richard Dawkins, the eminent biologist, stated that it was *our genes that define us* and that we exist only to facilitate the survival of those genes, we being little more than disposable survival machines (Dawkins, 1976). The family is the biological mechanism by which the survival of genetic material is facilitated.

Of all groups and teams it is the family that usually displays the strongest bonds. Parents can often appear irrational in their support for their children even when the child has committed an illegal act. The strongest of team/group bonds is love, not a concept that appears in many management texts and yet one that is of considerable interest to those studying groups, teams and leadership. St Paul's famous comments on love (1 Corinthians 13) make clear the almost unique nature of that particular emotion and it is love that is the main binding force within the family group. While the predominance of the family business declined during the second half of the twentieth century, there are still many organisations where family ties lie at the heart of the operations and philosophy of the organisation and thus decisions may be made and implemented that owe more to family ties and thus love, than to the products of rational decision-making models – a concept explored more fully in Chapter 9, which looks at the relationship between culture, teams and leadership.

Multiple membership

In real-life scenarios individuals may be members of a variety of groups and teams. This can cause some psychological difficulty for the individual if the values of one group or team are radically at odds with membership of another.

Members of professional groups may find that the values of their profession conflict with those of their employer or that the honesty required by their religious and spiritual beliefs cause a conflict if they discover something happening at work that they find abhorrent. Whistle-blowing on an employer has often resulted in the dismissal of the employee. While employers can, quite rightly, demand loyalty from employees and that commercially sensitive information be protected, this can cause a conflict of interest for an employee who discovers that a group of which he or she is a member (the organisation) is acting against the interest of another group they belong to. Where that other group is the society or nation, governments have begun to provide protection for the individual.

Although the USA has had legislation in place protecting employees who report their employer for illegal acts, UK employees received such protection only as a result of the Public Interest Disclosures Act of 1998 (HMG, 1998). Under this legislation an employee cannot be dismissed or disciplined for bringing to the attention of the authorities any action by the organisation that is a breach of the law. This is a new type of legislation for the UK, and it will be interesting to see how employers receive protection against malicious accusations – and, indeed, whether having blown the whistle the employee would want to carry on with the same organisation.

In the main, individuals tend to associate themselves with groups and teams that reflect their individual norms and values. To do otherwise is to invite a degree of *dissonance* that can lead to considerable stress. Fortunately for human beings, our brains appear well developed when it comes to rationalisation. The football supporter who is shouting abuse at a rival player one week appears perfectly able to cheer that player on when representing the national side a few days later.

George Orwell's classic novel *1984* had a scenario in which the three power blocks of the world shifted alliances so that two were always at war with the third but with no constancy of the alliances – i.e. one week it was A and B against C and the next B and C against A. The world's population was brainwashed into accepting this apparent contradiction.

The advantages and disadvantages of team work are considered in Chapter 4 on Synergy and Groupthink.

SUMMARY

- Various authorities have sought different methods of *defining groups and teams*
- In general terms groups and teams can be defined in terms of *common objectives, interdependency, psychological awareness* and a perception of *membership*
- Teams are groups focused on *specific tasks*
- Teams vary according to their *size* and *task*, some being more permanent than others
- Membership of teams can be described in terms of a fairly stable *core* and more fluid *ancillary membership*
- The *family* can be considered as a team, albeit one that may behave differently to teams found in the workplace
- Individuals may be members of a number of teams, and this can cause a *conflict* if the teams operate to different sets of norms and values.

QUESTIONS

1 What do you understand by the terms 'group' and 'team'? In what ways do they differ from mere collections of individuals, and under what circumstances might a mere collection of individuals become a group as defined in this book?
2 How might membership of one team conflict with membership of another?
3 In the typology of teams, how might the differences in behaviour between the different types be manifested?

Recommended further reading

John Adair, *Effective Teambuilding* (1985), and W. J. H. Stott, *Human Groups* (1958, one of the first popular texts on the subject), will provide useful and interesting further reading.

■ M̄ 4 Synergy and groupthink

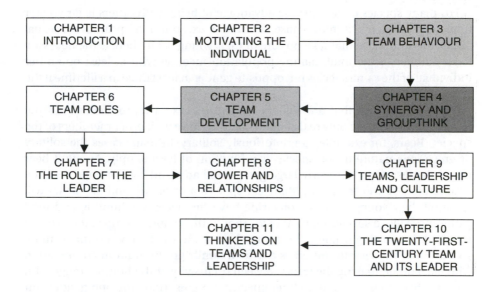

| CHAPTER 1 INTRODUCTION | → | CHAPTER 2 MOTIVATING THE INDIVIDUAL | → | CHAPTER 3 TEAM BEHAVIOUR |

| CHAPTER 6 TEAM ROLES | ← | CHAPTER 5 TEAM DEVELOPMENT | ← | CHAPTER 4 SYNERGY AND GROUPTHINK |

| CHAPTER 7 THE ROLE OF THE LEADER | → | CHAPTER 8 POWER AND RELATIONSHIPS | → | CHAPTER 9 TEAMS, LEADERSHIP AND CULTURE |

| | | CHAPTER 11 THINKERS ON TEAMS AND LEADERSHIP | ← | CHAPTER 10 THE TWENTY-FIRST-CENTURY TEAM AND ITS LEADER |

Learning outcomes – Advantages and disadvantages of group membership and team work – Advantages of team work – Disadvantages of group and team work – Synergy 'groupthink' and unacceptable behaviour – Mitigating against the effects of groupthink – Group dynamics: a summary of the history – The team as an entity – Summary – Questions – Recommended further reading

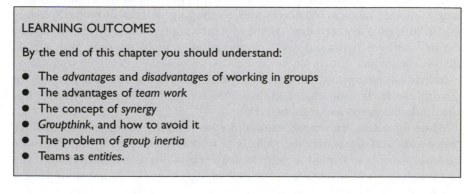

LEARNING OUTCOMES

By the end of this chapter you should understand:

- The *advantages* and *disadvantages* of working in groups
- The advantages of *team work*
- The concept of *synergy*
- *Groupthink*, and how to avoid it
- The problem of *group inertia*
- Teams as *entities*.

Advantages and disadvantages of group membership and team work

Why be a member of a group?

Given that belonging to any group or team involves a sacrifice of at least a degree of individuality there must be very good reasons why people join with others. As was shown in Chapter 1, humans are *social animals* and the individual sacrifices of freedom of action are compensated for by the benefits of being and working with others.

For many species of animals the advantage of being with others is far greater than any problems it may cause. With the exception of primitive asexual organisms and those that take no care of their young at all, there is the necessity for a number of the total, mature population meeting with at least one other individual of the same species but opposite gender at least once in a lifetime if the species is to continue.

For many species that are solitary by nature, sexual reproduction and the rearing of young is the only real contact that they have with other members of the species. Bears, for example, are notoriously solitary. In many cases the solitary or gregarious nature of the species is a function of food supply. An adult bear needs the resources of a fairly large geographic area and cannot cope with the competition of another adult. Many cat species are solitary and like bears will drive off their young once the offspring have the necessary hunting and food gathering skills to survive on their own. Should the offspring return, they will be attacked. Interestingly, lions also a member of the cat family are much more sociable and the females (often as part of a family group) hunt in co-operation with each other, making the trade between exclusivity of the hunting range with the benefits of co-operation. Other species are gregarious for one gender but solitary for another. It is often the males that have to lead a solitary existence.

Dogs and other pack animals including many primates and large aquatic mammals such as whales and dolphin have developed complex social systems, hierarchies and communication methods to enable a large group to live together. In this way they can develop effective *group hunting strategies* taking prey (and then sharing it, usually in order of the hierarchy) that would be difficult for an individual to catch without the assistance of the pack.

Even herbivores can gain protection by being just one of the crowd. While a single antelope might make an easy prey, a galloping herd can be both distracting and intimidating to a predator. A number of insect species have developed clearly defined societal behaviour with co-operation, mutual support and a rigid division of labour.

Individuals gain protection from being a member of a group and in return for sharing receive benefits that might be difficult to access on their own. It is this that underlies group and team behaviour.

While there has been much work undertaken on the promotion of effective team work and team building skills it is important to realise that there are disadvantages as well as advantages to team operations. It is quite possible for a factor to be both an advantage and a disadvantage, as will be demonstrated in the following sections. Working within a team nearly always involves some form of sacrifice by the individual in order to gain an advantage in another area. For example an individual may be able to programme tasks according to their personal agenda. As soon as a team becomes involved it will be necessary to sacrifice individual flexibility in order to accommodate the needs of other team members.

The advantages will be examined first, followed by the disadvantages. It needs to be realised, however, that there are no clear-cut distinctions in this analysis of team work. The advantages and disadvantages will always be there but if the team realises their presence, advantages can be maximised and the effect of disadvantages mitigated against.

Advantages gained by the group

It is not just the individual who gains out of being a member of a group, or team but also the other members. First they gain extra skills and all the advantages that are covered in the next section of this chapter.

Second, as will be expanded on in Chapter 5, the group or team and society in general gain from the *social control mechanisms* offered by groups and teams. The behaviour of the individual becomes adapted to the values and norms of the other members acting collectively. The downside to this occurs when the behaviour of the group or team is at variance to that of the wider society. In cases such as this the group may be ostracised or may emigrate to a society more in tune with its values. The emigration of the Pilgrim Fathers on the Mayflower in the seventeenth century is such an example. Their religious beliefs were not accepted by much of the population of England and in turn they spurned the behaviour of others in wider English society. Finding that they did not fit into English society any more but wanting to retain links with the land of their birth they emigrated to one of the English colonies in what is now the USA. As stated earlier, social control through groups and teams forms part of Chapter 5, but it needs to be stressed at this point that anybody who wishes to be a member of a society needs to conform (at least in a visible manner) with its norms and values. In some societies (ranging from groups such as Masonic Lodges through to whole counties) these may be codified through rituals such as 'pledging allegiance to the flag', as occurs daily in US schools.

Advantages of team work

Support

Perhaps one of the most obvious advantages of team work is that of mutual support for team members. As discussed in Chapters 1 and 2 of this book, *support* and *esteem* are psychological needs for a social animal such as humankind and form an important part of the individual motivational process.

Working within a team allows the individual to receive support both for the task in hand and for outside events from other team members. It is often at times of great emotional stress – for example, bereavements or relationship problems unconnected with the job role – that the support and understanding of other team members becomes a key factor in the continuing effective function of the individual. By taking up and sharing duties the team can help provide a breathing space for the individual. The psychological contract is that the individual will provide similar support for other team members when required.

It is often other team members who first notice that an individual is having a problem. This is facilitated by the *psychological awareness* introduced earlier. Other team members become attuned to nuances and can spot the onset of problems much more quickly owing to the closeness of the relationship.

While they may not be trained for the task of counselling, other team members often perform a vital, unofficial counselling role for their team colleagues. It is likely that a team member with a problem will be far more likely to discuss that problem with somebody from his or her team. The role of the leader in supporting subordinates will be covered later in this book and other team members can become a useful extension of the leader in these particular circumstances.

Confidence

In many cases it is not a question of whether a person possesses the skills and aptitude to undertake a task, but whether they have confidence in their own ability. Working as a member of a team helps boost confidence owing to the mutual support discussed in the previous section. There is no doubt that having supportive team members around, especially when attempting a task for the first time or after a previous failure, is likely to boost confidence. The disadvantage is that the team member may become overconfident and attempt to do something as an individual that they should be doing in a team situation.

In Chapter 7 the Adair *team leadership model* will be introduced, and it will be stressed that there is an important balance between individual, team and task needs. An effective team leader is aware that the confidence of the individual needs to be considered and boosted in both an individual and a team context, and that his or her limitations need to be addressed.

Limitations (these will be met again in Chapter 6 when the allowable weaknesses associated with team roles are introduced) form part of the *confidence balance*. To be truly confident an individual also needs to know his or her limitations. This is best accomplished in a team situation where the support of others is available. Provided that a limitation is only individual and does not apply to the team then the impact on fulfilling a task may be negligible.

The confidence balance is a vital success factor as both over confidence and underconfidence in an individual can lead to failure, and even disaster. Captain Smith of the Titanic was overconfident. Newspaper interviews he gave before the disaster showed that he underestimated the danger that natural conditions could cause to a ship of the *Titanic*'s size and that he believed that he could overcome any natural phenomenon (Davie, 1987). That he was not on the bridge of the ship as it sped towards a reported icefield shows also that he was overconfident about the capabilities of his team.

Equally, underconfidence can be a problem with the inability to act leading to vacillation and mistakes. If a team is not supportive it may well be that the presence of others can undermine confidence by making the individual nervous about receiving undue criticism. Again a delicate balance needs to be struck. Team members can and should be critical but in a constructive manner ensuring that they also say something positive about the individual.

Flexibility

One of the major problems faced by every one-person or small business is that of compensating for the illness, holidays and domestic issues of a key person. In the case of a very small business this may mean that operations need to be suspended for the duration. As the members of a team work together they develop an understanding about each other's role so that it is likely a team member could substitute for a colleague, albeit for a short period and possibly less effectively. It may also be the case that while a part of the operation may need to be suspended, the team can rearrange tasks in such a way as to ensure some continuance. This flexibility gives teams a considerable advantage over an individual, or even a group of individuals not working as a team. Team work involves a knowledge of one's colleagues that allows for substitution and flexibility.

Skill mix

Within a team there is likely to be a mix of skills.

If one member of the team has not acquired a skill, another probably has, and – of equal importance – can pass that skill on to team members. Effective teams are *learning teams*. By working as a team, individual skills are enhanced and honed. As members become multi-skilled this aids the flexibility discussed in the previous section.

If no member of the team possesses a necessary skill it will be necessary either to train somebody up in the skill – and that takes time but ensures that the skill base is enhanced – or recruit a new team member. If the skill is going to be needed again, a permanent appointment may be made and the issues involved in team recruitment are covered in Chapter 7. If it is a temporary skill that is required, a *temporary secondment* to the team may be made from outside. In this case, it will be important that the secondee is inducted into the team and not excluded by the use of language and culture – issues to be addressed in later chapters.

Norms

The setting of *group/team rules or norms* is an important advantage as it allows the group/team to become self-policing. However as Yablonsky's classic study of Chicago street gangs (1962) showed, the rules that are sometimes adopted are not those that are always acceptable to the wider society. The street gangs displayed considerable loyalty, a rigid hierarchy and a strong adherance to the gang's rules

– however the rest of Chicago did not accept such rules as they were deemed (and were) anti-social, but rules they were.

Risk-taking

At first sight risk-taking may seem a strange advantage. However, just as underconfidence can be as dangerous as overconfidence so a too cautious approach can be less effective than a risk. Indeed confidence and risk-taking are linked. To take a risk one needs to be confident in oneself, one's colleagues, one's materials, one's subordinates and one's superiors.

Very few activities are without risk. The risks may be physical, emotional or financial and while the consequences of taking a risk may be great, the rewards if it pays off may be even greater. Not for nothing is 'Who dares wins' the motto of the British Special Air Service (SAS). Boeing took a huge risk in committing some 80 per cent of the company's worth to developing the first commercial wide-bodied airliner, the Boeing 747 Jumbo in the late 1960s (Irving, 1993). The risk paid off and Boeing virtually controlled the market with little competition. It was only in 2001 that Airbus Industrie announced that they too would build a very large commercial airliner to compete with the Boeing product. It could have gone wrong and for a time in the 1960s prior to the 747's introduction into service, Boeing went through some torrid financial times. The marketing managers had performed their forecasts correctly however, and the aircraft sold, but nevertheless it was a risky venture.

Teams (and groups) are better at taking risks than most individuals. The exception perhaps is the very charismatic leader who is very confident in their own ability (see Chapter 7). Most individuals are more cautious when on their own than when in a group. The reason is fairly obvious. In a group blame can be spread rather than being carried solely by one individual. There is the phenomenon of finding a scapegoat but that often involves somebody outwith the team or an individual the team wishes to be rid of.

While risk-taking is an advantage of team work in that it gets things done that individuals would not do, as will be seen under disadvantages below, it is also a disadvantage as the risks associated with a wrong decision may spell disaster.

Working as a team allows the risk and therefore the consequence of failure to be spread among the members. Pettinger (2001) has commented on the 'blame culture' and its effect on organisations. It is an unfortunate fact that it is becoming more and more usual for the hunt for somebody to blame to take precedence over finding out precisely what went wrong, and how to prevent a re-occurrence of the event.

Synergy

The advantages of team work can be expressed in one word – *synergy*. Synergy can be described as:

'The sum of the parts being greater than the whole.'

A few examples may assist in explaining the concept:

- Two work teams with members of similar experience, skills and intelligence produce widely different results. Both teams consist of six members but one seems to produce an output suggesting it actually has seven members while the other appears to have only five.
- A Premiership football team is playing in a round of the FA or Scottish Cup against a team from a much lower division and are soundly beaten. All the pundits, who base their predictions on past record, skill (and even cost) of players are proved wrong. The second team appears to be playing well above its abilities.

If a team is *well constructed* (team roles being the subject of Chapter 6 and recruitment that of Chapter 7) then the effects of mutual support, confidence, flexibility, skills and risk-taking are likely to result in a performance that is above that predicted based on a consideration of the individual members of the team. If the team is badly constructed then personal chemistry may result in the opposite effect and performance will be less than could be gained from a well-constructed team and even less than predicted when considering the team members as individuals.

Synergy is a wonderful thing. It means that a well-constructed team is able to do something that is theoretically impossible in the physical world – provide something for nothing. However, there is always a trade-off between advantages and disadvantages. The very factors that provide synergy in a well-constructed team may be major disadvantages in a team that is not properly balanced or one that has forgotten the organisational purposes for which it was set up – a team that has in fact outgrown its organisation.

An excellent example of synergy was provided by a comment made during the televising of Scottish football's CIS Cup Final in March 2001. Both the teams involved were well-known names, Celtic and Kilmarnock. Just after half time Celtic opened the scoring but then had a player sent off for a foul. It was therefore 10 players against 11. Celtic went on to win the match (and the cup) 3–0. During the latter stages, one of the television commentators asked the rhetorical question, 'Which of these teams has only 10 men?' In fact the mutual support shown by the Celtic players suggested that they were the team with the player advantage – synergy in action!

Mathematically speaking $1 + 1 + 1 + 1 + 1$ always equals 5, however in team work, $1 + 1 + 1 + 1 + 1$ can actually equal 6 (or above) if the team is properly constructed and the team works well together. The converse is also true $1 + 1 + 1 + 1 + 1$ can equal 4 (or be less than 4) if the input of one or more team members is nullified by poor construction and personal chemistry.

The **synergy gain** can be defined as:

'The extra performance, over that the individuals working on their own, gained by the team working together.'

The **synergy loss** is likewise defined as:

'The diminution in performance, over that the individuals working on their own, displayed by the team working together.'

In a synergy gain each of the advantages in team work provides a component of the gain. In a synergy loss it is likely that there will be a major factor causing the effect. This factor is often on the personal level and will be considered in more detail in the introduction to team roles in Chapter 6.

Think/discussion point

- Using your own experience, analyse teams with which you are familiar to show the factors that have led to a demonstration of synergy.

Disadvantages of group and team work

Despite all of the advantages quoted above, there are disadvantages attached to group and team work. While in most instances the advantages far outweigh the disadvantages there have been occasions in history when the problems associated with teams have become so great as to threaten the existence of nations and in the case used to illustrate the phenomenon of groupthink at the end of this section, the very planet itself.

Risk-taking

As discussed above, risk-taking can be a considerable advantage allowing decisions to be made in a group/team situation that an individual might not make purely because of the risks and the personal accountability involved.

The taking of risks is acceptable provided that the decisions are the right ones and that a proper *assessment* of the consequences of risk has been carried out.

In Chapter 6, the team role of Monitor–Evaluator (Belbin, 1981) will be introduced. Monitor–Evaluators have an important role in ensuring that team members weigh up the consequences of their collective actions, thus performing an in-built risk-analysis role. The point will be made in Chapter 6 that Monitor–Evaluators behave in this way as a result of their personalities and that this wish for further consideration and a degree of caution is one of the biggest assets they bring to a team, however much other team members may resent having their ideas questioned.

Huczynski and Buchanan (1991) have made the point that the degree of risk that is acceptable may be a cultural factor. Trompenaars (1993) in his classic work on national cultures and their effect on how business is carried out, has drawn attention to the diversity of belief systems around the globe. Among the factors he considered was the balance between the power of the group and that of the individual and perceptions of legal fairness and equality. The importance of not losing face in many Eastern cultures has a direct bearing on the amount of risk that can be accepted (and on who takes the blame). Not all groups and teams will be encouraged to take risks. Those working within organisations that display a punishment-centred or a blame culture are likely to take smaller risks than those in cultures where risks are accepted for the sake of the possible benefits. What can be said is that on a level playing field, a team is more likely to accept a risk than an individual.

Invulnerability

The longer a group or team is together, and provided that the members achieve both collective and individual success, the more collective and individual confidence will grow. The gaining of confidence through mutual support, as stated previously, is one of the advantages of team work. Indeed it may well advantage both the individual and the group and thus is to be welcomed.

There can come a point however, when confidence becomes overconfidence and this can lead the group to perceive a degree of *invulnerability* to its decisions and actions. Combining feelings of invulnerability with a propensity to take more risks than an individual can lead to a very dangerous situation indeed, as the Bay of Pigs (on the coast of Cuba) incident, to be covered later in this chapter, will show.

Overconfidence can easily lead to arrogance. Arrogant individuals and arrogant teams are usually reluctant to listen to advice. An overconfident leader with a perception of personal invulnerability coupled with a team lacking confidence can also be a recipe for problems.

Sooner or later the actual vulnerability of the team will be exposed and a team that has considered itself invulnerable is likely to be at a disadvantage when so exposed as it will be unlikely to have developed the necessary strategies to *cope with failure*. Failure is very difficult for teams (and individuals, especially leaders) to deal with if they have perceived themselves to have developed a high degree of invulnerability.

Sacrifices of the individual

The importance that is attached to individual behaviour and responsibility has already been discussed in the earlier chapters of this book. Team membership, for all the support that it brings, involves the repression of at least some part of individuality. It may be conscience, dress (team members may have to wear a uniform or adhere to a particular dress code), language (using team words and phrases instead of the individual's usual idioms) or even social activities. Bringing the team or group, or firm or profession into disrepute by one's behaviour outwith the work situation is usually considered a bigger crime than the individual bringing themselves into disrepute.

Human beings and other animals accept this subjugation of the individual because of the advantages of group membership discussed at the beginning of this book. As was shown in Chapter 2, self-actualisation, a motivational concept closely linked to individualism, is a higher-order need than belonging and it should be expected that group membership will be more important than the expression of individualism.

'Groupthink' and unacceptable behaviour

The author first became interested in group dynamics and team behaviour during a visit to Eastern Europe in the 1980s. Together with other members of his tour group he was visiting the site of one of the Nazi concentration camps. Attached to the site was a small memorial and while reading of the horrific acts performed against innocent and unarmed men, women and children another member of the group (an American by nationality) came up to him and said 'Gee how horrific, I could never have done those things – could you?'

The rational and logic answer is, 'No, of course not.' However, the author still remembers wanting to say that, but finding that the words would not come out. Who knows what they are capable of unless put in that particular situation.

To this day (and the author does not like thinking about it too deeply), he is sure that as an individual he could not act so barbarically, but as a member of a group and with everybody else treating barbarity as normal? What effect would peer pressure have? The author certainly hopes that he would resist, but one can never be sure.

Janis (1982) made an in-depth study of US foreign policy decisions from the end of the Second World War, particularly in relation to the policy on Cuba. In 1959, the communist revolutionary Fidel Castro overthrew Batista (a right-wing, US-supported dictator) to the consternation of the USA. The initial US response was first for President Eisenhower to break off diplomatic relations with Castro and then, following the election of President John F. Kennedy, to assist in the retaking of Cuba by using the Central Intelligence Agency (CIA) to train and arm Cuban exiles. The USA then decided to provide limited air and sea support for an invasion of the Island. On 17 April about 1,300 exiles, armed with US weapons, were landed at the Bahía de Cochinos (Bay of Pigs) on the south coast of Cuba. Hoping to find support from the local population, they intended to cross the island to Havana, but were quickly stopped by Castro's army. By the time the fighting ended on 19 April, 90 had been killed and the rest were prisoners. The failure of the invasion seriously embarrassed the Kennedy Administration, which was blamed by some for not giving it adequate support and by others for allowing it to take place at all. The captured exiles were later ransomed by private groups in the USA. All in all a small communist state had managed to embarrass one of the world's superpowers, but a much more deadly danger was to come.

Following this failure, Cuba developed increasingly closer ties with the USSR (the Former Soviet Union or FSU) and agreed to the stationing of Russian troops on the island eventually to be equipped with nuclear armed missiles capable of devastating large parts of the southern USA. When US reconnaissance aircraft uncovered the existence of these missile sites in 1962, the US government under President Kennedy decided that this was unacceptable. (As an aside, it must be remarked that NATO (of which the USA was a major member) had had no qualms about stationing nuclear weapons in Turkey, a NATO member having a direct border with the USSR.)

Kennedy and his advisors determined on a blockade of Cuba to prevent Soviet ships delivering the missiles and warheads. They announced that they were prepared to sink any Soviet vessel attempting to run the blockade. The Soviet President, Khrushchev then announced that such a sinking would be treated as an act of war. NATO and its Soviet equivalent, the Warsaw Pact, became involved in a stand-off with each side equipped with weapons of mass destruction. Those readers who were alive at the time may recall how close we all believed we were to nuclear war.

Communication between Khrushchev and Kennedy was opened through diplomatic channels. On 28 October Khrushchev acceded to the US demands; Kennedy halted the blockade and gave assurances that the USA would not invade Cuba. The Soviet retreat was considered a personal and political triumph for Kennedy. (It has been rumoured for some time that both the USA and the UK had a highly placed spy in the Kremlin who was able to give advance information of the Soviet moves and responses, and that war was perhaps less likely than feared at the time.)

In retrospect, it is clear that the missile crisis had its roots in the abortive Bay of Pigs invasion. How could such an invasion have been sanctioned? All the experience of amphibious landings from the Gallipoli campaign of the First World War, through the Pacific invasions of the 1940s and the Italian and D-Day landings of June 1944 and the more recent landings at Inchon during the Korean War (1950) had pointed to the need for effective gunnery support from ships offshore and adequate air cover. The USA had participated in all but the First World War landings at Gallipoli (this was a failed UK, Australian, New Zealand campaign against Turkey) so there should have been a collective knowledge in the US armed forces of what was required. Nevertheless, seemingly intelligent and experienced officials launched an invasion with inadequate support, one that hindsight suggests could never have succeeded.

When examined by authorities such as Janis (1982), it became apparent that in the case of a very cohesive group, consensus was obtained by members agreeing to things they disagreed with privately in order not to break the group consensus and appear out of step with their peers. Janis termed this phenomenon, 'groupthink'. The major problem with groupthink is that dissent is discouraged, with the result that very bad decisions can be made. As has been demonstrated, groups can perceive themselves to be invulnerable and are more prone to taking risks than individuals. A risky decision (perhaps the wrong one) made by an overconfident group can spell disaster.

Huczynski and Buchanan (1991) have pointed out that the very cohesiveness that makes team work an advantage is in many cases directly responsible for groupthink. It should also be remembered that silence does not necessarily give consent; silence is precisely that – an absence of consent.

Think/discussion point

In many years working with groups and teams in a seminar situation, the author has often observed the following scenario:

The trainer makes a point and then asks:

'Did you all understand that?'

There is usually a nodding of heads around the room and discretely muttered affirmations.

If the group is lucky, one hand is tentatively raised and a small voice says something along the lines of:

'I may be a little dense but . . .'

A collective wave of relief goes around the group, because that person has just asked the question that everybody wanted to ask but nobody dared for fear of showing him or herself up.

- Have you ever experienced that?
- How did you respond?

The two types of groupthink

Groupthink as a phenomenon has two major causes and an opposite effect – *group inertia.*

The two causes of groupthink are:

- Peer groupthink
- Hierarchical groupthink.

Peer groupthink

Peer groupthink stems from the psychological need for cohesiveness among the group members. As was pointed out in Chapter 2, belonging is a fairly basic need for primates, including human beings. Individuals are unlikely to take a stance that sets them apart from their peers unless there are compelling reasons, often of an ethical/religious nature to do so.

Peer groupthink can explain much of the unacceptable behaviour seen in war. While the rationalisation might be 'I was just obeying the orders of my leader', in reality the truth may be more complex. The leader has a role, as will be demonstrated below, but it may be pressure from peers that is the most decisive factor. Peer pressure probably accounts for the behaviour of football hooligans – when did you last see a football hooligan – i.e. acting purely on his (or her) own with no peers in the vicinity?

The importance of peer pressure in advertising and purchase decisions has been discussed by Cartwright (2001), who has stressed that the benefit conferred by a purchase may be more related to the degree of conformity with peers and their acceptance of the individual through the artefacts used by that individual than the more tangible uses for the product. There are many brands of training shoe available but some of them have become a team/group uniform and are thus bought for their logo rather than comfort and practical use.

Group cohesiveness dictates a considerable degree of peer conformity. The problems occur when the behaviour required by the group becomes unacceptable to the wider community.

A team may be considered as being surrounded by a **boundary of conformability**. This is a flexible boundary but the flexibility goes only so far. If a team member attempts to stretch the boundary too far then peer pressure will pull them back. The closer a team member comes to breaking out of the boundary, the stronger the pull from the team to bring that member back into the centre. If however the member is influential it is possible that the whole team can be pulled over the boundary in a form of mass defection.

It is often useful in cases of mergers and take-overs to identify the most influential member of any team that appears resistant to the new regime and to work on that member so that they will bring the whole team across the boundary and thus provide a functioning team in a new scenario.

In biological terms the team boundary acts like a semi-permeable membrane, as it will allow for limited movement of members and also of ideas both into and out of the team.

Chapter 5 considers how individuals cope with the membership of different teams and it is important to realise that each team will have a boundary and that it can be difficult for an individual to move easily across boundaries especially if the objectives and culture of the various teams they belong to are at variance with each other.

Hierarchical groupthink

Later chapters of this book consider the importance and roles of leadership. While the Prime Minister of the UK may be termed *primus inter pares* – i.e. first among equals – it is a fact that primate and many other animal societies need a recognised leader and thus have a hierarchical structure. The effect of the wishes and belief system of the leader must be taken into account when considering groupthink as a phenomenon.

The influential force for cohesion that the leader can bring to bear on an individual or a grouping of individuals within the team is likely to be stronger than that between those lower down in the hierarchy. Indeed if it were not, the leader's position would be very precarious as shown by the leadership rules put forward by Morris (1969), to be discussed in Chapter 8.

Fear of or an attempt to curry favour with the leader is an important component of groupthink. Leaders often have very strongly held ideas and it may be a brave team member who is prepared to criticise the leader's proposed course of action. Nevertheless, as Chapter 6 will show, when considering team roles, an effective leader will nourish and control constructive criticism rather than subjugate it.

In 1930 the British Airship R101 crashed in France early on its first voyage from the UK to India. Stewart (1986) makes the point that the airship's commander, Flight Lieutenant H. C. Irving, could hardly have been unaware of the dangers facing the craft on its voyage and of the previous problems of weight and construction. It is interesting to note that Stewart lists the passengers on that fateful voyage who included:

- Brigadier General, The Right Honourable Lord Thompson – Secretary of State for Air and Viceroy of India (designate)
- Sir W Sefton Branker – Director of Civil Aviation
- Wing Commander R. B. B. Colmore – Director of Airship Development.

Major G. H. Scott was also on board and was technically in charge of the flight but not of the running of the craft. While this may seem strange, it is a device for dividing responsibility often used in commercial and military organisations. An admiral will be in charge of a fleet but is not allowed to give orders to a sailor on board the flagship unless that sailor is a member of the Admiral's staff. The ship remains under the command of its Captain. Large capital ships used to be built with two bridges, one from which the captain commanded the ship and the other from which an admiral could command the squadron or fleet.

As none of the senior staff survived, one can only surmise the hierarchical pressure that was placed on Irvine to continue a flight against what Stewart considers must have been his better judgement. Lord Thomson appeared determined to travel to India on the R101 to a timetable dictated by political rather than safety considerations. Such risk-taking and a belief in invulnerability is, of course indicative of groupthink.

It can be seen that there are two components acting on an individual to conform, *peer pressure* and *hierarchical pressure*. It is possible that a situation can arise in which nobody agrees with the decision, and yet it is carried out. It may even be that the leader is not sure and yet feels that something must be done or else s/he will appear weak and ineffectual. The authority of leadership, as discussed earlier in this book, may be such that team members are unwilling to voice their concerns in public. The result is often that the team goes along with the decision but that individuals record their reservations privately (often in writing) so as not to be judged too harshly in any future analysis of the situation.

Think/discussion point

This is an activity to try when you are chair of a meeting or leader of a group.

- Express a firmly held opinion and see if the discussion ends up with the team members agreeing with you.
- Now, change your mind, and argue for a different course of action. What happens?
- How many team members change their minds?
- Discuss this with your team and record their rationalisation of their change of mind.

Group inertia

A group that is overwhelmed with a need for important decisions may suffer from such an overload that it either fragments or ceases to function and operates in a dream world. The behaviour of the senior members of the Argentinean Government following Britain's response to their invasion of the Falkland Islands in 1982 is such an example (Hastings and Jenkins 1983). What had been a very decisive, focused team suddenly became, almost overnight incapable of producing a rational decision. In many ways this inertia is the opposite of synergy, and can occur when a previously successful team is confronted with a major failure.

Janis also demonstrated that in addition to invulnerability and the *self-censorship* of group members that made them unwilling to speak up, groupthink also manifested itself in three other ways:

Rationalising away data that conflicts with the group's own beliefs

This is a common trait: 'if we don't believe it, it doesn't matter.' The sinking of the *Titanic* mentioned earlier is all the more remarkable because of the fact that the senior team on board had received a number of ice warnings during the day of the collision. They chose to either ignore them completely or to take inadequate steps to protect the ship.

Janis also introduced the concepts of 'mind guard', often senior members of the group whose role it is to prevent unacceptable information reaching the group. In a small team this may be a very unofficial and unplanned role but in governments it may be formalised through official censorship. Unbelievable as it may seem, in 1914 the British Admiralty attempted to suppress the fact that the new battleship *HMS Audacious* had struck a mine and sunk off the coast of Northern Ireland. The *Audacious* took nearly 12 hours before she eventually blew up and sank. During that time the White Star liner, RMS Olympic (the sister of the *Titanic*) had assisted in the rescue operation and a number of the US citizens on board the *Olympic* had taken photographs. Nevertheless, the mind guards in the British government believed that they could keep the sinking secret, less for fear of the Germans knowing but because of the effect on their own citizens. Needless to say the censorship attempts failed.

That mind guards are still in place is shown by the attempts to stop the publication of books and articles deemed detrimental to the state, often for fear that they will provide members of society with unpalatable facts. That governments persist in such actions in the era of the Internet is testimony to the wish to control what the group hears and sees.

An almost unshakeable belief in the inherent morality displayed by the group

Teams need outside scrutiny not only on what they do but also on the value system that underlies actions. Much ethical behaviour is cultural in origin. What one team or group do in a particular culture may be unacceptable if performed in another country. The morality aspect is important to understanding how individual and team behaviour can differ. If members of the team believe something is acceptable then the individual is actually behaving in an ethical manner, as defined by the team, in conforming. Yablonsky's classic study of Chicago street gangs showed that members obeyed a very rigid set of rules and had a definable moral code – it was just that it was a different moral code to those sharing society with them! As Chapter 5 will show, rules and values are very important components in team development.

Stereotyping

Groups and teams often stereotype non-members and members of other groups and teams in a derogatory manner. The 'hate' shown by members of opposing football teams can be testimony to this. Demonising an enemy has long been a military tactic and is even applied to commercial competitors.

When one team begins to believe that they are somehow better in all respects than another then behaviour patterns may begin to reflect that perception. The demonisation of racial groups by the Nazi regime in Germany (and others since, notably in Rwanda and the former Yugoslavia) brings about the appalling spectre of one team believing it has the moral authority to eliminate another due to its supposedly superior belief system.

Think/discussion point

- Have you ever been affected by or the victim of groupthink?
- How did the phenomenon manifest itself?

Mitigating against the effects of groupthink

Groupthink can be militated against by sensitive leadership, effective communication between team members and the encouragement of mutual trust.

If members feel that they can express an opinion that may be contrary to that they perceive as being held by their colleagues and not then suffer for their views, it stands to reason that they will be more likely to be forthcoming. The leader needs to encourage an atmosphere where constructive disagreement can occur. Naturally there need to be rules as to how such disagreements are introduced, debated and resolved, to ensure that no member of the team feels that they are being ignored or browbeaten.

A relatively simple but effective step that can be taken to counteract any tendency to groupthink is for the leader to ask for opinions from more extreme subordinates before the more senior team members. If a newly joined member has heard the leader express opinion A followed by agreement from the senior members of the team, he or she will be under considerable pressure to concur and not to express opinion B. If they were asked first without the leader or senior team members expressing a view, they might be more forthright.

The importance of achieving WIN–WIN situations will be discussed in Chapter 10 and such mutually beneficial conflict resolution will help to generate an atmosphere that mitigates against groupthink.

The leader also has a major role in ensuring that the team's language and behaviour respects other groups and teams and should not encourage the scapegoating of groups outwith his or her team. Unfortunately leaders have often encouraged members of their group to turn on others as a means of deflecting criticism of their leadership.

Finally, any team building exercises should include a study and analysis of groupthink. The author's experience working with a large number of organisational teams suggests that if teams are aware of the dangers of groupthink they can guard against them. The biggest problem comes when the members are unaware that the phenomenon exists and thus take no steps to protect themselves against its manifestation.

Group dynamics: a summary of the history

In the years 1918–39, and especially following the conclusion of the Second World War, a considerable degree of research began to be undertaken into the difference between group behaviour and that of individuals, and a new vocabulary grew up related to the ideas of group dynamics. Researchers looked at the advantages and disadvantages of working in groups and a set of clear ideas began to form. Sherif (1936) was one of the first to use the concept of *social control* through group norms. His experiments using moving lights in dark rooms to produce an autokinetic effect showed how individual perceptions were modified by other members of the group so as to produce a group result – i.e. members of the group saw a light moving in the same way despite differences in vision and perception. Following on from Mayo's work at General Electric covered in Chapter 2, Roethlisberger and Dickson, writing in 1964, concluded after studying a series of work groups that deviance by individuals was carefully regulated by the group and that the mechanisms by which internal control was exercised varied. Perhaps the most important were sarcasm, 'binging' and ridicule. Through such devices pressure was brought to bear upon those individuals who deviated from the group's norm of acceptable conduct. Handy (1976) has catalogued the manner of socialisation used within the US Coast Guard Academy, with its concentration on the subjugating of the individual to group values and culture.

The ease with which a group is able to obtain conformity from its members, can of course be of considerable disadvantage. Asch's 1951 experiments, whereby participants appeared willing to back incorrect statements which emanated from the group, especially when the individuals perceived themselves to be of lower status, highlighted the strength of adherence to group norms.

Yablonsky's classic study of street gangs (1961), cited earlier in this chapter, showed how clearly the power of the group manifests itself, and not only for good. He found that adherence to the gang's norms could easily transcend other accepted societal norms, sometimes with tragic consequences, and that fear of retribution from other gang members, especially rejection, could easily produce aberrant behaviour.

That human beings are a social animal and are thus subject to group as opposed to personal pressures has long been known. It was the Count d'Cavour writing in the nineteenth century who said: 'What scoundrels we would be if we did for ourselves what we do for Italy.' Such an excuse has been used by war criminals ever since: we were not acting for ourselves but for the group. Richard Dawkins (1976) argues that the innate group response whereby individuals subjugate themselves to the group and will even sacrifice themselves for the good of the group is really a form of selfishness and that group membership is the ultimate in selfish individual behaviour, whereby, at the end of the day, the individual is really interested only in *self-survival*; if all the individuals in a group act this way, then the group itself is likely to survive and be a strong group.

Given that the group 'instinct' is so strong within the primates, it is of little surprise that it has become the subject of considerable interest in regard to the study of human behaviour, especially in the fields of psychology, sociology and organisational behaviour.

The post-Second World War studies of groups have shown that groups are far more prone to risk-taking than individuals. This can be both an advantage and a disadvantage. In a fast-moving business environment, an increased propensity to take risks may give an organisation a considerable strategic advantage. The success of many Japanese businesses since 1945 has been attributed in part to their willingness to experiment and take risks compared with their Western competitors (Pascale and Athos, 1981). The degree to which groups can take risks is perhaps contingent upon the culture of the organisation. A machine or professional bureaucracy, with its tight structure and rules, is less adaptable to both change and risk-taking.

Mintzberg (1983) saw bureaucracies in terms of a clear basic organisational configuration. He saw the main characteristics as highly specialised, routine operating tasks, formalised procedures, a proliferation of rules, regulations and formalised communications throughout the organisation. He believed that such organisations developed large-sized units at the operating level with reliance on functional roles for grouping tasks and a relatively centralised power structure for decision-making with an elaborate administrative structure, displaying a sharp distinction between line employees and staff members who fulfilled support duties.

Such a cultural environment is hardly conducive to taking risks whereas the more organic organisations, operating in less stable and rapidly changing setups, have needed to adopt less defined structures and a *matrix approach* where multi-disciplinary groups are able to flourish and be more entrepreneurial. Such organisations are found to the more organic end of the mechanistic–organic continuum proposed by Lawrence and Lorsch (1967). A propensity to take risks can lead to considerable advantage to such organisations, provided that the risk 'pays off'; if it does not then disaster can follow.

The team as an entity

Groupthink is a function of the team (or group) as an entity and not of its component parts. It is as though the team were the entity and not the individuals that make it up. The longer a team is together, the closer the bonds between members become and the more the team presents an unbroken, holistic image to those outwith its membership. This can present a problem for an organisation that has such a team in its midst as the team may begin to pursue agendas of its own and not those of its sponsoring organisation.

Friction with other groups

Organisations desire that teams should be strong and cohesive. However if the team becomes too cohesive it may (collectively) see other teams within the organisation not as colleagues but as threats.

Sherif and Sherif's (1956) experiments using two groups at a US boys' camp highlighted the dangers that too strong a team identity can cause. Two teams, Blue Dogs and Red Devils were formed, each having its own bunkhouse. By deliberately manipulating the situation so that the Blue Dogs team always had an advantage over the Red Devils, within a short period of time there was considerable friction between the teams, eventually leading to fighting. Such experiments should be conducted with care, as it then took two days to bring about a degree of harmony.

The sponsor

It is rare to find a team that does not have a sponsor outwith its membership ranks. While the designated team-leader is a member of the team there may well be a more senior individual elsewhere within the organisation who is responsible for setting tasks and targets and providing resources for the team. A key task of the outside sponsor is to ensure that the team remains in tune with and operates according to organisational goals and norms.

There may be times when it is necessary for a team to operate outwith the normal procedures of the organisation. The so-called 'skunk teams' defined by Peters and Waterman (1982) were used by US companies to spearhead groundbreaking research and development. One US company set up a team to develop a major product that promptly ran up a skull and crossbones over the entrance to the team's dedicated premises to demonstrate their independence from corporate bureaucracy and the piratical (but completely legal) nature of their operations. Many special forces teams such as those operated by the British Army's Special Air Service (SAS) and the Royal Marine's Special Boat Service (SBS) operate in a manner far removed from more conventional military traditions. In doing so they are intensely disciplined and accept rigorous internal controls so as not to be at variance with the core objectives of their parent organisation.

A team that has come to believe that it is more important than the organisation may have outlived its usefulness. The longer a team is together without variation in its membership, the more it will develop an entity of its own and the greater the danger of variance with its organisation's objectives.

An effective team is one that listens to those from outside as well as to its members. Conflicts of interest can be avoided if the team is aware of its role within the organisation and the part it is to play in fulfilling the objectives of that organisation.

An organisational team has had a major success. To celebrate the team have planned a night out.

- Unfortunately, senior management want to present the team's work to a client that same evening and demand that the team attend.
- What should the team do?

Hypothetical situations such as this are always difficult to resolve without a knowledge of all the factors involved. However it is unlikely that the team will have achieved their success without the assistance and co-operation of others from the organisation. Important as celebrating success may be, the team should bear in mind the future business opportunities that a meeting with the client may produce. If the team insist on their night out, this might be perceived as saying to the organisation that the team considers itself to be more important than those who sponsor it.

SUMMARY

- The advantages of team work can be combined to form the concept of *synergy* in which the whole appears greater than the sum of the parts
- The disadvantages of group membership and team work manifest themselves through *groupthink* in both its peer and hierarchical forms
- Groupthink can be very *dangerous*, as history as shown, and needs to be guarded against.

QUESTIONS

1 Groups have both advantages and disadvantages – describe what these are, and how they may have implications in both work and social situations.
2 Explain what is meant by 'synergy' and describe the factors that combine to produce synergy in a well-constructed group.
3 'Groupthink is the price paid for synergy.' Discuss this statement, showing the factors that combine to produce groupthink and how its effects can be countered.

Recommended further reading

Further information on groupthink can be found in I. Janis, *Groupthink* (1982), and Paul Hart (ed.), *Beyond Groupthink* (1997).

■ ⋈ ◢ *5* Team development

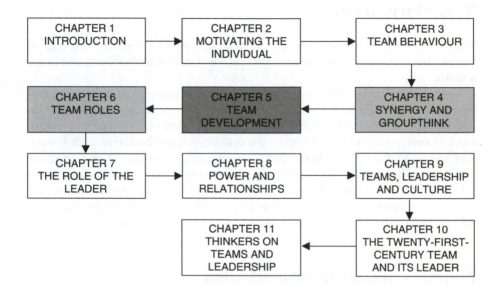

CHAPTER 1 INTRODUCTION	CHAPTER 2 MOTIVATING THE INDIVIDUAL	CHAPTER 3 TEAM BEHAVIOUR
CHAPTER 6 TEAM ROLES	CHAPTER 5 TEAM DEVELOPMENT	CHAPTER 4 SYNERGY AND GROUPTHINK
CHAPTER 7 THE ROLE OF THE LEADER	CHAPTER 8 POWER AND RELATIONSHIPS	CHAPTER 9 TEAMS, LEADERSHIP AND CULTURE
	CHAPTER 11 THINKERS ON TEAMS AND LEADERSHIP	CHAPTER 10 THE TWENTY-FIRST-CENTURY TEAM AND ITS LEADER

Learning outcomes – Team formation – The six factors of a team – Means of Communication – The team life cycle – The learning curve – Team building – The 'invisible team' – Loyalty – High-performance teams – Summary – Questions – Recommended further reading

---

LEARNING OUTCOMES

By the end of this chapter you should understand:

- The ways in which teams are *formed*
- *Cohesiveness*
- The importance of *communication*
- The need for a *sponsor*
- The steps that need to be taken before teams can *perform effectively*
- The concept of the *team life cycle*
- How team performance can *change* due to altered circumstances and new members

- *Team building* activities
- The *invisible team*
- The problems of *disbanding* teams
- *High-performance* teams
- *Sequential/dispersed* teams.

Team formation

Teams do not just appear, they are *formed*. Just putting together a group of people together, even if they have shared interests and objectives, will not make a team.

A team, as discussed earlier in this book, not only has common interests and shared objectives but is also bound together by a sense of *belonging*. Belonging is a temporal activity in that it takes time to manifest itself. Meredith Belbin, whose work is covered in detail in Chapter 6 has distinguished between work groups and teams. In *Beyond the Team* (2000) he concludes that size is an important determinate between groups and teams, as is selection (teams tend to be actively selected whereas it is much easier to become a group member. While the members of a group may have shared objectives, it is the *interdependence* of team members on each other that makes teams much more cohesive.

Purpose – organisational motivation

The reason organisations set up teams is to gain *synergy* from the particular grouping of people. Organisations want value for money, and the synergy of a well-constructed team gives just such value for money. It is also often easier to control a team than a set of individuals, but paradoxically if the team becomes too inward-looking it may then be difficult to control.

Individual motivations

Organisations set up teams to fulfil specific objectives. Individuals join teams for reasons that may or may not be connected to those objectives. Each person will have his or her own agenda for what they want to achieve through membership. They may wish to gain skills, interact socially or enhance promotion prospects. One of the tasks of the team as an entity is to ensure that these motivations can be achieved without disadvantaging other team members or detracting from the team's main objectives as defined by the organisation. The cohesion of a team comes as the objectives of the individuals coalesce with the team's objectives. At this stage the team begins to appear as an *entity*.

The six factors of a team

In any team, six factors are in operation:

- The *team's objectives*
- The *members' objectives*
- The *personalities* of the members
- The *skill mix* of the members
- *Communication*
- Outside *sponsorship*.

Objectives

Objectives were discussed above. The team's objectives will be its guiding force – they are what it will have been set up to achieve and while the team may be able to modify them in the light of experience they will probably have been set externally in the first instance, and in line with the organisation's overall objectives.

Individual objectives will vary with the motivation of the individual team member but it is important that they should not conflict with the team's objectives. A team member with conflicting objectives is likely to detract rather than add to team effectiveness.

Like all objectives they should be in C-SMART criteria (Cartwright, 2000):

- Customer-centred
- Specific
- Measurable
- Agreed
- Realistic
- Timely (i.e. with deadlines and timescales attached).

Think/discussion point

Referring to a team of which you are a member:

- What are its main objectives?
- Why are you a member?
- What do you get out of membership, professionally and personally?
- Do any of your own objectives conflict with any of the team's?

Personalities

After team and individual objectives the third team factor is the personality of the team members. So important is this factor in the success or otherwise of a team that it forms the basis of Chapter 6 of this book.

Skills

Every work role has a particular set of skills attached to it, whether they are technical, administrative, scientific, manufacturing, financial, etc. It is important that an effective team is able to offer a mix of the relevant skills.

Where the skills are not available from within the team they will need to be outsourced. It is vital that anybody brought into a team for a temporary period to cover a skill gap is made to feel welcome and a member of the team.

Think/discussion point

- How does a team you are a member of compensate for any gap in the skills mix of the members?

Communication

One of the most frequently heard complaints within any organisation is a lack of communication. Teams need to communicate both internally among team members and externally to the rest of the organisation and beyond.

Internal communication

If the team is operating in a regular face-to-face manner, communication should be relatively straightforward. Indeed as the team grows in cohesiveness it may be that members are able to anticipate each other's wishes. However at the very beginning, effective internal communication is vital.

One of the first people to look seriously at the way teams communicate was Alex Bavelas (1948, 1950), a follower of Kurt Lewin (see Chapter 11). The types of communication processes that can be applied are shown in Figure 5.1.

Handy (1976) states that the wheel will produce the quickest solution or conclusion and the circle the slowest. The all-channel is best for dealing with complexity and also provides the greatest satisfaction for team members as there is maximum involvement.

Both the circle and the all-channel, like the wheel, involve a key co-ordinating figure and if these mechanisms are used it is imperative that this person ensures that communication flows through them rather than stopping at them and

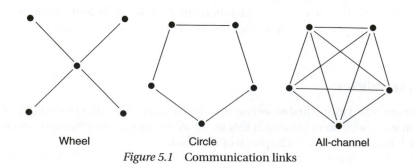

| Wheel | Circle | All-channel |

Figure 5.1   Communication links

that they do not abuse the power that being the information collecting point gives them.

Stott (1958) actually provides mathematical examples showing the effectiveness of each mechanism depending on an individual's position within the mechanism and his work is part of the recommended reading at the end of this chapter.

Think/discussion point

- Which of the communication mechanisms quoted earlier is the main one used in your team?
- Could communication be more effective if another mechanism were employed?

The importance of feedback

The way to ensure that a message has been understood is to request *feedback*. Just asking, 'do you understand?' is a very closed question and often receives a 'yes' response because the recipient believes that they have in fact understood. This can be a form of groupthink, as the recipient may believe that other members of the team have understood the message when in fact they haven't.

It is often illuminating to ask, 'In your own words, what have you been asked to do?' It is often possible to gauge understanding by analysing the subsequent conversation to see if both parties have ascribed a similar meaning to the message.

Noise

Communications both within and outwith teams are often misunderstood because something interferes with the process. Anything that interferes with communications is called noise. It may be actual physical noise that distorts the message or it may be bad handwriting, conflicting meanings – e.g. the old chestnut about the two builders, 'I'll hold the nail and when I nod my head hit it with the hammer!' Hit what? The nail or the person's head? Noise can be the use of dialect that only one of the people understands or it could be the differences between an apparent common language, British English ascribes different words and meanings than American English to certain things. As teams become more and more global in nature, these differences gain in importance. *Divided by a Common Language* by Christopher Davies (1997) is a useful guide to the differences between British and US English (Canadian, Australian and New Zealand versions of English are different again). Anything that distorts the message or prevents reception or disrupts decoding is noise. In any communication either between team members or with those outwith the team, noise should be kept to a minimum or eliminated altogether. This involves checking that the receiver can actually follow and understand the message. As will be shown in the next section on external communication, the use of acronyms and jargon are typical examples of noise. Professions and high-tech

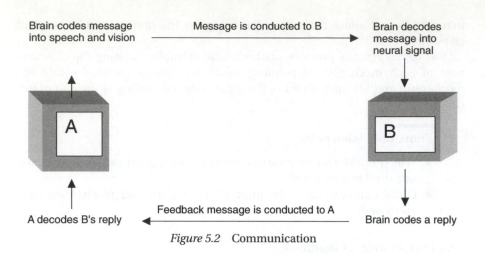

Brain codes message into speech and vision — Message is conducted to B → Brain decodes message into neural signal

A

B

A decodes B's reply ← Feedback message is conducted to A — Brain codes a reply

Figure 5.2 Communication

suppliers can often be accused of using 'in-terms' that they understand but outsiders don't (Figure 5.2).

External communication

Teams can become very insular and while having very effective internal communications, they may have difficulty getting their message across to those outside the team. As teams exist to fulfil organisational objectives, there is a need for an information flow both to and from the team.

One method teams use, often subconsciously to exclude outsiders, is in the language they use. Specialist phrases, technical terms, jargon and even in-jokes can serve to exclude outsiders and strengthen group bonds. This can be highly destructive to external communication as it can alienate those outside the team who nevertheless have to interface with it.

Fortunately people can often gain a sense of the meaning of unfamiliar terms and phrases by using the preceding and following phrases to set the term in some form of context. Human nature being what it is, people are often very reluctant to show their ignorance and ask what the term means and thus misunderstandings can and do occur. Anything that makes the receiver look foolish should be avoided, especially if the receiver is a customer, as a foolish-looking customer soon becomes an ex-customer. Plain English and jargon-free terms are the best way to build up relationships. Governments, both local and national, have gained a reputation for writing documents in a manner that makes them indecipherable to the average person and organisations such as the Campaign for Plain English have waged a battle on behalf of the man and woman in the street, in order to have official documents in a more readable and understandable style and format.

Language

As Trudgill (1975) has pointed out when referring to the work of Bernstein (1961), we all speak a number of languages, even if we claim not to speak a foreign language. We have a language type (or *register*) that we use at home, one for work, and one when with our friends. An individual may have a different language register for a whole variety of situations. Using the wrong language register can have damaging consequences – a person who used their 'drinking with friends' language register when talking to their senior manager would be in danger of creating the wrong impression. It is important that team members can use the language register of the people they are dealing with outwith the team, rather than relying on them, to learn and understand the language register of the team.

Think/discussion point

- How many languages do you speak?

  Include your native language and any dialects, foreign languages and language registers used at work, at home, on the sports field, in the bar, in your own thoughts, etc.

- What are the differences between your language registers?

Sponsors

When one examines the source of a team's power and authority it is often derived from somebody else in the organisation, usually in a high position within the hierarchy but not actually a member of the team.

As Colin Hastings and his team from the Ashridge Management Centre (1994) have pointed out, the sponsor of a team is a very important person as they can act as the mentor, godfather, smoother and resource-provider for the team. A sponsor with power within the organisation is able to transfer part of their power to the team and provide the members with authority that their individual positions may not allow for. A team sponsored by a powerful person will find that it has part of that power but it may also find that its actions are constrained by having to conform to any personal agenda that the sponsor may have.

Means of communication

Modern technology has greatly increased the speed and methods by which both internal and external communications can be accomplished. The advent of Email has meant that distance is no barrier to communication and thanks to the computer and the facsimile machinetime-zone differences have been made of little account. Whatever means of communication is used, however, the medium must suit both the *transmitter* and the *receiver* and relationships must be developed between people not machines. At the end of this chapter there is a consideration of dispersed teams. Technology has aided the involvement of people in team work even when separated by great distances. Whatever the communications technology used, social skills are often actually more important than technological ones.

The team life cycle

All living things and many concepts have life cycles – the product life cycle is a well-known example from the world of business.

Teams, as entities, also possess a life cycle. Early studies suggested a rather simplistic life cycle arranged around the 'orming' model of Forming–Storming–Norming–Performing. The author's experience with a wide range of work teams suggests that this is too simplistic, and that three other stages are also present – Dorming, Re-forming and Adjourning (the latter suggested by Bedian, 1993) or Mourning (Yeung, 2000).

The actual times and intensity for each stage of the life cycle will vary from team to team but the basic principles hold good for the vast majority of team situations.

The model starts prior to the formation of a team and in its revised format covers changes to team membership and the decline of the team when its purpose has been served.

To aid the illustration of the model, Figures 5.3–5.10 plot team performance against time, although it must be stressed that these are illustrative and not quantitative. Negative performance (when the life cycle line drops below the time axis) can be defined as a time when the output of the team is less than the inputs into it. In manufacturing terms, this can occur when more defective items are produced than correct ones.

Forming

The first meeting of any members of a potential team can be crucial. It is often tense. It may be that the prospective members do not know each other and even if they are acquainted either professionally or socially they may never have worked as a team before.

The key issues will be of communicating the team objectives, orientation and socialisation. Icebreaker activities may be performed as a means of the team communicating information about themselves. While there are likely to be many questions that the team members require answers to, it is also likely that individuals will wait rather than be the first to ask a particular question. A team leader may well have been appointed before the members are brought together and even if this is not the case it would be wise for a temporary co-ordinator to be appointed in order to give form and focus to the team.

The Forming stage is not usually very productive. Any 'performance' that there is will be due to individual rather than team efforts.

While the Forming stage may be relatively unproductive in terms of task objectives, it is a very important part of the team life cycle and cannot be omitted. Time needs to be made to ensure that the social relations within the team can begin to develop. Forming is best accomplished without any task demands being made. It can be quite helpful if a social occasion can be arranged to bring the team members together to meet in an informal atmosphere. Too little attention paid to the Forming aspect of the team life cycle may mean that the next stage,

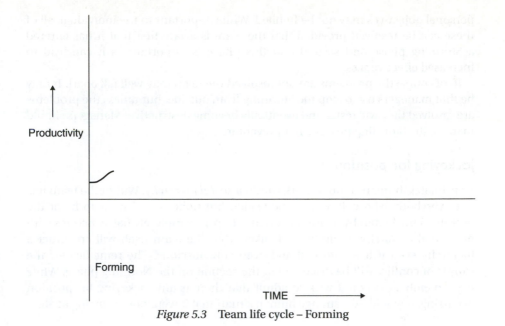

Figure 5.3   Team life cycle – Forming

Storming, lasts longer than necessary and that will be detrimental to the accomplishment of the objectives the team has been formed to meet.

The major process involved in the Forming stage involves development of bonds between the team members, the exchange of both professional and personal general information and the beginnings of individual orientation within the team. Forming is characterised by its social nature, politeness and the tendency to silence rather than discussion, as team members sort out the various positions and expertise held by the other members (Figure 5.3).

Storming

Storming can be the most worrying period of the team life cycle. In the most extreme cases it can appear that, almost at its inception, the team is riven with internal conflicts and falling apart. Paradoxically it is the internal tensions that, properly managed, will enable the team to emerge as a strong entity and that will aid later performance.

As Figure 5.4 (p. 71) shows, there can be a burst of performance following the Forming stage but in many cases it is a false dawn.

Due to the fact that at the Forming stage, what is called the team is in fact just a collection of individuals with their own agendas, preferences and ways of doing things, it is perhaps inevitable that conflicts will arise. Conflict is often considered destructive but in the work situation, properly managed and resolved, conflict can lead to increased effectiveness.

Conflict in teams occurs at this stage due to a jockeying for position among team members, inappropriate behaviour by team members and a feeling that personal objectives may not be fulfilled. While important to the individual, all of these can be resolved provided that the team is aware first that it has entered a Storming phase and second that this phase is important as it can lead to increased effectiveness.

If, of course the problems are not resolved the team may well fall apart. It may be that managers try to stop the Storming from outside, but unless the problems are resolved they will fester and eventually become destructive. Managers should manage the Storming process, not prevent it.

Jockeying for position

As primates, humans tend to work within a *social hierarchy*. Within the team it is not everybody who will want to be leader, but nobody will want to be at the bottom of the hierarchy. Teams are often set up as completely flat structures with no formal hierarchy at all, but it is likely that the team itself will construct a hierarchy even if it is informal and even subconscious. The remedies for the causes of conflict will be discussed in the section on the Norming phase. While team members may not wish to admit that there is any jockeying for position occurring, it would be a strange human situation if it were not occurring at all.

Inappropriate behaviour

Inappropriate behaviour can cover a multitude of sins, for example smoking in the company of non-smoking team members, offensive language, inappropriate dress and even sexual/racial harassment (both of which are not only in-appropriate but against the law in most jurisdictions). Whatever the form of behaviour, if it causing offence it needs to be dealt with.

One of the problems may well be that one person's normal behaviour may be deemed offensive by another. The importance of discussing such issues in the Norming phase will be discussed later.

Personal objectives not being fulfilled

While it may be presumed that all of the team members have bought in to the overall team objective they will each have their personal objectives that they wish to fulfil and an agenda to accomplishing this. If team members find that membership is not assisting them personally, this can be a considerable source of conflict. While team members may be unwilling to share their personal objectives and agendas, the team and its sponsors should ensure that an atmosphere exists in which people can feel free to express themselves. Norming (the next section) provides a mechanism for long-term conflict resolution and should lead to the Performing phase.

While conflict is on going in the Storming phase, whether it is outright aggression or more subdued, there are important things that the team can do to ensure that it does not become out of hand and relationships permanently soured. Too much conflict can sap morale and destroy a person's confidence and this leads to diminished performance. In extreme cases a disgruntled team member may even attempt to undermine the team's work.

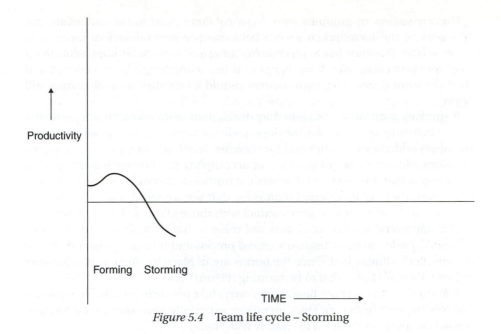

Figure 5.4   Team life cycle – Storming

From the team leadership point of view the aim in the Storming stage should be to bear in mind that:

- Conflict, if managed can be productive
- People who disagree on issues can still respect each other
- Openness aids resolution
- Listening is usually better than talking.

If these points are kept in mind during the Storming stage it is likely that it will be short. It may well be a painful period for the team but it will also be a learning experience.

Performance is likely to slump during this phase, as shown in Figure 5.4.

In the Storming phase the major processes are competitive, procedural and personal disagreements and even out-and-out conflict. This phase can be characterised by low morale, a feeling that the team will never work, impolite behaviour and even hostility.

The resolution of work conflict is covered by Ronald T. Potter-Efron (2000) in his book *Work Rage – Preventing Anger and Resolving Conflict on the Job,* a text that forms part of the recommended reading at the end of this chapter.

Norming

During the Storming phase morale may become very low. It will be clear that if the team is to fulfil its objectives then it will have to find a way of moving away from Storming towards Performing. This is accomplished by a process or phase known as Norming, a name derived from the setting of norms (or rules).

For any society or group to work together there need to be a set of norms, accepted by the members to govern behaviour. In general society we refer to these as laws. Storming has to precede Norming as it is probably impossible to set rules for every eventuality. What happens is that something causes a conflict and then the team decide how such matters should be resolved and what rules will apply.

If smoking is an issue, the team may decide that smokers can use a particular area. There may be norms for the dress code for the team, for the way in which members address each other and for meeting deadlines. Any part of the team's activities will have a set of norms that accompany it. The constructive part of Storming is that it is the team that sets the norms, and people are more likely to obey rules they set themselves than ones that are imposed from outside. The team's norms must not, of course conflict with those of the wider organisation.

The important function of norms and rules is that they allow conflicts to be resolved by reference to a *mutually agreed process* and thus the 'personal' part of the conflict is diminished. Once the norms are in place the team is in a position to begin its main task – that of Performing (Figure 5.5).

The team norms may not be written down and operate in an informal manner but it is imperative that all team members, especially new ones (se Re-forming below) are aware of the need to comply with them.

The main processes in the Norming phase are those of developing a working structure and relationships, the establishment of roles and the setting of mutually agreed norms. The phase is characterised by an easing of any tensions, the

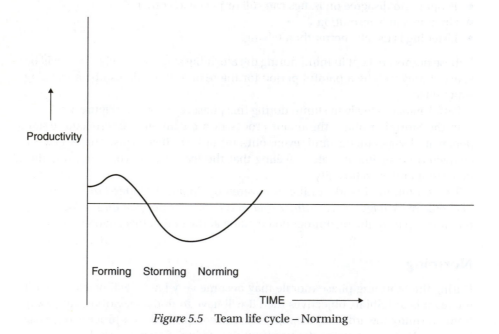

Figure 5.5   Team life cycle – Norming

seeking of consensus, a growing feeling of support between the team members and a feeling of unity.

Sanctions

As well as setting norms the team will need to decide how those transgressing the norms will be sanctioned and who will be responsible for it. In a well-constructed and formed team it may be that members will actually sanction themselves for breaches of the norms. It is necessary, however, to have a set of fair and practical sanctions in place. Often the feeling that one has let the team down is sufficient sanction.

Think/discussion point

Consider teams you have been a member of.

- Can you recognise the Forming, Storming and Norming phases?
- What type of issues caused conflict and what norms were adopted to deal with them?

Performing

Performing is what the team will have been formed to do. However, as has been shown it needs to go through the processes of socialisation, conflict and rule-setting before it can reach the stage where the team members can give the task in hand their full attention. In the Performing phase the focus is on achievement. The phase is characterised by a high task orientation and the smooth running of the team (Figure 5.6).

Teams that fail to perform will often revert to an almost continuous process of Storming. In these cases members may well attempt to leave the team as the atmosphere becomes difficult to work in.

Dorming

Many texts finish their discussion of the team life cycle at this point. The team is Performing and all is well. Even Bedian (1993) who has added Adjourning as a team life cycle phase has it following on from Performing. The author however, considers that there are two other highly important phases, the first of which he has entitled Dorming – from the word dormant.

However much management might wish it, performance cannot be continually improving. There is a stage when efficiency is either at its absolute maximum or has reached a plateau. Children in school do not learn at a regular rate. In one year there may be a huge progress made with less in the next and then another spurt. Plateaus are often psychologically necessary in order to consolidate information.

Obviously if the team remain on a plateau for a long period it has either reached its full potential or it has stalled in its growth. A plateau does not mean

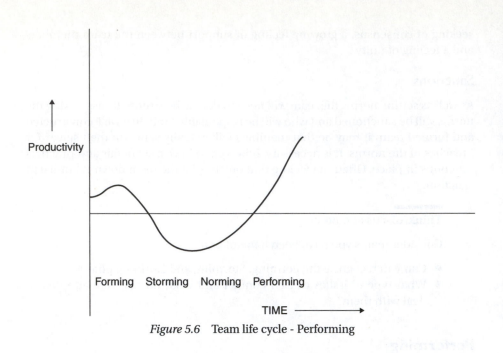

Figure 5.6   Team life cycle - Performing

that performance has decreased but that it has stopped increasing. If the level of performance reached is acceptable then no action is needed (Figure 5.7). It is only if it is clear that there is more potential to be gained that steps need to be taken to stir up the team to achieve higher performance (Figure 5.8).

A team that is self-aware may realise that it is in the Dorming phase and will be able to assess whether there is more potential for a growth in performance. If the team is not so self-aware then external managers will have to assess the situation to see whether full potential has been reached and, if it has not, what can be done about it.

A Dorming team may be very comfortable with itself and is characterised by very smooth operations but perhaps less dynamism than it displayed earlier in its history.

Re-forming

The problem the author faced with team life cycle models that ended at Performing was the issue of what happens when the team is disrupted in some way. While in an ideal world the team retains its original membership, in the real world members leave, new members join and sometimes old members who have been away owing to sickness, secondment and maternity re-join the team.

Working with a large number of teams the author found that what happens at Re-forming is that there are often mini-Forming, Storming and Norming phases before performance retains its original level or indeed, rises due to addition of new blood.

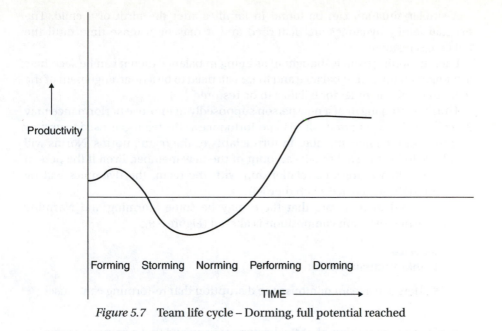

Figure 5.7   Team life cycle – Dorming, full potential reached

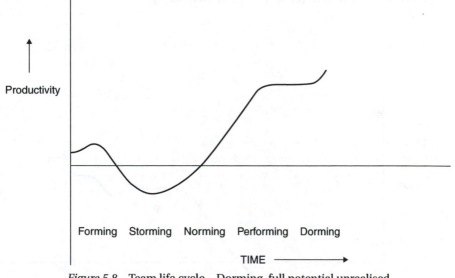

Figure 5.8   Team life cycle – Dorming, full potential unrealised

A similar situation can be found in families after the birth of a child. The original family dynamics are disturbed and it may be a tense time until the balance is restored.

If a functioning team is thought of as being in balance then it can be seen how a change can upset that balance and there will need to be a re-arrangement of the team dynamics in order for balance to be restored.

Thus the bringing in of a new person supposedly to improve performance may actually lead to a temporary drop in performance as the team gets used to its new member and the new member in turn adapts to the team's norms. Norms will also have to be adjusted to take account of the new member. Even if the person joining has had a previous relationship with the team, the dynamics will be different to those in place when they left.

Teams need to be aware that there may be some Storming and Norming required when the team composition is altered (Figure 5.9).

Think/discussion point

- How can a team minimise the disruption that re-forming can cause?

One of the simplest things that can be done is to ensure that a new team member or a returning member receives a proper and comprehensive *induction* into the team. Their role and the team objectives should be made clear and they should be given time to adjust to the team's mode of working.

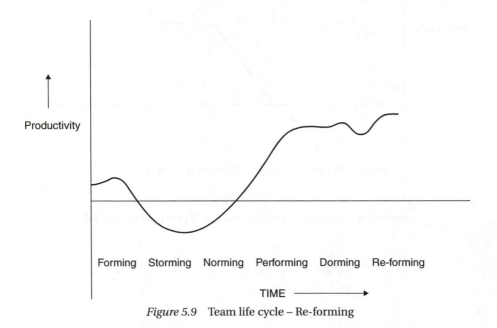

Figure 5.9   Team life cycle – Re-forming

Adjourning

While some teams may be permanent, albeit with different membership (the Manchester United football team of 2002 has no team members in common with that of 1982 but it is still Manchester United), having gone through a series of Performing – Re-forming – Performing – Re-forming stages, other teams reach a stage where they are disbanded.

Adjourning can be a difficult phase as the team is likely to have developed strong relations between the members. It is not unusual for these relationships to persist long after the team has been disbanded, with ex-members going to each other with problems rather than to their newer colleagues.

If a team is not meant to be permanent then this should be stated at the very beginning so that there is no doubt that it will be adjourned. This allows for members to concentrate on completing the tasks and fulfilling the objectives rather than diverting their energies into strategies for keeping the team alive.

If the team has been very successful there may be a feeling of euphoria about the achievements but as the final day approaches performance is likely to drop dramatically as the team members revert almost to a socialisation phase to get the last bit of comradeship from their colleagues. Once the team has been disbanded the greatest problem is its ex-members constantly referring to how good it was to be a member of that team, often to the annoyance of their new colleagues (Figure 5.10).

Yeung (2000) calls this stage Mourning, to reflect the fact that the breaking up of a long-established team can be quite emotional for its members.

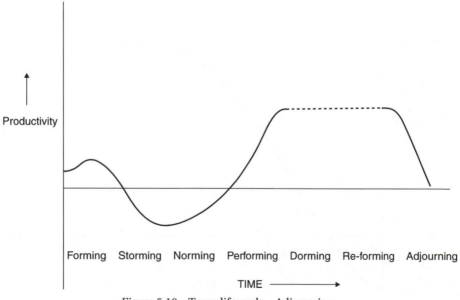

Figure 5.10   Team life cycle – Adjourning

The learning curve

We are all aware of the learning curve. The first time one carries out a task it takes an hour, by the hundredth time it takes 10 minutes. This is known as the *learning curve*, the time taken to do something decreases or the efficiency and quality increases over time as one becomes used to the task. As Clive Irving (1993) has reported, the first 50 Boeing 747 Jumbo Jets required a work force of 27,000 to build them while the 400th required a workforce of 7,500 and the smaller number could put the aircraft together quicker – that is the learning curve in action.

At the bottom of the learning curve a great deal of encouragement is required as it is probable that mistakes will be made. Mistakes are important to the learning curve as people learn more from things that go wrong than from those that are right first time. Negative productivity occurs when incorrect actions outnumber correct ones. The majority of learning occurs early on in the process, as shown in Figure 5.11. One of the advantages of team work is that the members can support each other through the learning process.

Team building

Like anything in life, the more that one puts in, the more one is likely to get out. Team building is a programmed activity designed to strengthen the team and aid performance.

There are whole texts purely related to team building activities, two of which are included as recommended reading at the end of this chapter.

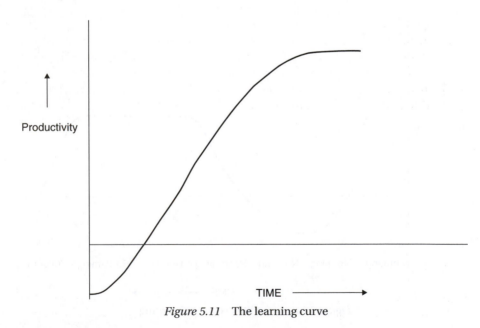

Figure 5.11   The learning curve

Such activities range from indoor construction and logic exercises to climbing mountains and using survival skills. While there are benefits from the latter there is a danger that the accomplishment of the task will become the objective rather than the team building aspects and that some team members will feel forced to carry out physical activities that are well out of their comfort zone. No doubt they will receive support from other team members but no team building exercise should cause fear in a participant. Psychological 'games' can also be dangerous. While they may encourage openness, they can also cause great discomfort.

It is well worth employing the services of an expert in team building, as he or she will be able to relate the activities to the objectives of the organisation and the team in addition to grounding them in the concepts and theory of team work and group dynamics.

The invisible team

On of the points made by Hastings *et al.* (1994) is the importance of the so-called 'invisible team'.

While the main team members may form a clearly defined entity, there will be others who have a relationship with the team and may be crucial to its success but are not immediately recognised as members of the team.

No team works in isolation. Everybody from administrative staff through to cleaners help the team fulfil its objectives. For every team member there may be a large number of members of this 'invisible team' (a team that can also include family members supporting the team member). Team members need to be aware of the contribution of the invisible team and to ensure that when praise and thanks are being given out that they are included. It can work wonders for their motivation. Just a simple thank you to the cleaning staff can ensure a spotless working environment! No person's contribution is too small to be acknowledged.

Within the limits of commercial confidentiality it is also well worth letting members of the 'invisible team' know what is going on especially if an extra effort is required from them. The author was once involved in preparing a major conference and made a point of briefing the ancillary staff not only on what was required but why the conference was important to the organisation. The result was a superb effort by everybody as they felt that they had some 'ownership' of the event and could see where their contribution fitted into it.

Think/discussion point

- Who are the invisible team that support your team?
- How much do you know about them, and how often do you thank them?

Loyalty

Teams rely on the loyalty of their members. A member who betrays the trust of the other team members faces being ostracised. Being ostracised is very damaging psychologically in view of the importance of belonging as a key factor in human motivation (see Chapter 2).

Teams engender loyalty but one of the issues with groupthink (see Chapter 4) is that loyalty to the team can sometimes override loyalty to the organisation. This is something that managers and team leaders need to be aware of and to guard against. The team should never be bigger than the organisation. A new member of the team will have to build up loyalty – it does not come as given, but must be earned.

High-performance teams

As will be shown when discussing the work of Meredith Belbin in Chapter 6, some teams perform badly, some are average and others are high-performance teams. The point will be made in Chapter 6 that the team composition and balance has an important role in assisting a team to become a high performance one but there are other factors.

Colin Hastings and his colleagues from the Ashridge Management Centre (1994) have postulated a series of factors leading to the development of what they have termed 'Superteams' (their work forms part of the recommended reading at the end of this chapter.

The important factors that they considered lead to a high-performance team were:

- Negotiating success criteria
- Managing the outside
- Planning the what
- Planning the how
- Leading the team
- Membership
- The team together
- The team apart.

Negotiating success criteria

High-performance teams know what their success criteria are. They may have been imposed from above but the team will have negotiated with their sponsor to ensure that they can be met and that they are in the C-SMART criteria introduced in Chapter 2. The team will also have monitoring procedures in place so that members can judge how they are doing.

There is no doubt that success breeds success. A degree of failure can be tolerated, but too much failure leads to demotivation. If success criteria are specified in advance then every team member should know what is expected of them. High-performance teams set high achievement targets and expect team members to meet them. They are also excellent at supporting those who are having problems, provided that they show potential.

Connected with this is the psychological contract between team members.

Psychological contracts were discussed in Chapter 2 and are very important in the relationship between team members. Usually unspoken, they are nevertheless the glue that motivates team members not to let the team down.

Managing the outside

High-performance teams understand the importance of managing the outside environment and the importance of the *interface* between the team and the rest of the organisation. As covered earlier, such teams will also be aware of the role played by the 'invisible team'.

Loyalty, as described earlier is a very important facet of team behaviour but the danger of creating a 'them and us' or 'insider/outsider' situation should be guarded against.

The management of the external environment also means building up a network of connections and ensuring that there is sufficient flow of resources into the team. Resources are often under the ultimate control of somebody outside the team and the building of relationships with *key resource suppliers* is a priority.

Planning the what

There is a maxim in military circles that 'Proper prior planning prevents poor performance'. Hastings *et al.* (1994) state that high-performance teams start their planning from a belief that they will be successful and that any mediocrity in the team is immediately challenged.

The team will (as mentioned earlier) have set targets along the way to enable progress to be monitored and evaluated. One of Hasting *et al.*'s most important phrases is 'Milestones not Millstones'. The goals should be those that are *challenging but achievable*, and not become a millstone around team members' necks, so vast or unreachable that they feel automatically doomed to failure.

Resources will be marshalled well in time but not so far ahead that they will be lying around unused. High-performance teams not only have a clear idea of where they want to go, they have *planned the route*. Like all good travellers they will also have *contingency plans* in the event of things going wrong.

Planning the how

The how is about the dynamics that the team will employ:

- How will members be motivated?
- How will team bonds be reinforced?
- How will the team members communicate with each other?
- How will the team communicate to the outside world?
- How will the relationship with the sponsor be managed?
- How will conflict be handled?

A high-performance team will rapidly develop the strategies required to deal with this issue.

Leadership

Effective leadership is the key to team effectiveness and as such is the subject of Chapters 7–10 of this text where the whole issue is covered in detail.

Membership

The team role aspect of membership forms the content of Chapter 6 but high-performance teams also need to consider:

- The skill mix
- How new members are recruited
- How temporary members are made to feel a part of the team
- What happens when a team member wants to leave?

All important issues that need strategies in place if they are not to present major problems.

The team together and the team apart

While it is easy to envisage the team dynamics when the members are working face to face, modern teams may often be widely dispersed. Information and Communication Technology (ICT) using computers, video links and email has made it possible for dispersed teams to operate more effectively than in the past.

Adair (1986) differentiates between teams that operate, to a degree, in concert between the members who are closely located in space, and sequential teams where actions may occur one after the other or sequentially. Of critical importance is that a team member must be able to rely on another member of the team to have completed something so that s/he can carry out the next phase. Communication is a priority, but so is the development of a relationship of *trust* between team members who may meet only occasionally.

Team building activities at the start of the team and throughout its existence are a priority for sequential teams, as they allow the personal relationships upon which effectiveness will depend to be rebuilt and strengthened. The role of the leader, important in all teams, is even more important in sequential, dispersed teams as it is also a central linking role across space as well as within the dynamics of the team.

Think/discussion point

Is your team a high-performance one?

- If *yes* – why do you think it is so effective?
- If *no* – what needs to be done to transform it into a high-performance team?

Planning and diverse teams are also considered in chapter 10 – The Twenty-first century Team and its Leader.

SUMMARY

- Teams are formed for a specific purpose and should have clear objectives and success criteria
- Individual team members will have their own motivation for membership and a personal agenda
- The 6 main team factors are:
  - The team's objectives
  - The member's objectives
  - The personalities of the members
  - The skill mix of the members
  - Communication
  - Outside sponsorship
- Teams must have internal and external communication strategies
- Teams can often adopt their own language that can be uncomfortable for outsiders
- Teams have a lifecycle of FORMING – STORMING – NORMING – PERFORMING – DORMING – RE-FORMING – ADJOURNING
- Each phase of the life cycle is important
- Loyalty plays an import role in team effectiveness
- Teambuilding is used to form and strengthen the team
- Never forget the invisible team
- High performance teams have strategies in place to deal with:
  - Negotiating success criteria
  - Managing the outside
  - Planning the what
  - Planning the how
  - Leading the team
  - Membership
  - The team together
  - The team apart

QUESTIONS

1 What do you understand by the invisible team and why is it so important to overall team effectiveness?
2 Describe the various stages in the team life cycle. Why is each important and how can each be managed?
3 What are the attributes of a high-performance team? How can such teams be developed?

Recommended further reading

For a consideration of the management of work conflict you are advised to consult Ronald T. Potter-Efron, *Work Rage – Preventing Anger and Resolving Conflict on the Job* (2000).

Useful texts on team building are Robert B. Maddox, *Teambuilding – An Exercise in Leadership* (1986), John Adair, *Effective Teambuilding* (1985), David and Frank Johnson, *Joining Together – Group Theory and Group Skills* (1987).

An excellent guide to high-performance teams is Colin Hastings *et al.*, *Superteams* (1994).

◼ ⩔ **6** Team roles

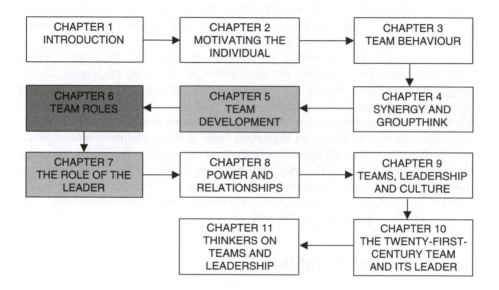

| CHAPTER 1 INTRODUCTION | → | CHAPTER 2 MOTIVATING THE INDIVIDUAL | → | CHAPTER 3 TEAM BEHAVIOUR |

| CHAPTER 6 TEAM ROLES | ← | CHAPTER 5 TEAM DEVELOPMENT | ← | CHAPTER 4 SYNERGY AND GROUPTHINK |

| CHAPTER 7 THE ROLE OF THE LEADER | → | CHAPTER 8 POWER AND RELATIONSHIPS | → | CHAPTER 9 TEAMS, LEADERSHIP AND CULTURE |

| CHAPTER 11 THINKERS ON TEAMS AND LEADERSHIP | ← | CHAPTER 10 THE TWENTY-FIRST-CENTURY TEAM AND ITS LEADER |

Learning outcomes – The difference between functional and team roles – Eligibility and suitability – Team-role theory – The team wheel – Belbin's work on team roles – Belbin's eight team roles – The balanced team – An extra role? – Team size – The Apollo Syndrome – Team-role sacrifice – Testing for team roles – Is one role better than another? – Team roles and recruitment/selection – The importance of team and work roles in the recruitment/selection process – Summary – Questions – Recommended further reading – Answers to the team-role pictures

---

LEARNING OUTCOMES

By the end of this chapter you should understand:

- The difference between *functional* and *team roles*
- *Team role theory*
- The importance of team roles in team *formation* and *maintenance*
- The preferred *team roles* of your colleagues
- The *allowable weaknesses* of your colleagues

- *Your* preferred team role and your allowable weaknesses
- The importance of a consideration of team roles in the *recruitment and selection process.*

The difference between functional and team roles

While some organisations still recruit general-duties employees who are involved in a wide range of activities, the trend since the middle of the twentieth century has been towards ever-increasing specialisation.

People are given quite specific work and team roles, with these often being formalised through a detailed *job description*. While many employees find a degree of security in having a detailed job description, Meredith Belbin, the international authority on team roles, has commented (1996) that in a fast-moving world, job descriptions and job specifications are often obsolete before they are even issued. This is an important issue. A job description cannot cover any eventuality and should therefore be general rather than specific. As roles and circumstances change, so the work employees undertake changes and there may not be time to issue new, detailed job descriptions and specifications. Far better to have an *empowered workforce* than one whose members need something to be in their job description before they will do it.

Eligibility and suitability

Traditionally people have been recruited based on their eligibility for a job on the strength of qualifications gained and skills acquired. In the modern, fast-changing world, skills and knowledge can quickly become out of date. Aptitude for learning new skills, personality and the ability to fit in with the organisation and the team may now be more important than measures of eligibility.

Team-role theory

As stated above, much of selection and recruitment has been concerned with finding somebody who has the necessary functional skills. Those responsible for recruiting have been preoccupied with the qualifications, experience and achievement of individuals to the exclusion of a consideration as to how the candidates will fit in with their colleagues. Even when this has been taken into account, too often it has been on the basis of an instinct. Some candidates may disqualify themselves through an obvious attitude problem or make it clear that they cannot work within the current organisational culture. Often, however, there may be those with similar attitudes and very similar qualifications and experience. How can recruiters chose between them?

It is likely that no one candidate will have every one of the functional attributes for a job plus all of the personal qualities the organisation requires. One of the advantages of a team is that while no single individual will ever be perfect, a well-constructed team may come much nearer to perfection. For this reason it is not the individual but the *team* that is the instrument of sustained and enduring success in management. A team can renew and regenerate itself by new recruitment as individual team members leave or retire, and it can find within itself all those conflicting characteristics that cannot be united in any single individual. It can build up a store of shared and collectively owned experience, information and judgement that can be passed on as seniors depart and juniors arrive. Provided that the members are aware of the team life cycle as discussed in Chapter 5, the team can exist much longer than its founding members. An individual may have only one lifetime but a team can have multiple lives.

Much of what people perceive as the reasons for team success is instinctive. People in organisations have a fund of stories about how often someone who has been highly successful within a team becomes a great disappointment when moved out of it. There are stories about effective teams destroyed by the promotion of individuals, without anyone ever considering the alternative of promoting the whole team or enlarging its scope and responsibility. There are few who do not recognise *synergy*, whereby a team produces a quality and quantity of work far higher than the sum of that which the separate individuals could have produced on their own.

What the work of Meredith Belbin, to be discussed throughout this chapter, has shown is that organisations, while not ignoring or neglecting the individual, should devote far more thought to teams: to their selection, development and training; to their qualifications, experience and achievements; and above all to their psychology, motivation, composition and behaviour.

Anthony Jay (1975) commented that the team, or work-group or hunting-band, was far more active in the modern organisation than most management sociologists or behavioural psychologists seemed to realise. However even having realised it, and having stressed the importance of building management structures around teams of 10 people or fewer, he believed that two central questions remained unanswered: How do you create a successful team? And why are some teams more successful than others?

The team wheel

Magerison and McCann (1985), Australian workers in the field of team roles, proposed that successful teams were structured in the form of a wheel as shown in Figure 6.1.

Under the team wheel concept, a successful team needs to contain individuals with the skills of innovating, promoting, developing, inspecting, advising, maintaining, organising and producing. This concept fits in well with the team role theory of Meredith Belbin that forms the subject of the bulk of this chapter.

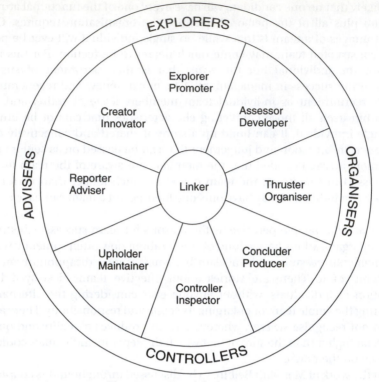

Figure 6.1 Simplified team wheel

Belbin's work on team roles

Meredith Belbin, while at the Industrial Training Research Unit at Cambridge, developed a concept that allows people to consider team in a new light. Basing his ideas on studies he had carried out at Henley. The work also provides a useful vocabulary for describing individual behaviour in respect of that individual's contribution to the team on a personal rather than functional level. Like Anthony Jay, the author of this book believes Belbin's work to be one of the most important single contributions of the late twentieth century in aiding the understanding of how human organisations work, and how to make them work better.

In 1981 when Belbin published *Management Teams – Why they Succeed or Fail*, the social climate was one that was tilted towards the individual and his or her motivation. The early ideas of Scientific Management produced at the end of the nineteenth and the beginning of the twentieth centuries had also concentrated on the motivation of the individual. The political/economic ideas surrounding Thatcherism in the UK and 'Reaganomics' in the USA (named for Margaret Thatcher the UK Prime Minister from 1979 until 1990 and Ronald Reagan, President of the USA from 1980 until 1988, respectively) also concentrated on the individual. The dominant political orthodoxy of the time stressed that people, as individuals, were responsible for their own destinies. These ideas, however, did not take into account the fact that individuals live and work in a society composed of groups and teams. Belbin's work showed the importance of a consideration of team behaviour, especially at managerial level.

Belbin's most important concept is that all members of a team have a *dual role*. The first role, the functional one, is obvious: an individual is recruited to a team because of his or her functional competence and skills – what they can do or know about. The second role, what Belbin refers to as the team role, is much less obvious, and yet in a sense we have all been aware of it, perhaps subconsciously, since we first started to work in teams. Most people would recognise that there are team members renowned for creativity, others for detail, others for their social abilities, yet others for being disciplined or challenging assumptions.

It is these team-role characteristics that formed the subject of Belbin's initial research. As first published, he identified and described eight roles as the only ones available to team members. The eight was later expanded to nine (to be described in full later in this chapter) as a result of more research with a large number of management teams. Belbin's work is supported by a huge volume of experimental and work-based evidence.

Belbin began his team role research at the Administrative Staff College at Henley in Oxfordshire, using the 10-week course for successful middle-managers with board potential programme as his research tool.

One part of this course was a business game in which eight syndicates competed against each other and periodically fed their decisions into a computer until finally the winner was found. In 1969 Belbin began to use this business game as a starting point for a study of team behaviour.

Having an interest in group as well as individual behaviour, but with no particular theories about teams, he enlisted the aid of three other scholars: Bill Hartston, mathematician and international chess master, Jeanne Fisher, an anthropologist who had studied Kenyan tribes and Roger Mottram, an occupational psychologist. Together they began what was to be a seven-year task. Over the years of his research, first at Henley and subsequently within the business world across the globe, Belbin learned to recognise those individuals who made a crucial difference to teams and to whose team types he gave descriptive names. 70 per cent of those observed fitted into the original eight team types, an indication that there was another type yet to be named.

Using psychometric tests to relate observed team behaviour to measured psychological traits and then to construct balanced teams, it became possible to predict team success or failure. The psychometric tests isolated four principle factors:

- Intelligence
- Dominance
- Extroversion/Introversion
- Stability/Anxiety.

It was the balance of ratings an individual achieved on these four scales, plus scores on a number of subsidiary measures, that determined which team role he or she would best fill. While everyone had a 'preferred' team role, most people had a 'secondary' team role they could display if no other team member had the role as their primary one.

Allowable weaknesses

One of the key concepts in Belbin's work is that of *allowable weaknesses*. Every team type has its strengths but each also has an 'opposite side of the coin' – weaknesses. Where these weaknesses are such that if they were removed it might also impact on the effectiveness of the strengths then they are allowable and need to be *managed* rather than removed. An example is the lack of attention to detail in the team type known as a Plant (see later). A Plant – naturally creative as he or she is – can be forced to concentrate on details but the danger is that the creativity will be lost. A more effective solution is to ensure that there is a team member whose strength is attention to detail (A Completer–Finisher) working alongside the Plant as this allows both to play to their strengths.

Think/discussion point

- In the discussion of each of the team roles that follow there is a picture with a 'thought bubble'.
- Try to work out why that particular thought has been associated with the team role. The answers are at the end of the chapter.

Belbin's eight team roles

The eight team types which Dr Belbin and his colleagues originally identified were:

- Co-ordinator
- Plant
- Shaper
- Monitor–Evaluator
- Implementer
- Resource Investigator
- Team Worker
- Completer–Finisher
- Specialist (added later).

Co-ordinator (Figure 6.2)

Co-ordinators was originally entitled 'Chairman', a term that was both misleading and would today be considered politically incorrect. It was misleading, as a strong coordinator may well not be the leader of their team. However, it is team leadership that such individuals are best fitted for. The name was later changed to Co-ordinator, a title that better expresses the nature of the team contribution.

Figure 6.2 Co-ordinator
Traits: stable, dominant and extrovert.

The Co-ordinator is the one who presides over the team and coordinates its efforts to meet external goals and targets. Co-ordinators are distinguished by their preoccupation with objectives and an ability to include all team members in discussions.

Co-ordinators are intelligent but not in any sense brilliant – and not outstanding creative thinkers: it is rare for any of the creative ideas to originate with them. They often display charisma, a concept to be considered in later chapters under leadership. Co-ordinators also possess natural 'people skills'. Co-ordinators are dominant, but in a relaxed and unassertive way – they are not domineering. They may, however tend to be manipulative, but in a covert manner. Co-ordinators tend to trust people unless there is very strong evidence that they are untrustworthy and they are singularly free from jealousy.

Co-ordinators have an ability to see which member of the team is strong or weak in each area of the team's function, and they focus people on what they do best. They are conscious of the need to use the team's combined human resources and synergy as effectively as possible. This means they are the ones who establish the roles and work boundaries of the others and also who see the gaps in the team wheel (see earlier) and take steps to fill them.

They are easy to talk to and comfortable with others. Their two-way communication is excellent. They are not compulsive talkers nor people of few words – they know how to listen actively.

One of the main roles of the Co-ordinator is to clarify the group's *objectives* and set its *agenda*. While they are responsible for establishing priorities in consultation with senior managers, they do not attempt to dominate the team's discussion of meeting the objectives. Their own early contributions are more likely to take the form of questions than assertions or proposals. They listen, they sum up group feelings and articulate the group's views, and if a decision has to be taken, they take it firmly after everyone has had their say.

Strengths of the Co-ordinator

Mature, confident, clarifies goals, uses available talents.

Allowable weaknesses

A tendency to be manipulative.

Think/discussion point

Consider those you work with.

- Is there a Co-ordinator among them?
- How does this person(s) manifest the role's strengths and allowable weaknesses?

Plant (Figure 6.3)

The title Plant was conceived when it was found that one of the best ways to improve the performance of an ineffective and uninspired team was to 'plant' a person of this team type in it. The Plant can also be thought of as the team role that scatters the seeds which the others nourish until they bear fruit.

The Plant is the team's source of original ideas, suggestions and proposals – i.e. the Plant is the ideas person. What distinguishes the Plant's ideas from those of their team colleagues is their originality and the radical-minded approach they bring to problems and obstacles. Plants are usually the most imaginative as well as the most intelligent member of the team, and the most likely to start searching for a completely new approach to a problem if the team starts getting bogged down, or to bring a new insight to a line of action already agreed. They are much more concerned with major issues and fundamentals than with details, and indeed they are liable to ignore details and make careless mistakes, an unfortunate allowable (if managed) weakness.

Plants tend to be uninhibited in a way that is fairly uncharacteristic of an introvert, indeed the first impression may be that they are extroverts. Plants are actually introverts masquerading as extroverts. The Plant can be prickly and

Figure 6.3 Plant
Traits: dominant, very high IQ, introvert.

cause offence to other members of the team, particularly when criticising their ideas. The criticisms Plants make are usually designed to clear the ground for their ideas and are usually followed by their own counter-proposals.

The danger with the Plant is that he or she will devote too much of their creative energy to ideas which may catch their fancy but do not fall in with the team's needs or contribute to its objectives. They may be bad at accepting criticism of their own ideas and quick to take offence and sulk if their ideas are dissected or rejected: indeed, they may switch off and refuse to make any further contribution. It can take quite a lot of careful handling and judicious flattery (usually by the Coordinator) to get the best out of them. But for all their faults, it is the Plant who provides the vital spark that can set a project in motion or the team in a new and profitable direction.

Strengths of the Plant

Creativity, ideas, good at problem-solving.

Allowable weaknesses

Communicating ideas and sticking to the objectives – can have a 'butterfly' mind that flits from one idea to another.

Think/discussion point

Consider those you work with.

- Is there a Plant among them?
- How does this person(s) manifest the role's strengths and allowable weaknesses?

Shaper (Figure 6.4)

The Shaper is full of nervous energy. He or she is outgoing and emotional, impulsive and impatient, sometimes edgy and easily frustrated. If they are not

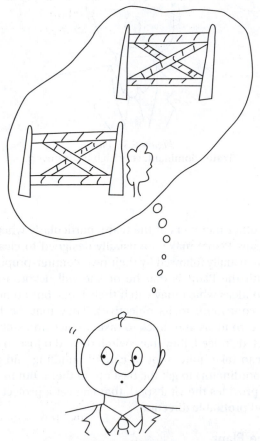

Figure 6.4 Shaper
Traits: anxious, dominant, extrovert.

the leader of the team they may constantly be vying with the appointed leader for that role. They are quick to challenge, and quick to respond to a challenge (which they enjoy and welcome). They often have arguments and rows, but they are quickly over and they do not harbour grudges. Of all the team, the Shaper is the most prone to paranoia, quick to sense a slight and the first to feel that there is a conspiracy afoot and that they are the object or the victim of it. The principal function of a Shaper is to provide shape to the team's efforts (hence the designation) and to provide challenges where necessary.

Publicly the Shaper exudes self-confidence although this often belies strong self-doubts. Only results can reassure Shapers. Their drive, which can have a compulsive quality, is always directed at their objectives. They are usually the team's objectives too, but then the Shaper, much more than the Coordinator, sees the team as an extension of their own ego. They want action and they want it now. They are personally competitive, intolerant of woolliness, vagueness and muddled thinking, and people outside the team are likely to describe them as arrogant and abrasive. Even people inside the team are in danger of being steamrollered by them on occasions, and they can make the team uncomfortable; but they do make things happen. The abruptness, rudeness and insensitivity are allowable weaknesses provided that the rest of the team understand them and realise that without a Shaper to make things happen the team will be less effective.

Strengths of the Shaper

Dynamic, outgoing, challenging, tenacious.

Allowable weaknesses

Prone to bursts of temper, insensitive.

Think/discussion point

Consider those you work with.

- Is there a Shaper among them?
- How does this person(s) manifest the role's strengths and allowable weaknesses?

Monitor–Evaluator (Figure 6.5)

In a balanced team it is only the Plant and the Monitor–Evaluator who need a high IQ, but by contrast with the Plant, the Monitor–Evaluator is much less creative. Monitor–Evaluators are likely to be serious and not very exciting. Their contribution lies in measured and dispassionate analysis rather than creative ideas, and while they are unlikely to come up with an original proposal, they are the most likely to stop the team from committing itself to a misguided project. Teams should always listen to a Monitor–Evaluator, for they are seldom wrong.

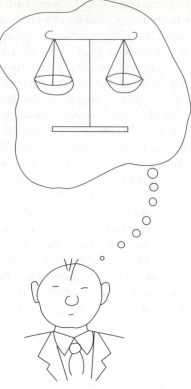

Figure 6.5 Monitor–Evaluator
Traits: high IQ, stable, introvert.

Although they are by nature a critic rather than a creator, they do not usually criticise just for the sake of it; only if they can see a flaw in the plan or the argument. Monitor–Evaluators are often the least highly motivated of the team: enthusiasm and euphoria simply are not part of their make-up. This, however, has the compensating advantage that ego-involvement does not cloud or distort their judgement. They are slow to make up their mind, and like to be given time to mull things over, but they are the most objective mind in the team.

Their most valuable skills are in assimilating and interpreting and evaluating large volumes of complex written material, and analysing problems and assessing the judgements and contributions of the others. Sometimes they can do this tactlessly and disparagingly, which does not raise their popularity, and they can lower the team's morale by being too much of a damper at the wrong time. Although they are not overly ambitious and have low drive, they can be competitive, especially with those whose skills overlap with their own, which means in most cases either the Coordinator or the Plant.

It is important for Monitor–Evaluators to be fair-minded and open to change, as there is a danger that they will turn depressingly negative and allow their critical powers to outweigh their receptiveness to new ideas.

Although they are solid and dependable, they lack warmth, imagination and spontaneity. Nevertheless, they have one quality that makes them indispensable to the team: their judgement is hardly ever wrong.

Strengths of the Monitor–Evaluator

Shrewd and objective.

Allowable weaknesses

May be seen as boring and lacking drive.

Think/discussion point

Consider those you work with.

- Is there a Monitor–Evaluator among them?
- How does this person(s) manifest the role's strengths and allowable weaknesses?

Implementer (Figure 6.6)

Originally designated with the title of Company Worker, the Implementer is the practical organiser. He or she is the one who turns decisions and strategies into defined and manageable tasks that people can actually get on with. Implementers are concerned with what is feasible, and their chief contribution is to convert the team's plans into an implementable form. They sort out objectives, and pursue them logically.

Implementers tend to be sincere and disciplined and known for their integrity and trustworthiness by their colleagues, and they are not easily deflated or discouraged; it is only a sudden change of plan that is likely to upset them, because they are less comfortable unstable, quickly changing situations.

As Implementers need stable structures, they are always trying to build them within the team. Given a decision they will produce a schedule; given a group of people and an objective they will produce an organisation chart. They work effectively, systematically and methodically but sometimes a little inflexibly, and they are unresponsive to speculative ideas that do not have visible immediate bearing on the task in hand, unlike the Plant who thrives on such ideas. At the same time they are usually perfectly willing to trim and adapt their schedules and proposals to fit into agreed plans and established systems.

The Implementer can be overcompetitive for team status, which can be damaging if it expresses itself in the form of negative, unconstructive criticism of suggestions put forward by other members of the team. Normally, however, they are close to the team's point of balance.

Strengths of the implementer

Disciplined, reliable and efficient.

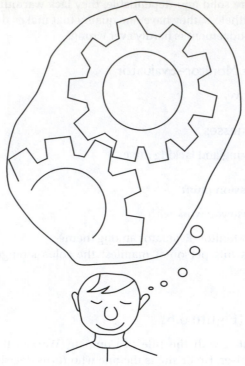

Figure 6.6 Implementer
Traits: stable and controlled.

Allowable weaknesses

Inflexible.

___

Think/discussion point

Consider those you work with.

- Is there an Implementer among them?
- How does this person(s) manifest the role's strengths and allowable weaknesses?

Resource investigator (Figure 6.7)

Probably the first team member to fill up their filofax and the one who is uncomfortable if parted from their mobile telephone or Internet connection. The Resource Investigator is probably the most immediately likeable member of the team. Resource investigators are relaxed, sociable and gregarious, with an interest that is easily aroused. Their responses tend to be positive and enthusiastic, though they are prone to put things down as quickly as they pick them up.

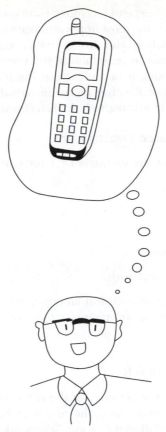

Figure 6.7 Resource Investigator
Traits: stable, dominant, extrovert.

The Resource Investigator is the member of the team who goes outside the group and brings information, ideas and developments back to it – hence their interest in communication's technology. They make friends easily and have masses of outside contacts. They are rarely in their office or workplace, and when they are, they are probably on the telephone, using email or surfing the Internet. They are the sales people, the diplomats and the liaison officers, always exploring new possibilities in the wider world outside. The ability to stimulate ideas and encourage innovation by this activity would lead most people to mistake them for an ideas person, but they do not have the radical originality that distinguishes the Plant: for all that, they are quick to see the relevance of new ideas.

Without the stimulus of others, for example in a solitary job, the Resource Investigator can easily become bored, demoralised and ineffective. Within the team, however, they are good improvisers and active and efficient under pressure. They can fail to follow up tasks they undertake in one of their frequent bursts of short-lived enthusiasm. Their range and variety of outside interests can lead them, like the Plant, to spend too much time on irrelevancies that interest them: nevertheless theirs is the most important team role in preserving the team from stagnation, fossilisation and losing touch with reality. The Resource Investigator has a vital role in maintaining the team's links with the external environment and preventing it becoming too insular. This role has grown in importance as teams have become more dispersed as new technology has allowed the formation of virtual teams linked electronically.

Strengths of the resource investigator

Gregarious, has many contacts, enthusiastic, good communication skills.

Allowable weaknesses

Easily bored.

Think/discussion point

Consider those you work with.

- Is there a Resource Investigator among them?
- How does this person(s) manifest the role's strengths and allowable weaknesses?

Team Worker (Figure 6.8)

The Team Worker is the most sensitive of the team – s/he is the most aware of individuals' needs and worries, and the one who perceives most clearly the emotional undercurrents within the group. Teamworkers also know most about the private lives and family affairs of the rest of the team. They are the most active internal communicators, likeable, popular, unassertive, the cement of the team. They are loyal to the team as a unit (though this does not mean they cannot take sides when there is a split) and support all the other members. If someone produces an idea, his or her instinct is to build on it, rather than demolish it or produce a rival idea.

They are good and willing listeners and communicate freely and well within the team, and they help and encourage others to do the same. As promoters of unity and harmony, they counterbalance the friction and discord that can be caused by the Shaper and the Plant, and occasionally by the Monitor Evaluator. They particularly dislike personal confrontation and tend to try and avoid it and cool down tempers in others.

When the team is under pressure or in difficulties, the Team Worker's sympathy, understanding, loyalty and support are especially valued. Their lack of competitiveness and dislike of friction may make them seem a bit soft and indecisive, but they also make them a permanent force operating against division and disruption in the team.

While the value of their individual contribution may not be as immediately visible as most of the other team roles, the effect is very noticeable indeed when they are not there, especially in times of stress and pressure.

Figure 6.8   Team Worker
Traits: stable, extrovert, low in dominance.

Strengths of the Team Worker

Makes excellent relationships, accommodating, non-threatening.

Allowable weaknesses

Can be indecisive.

Think/discussion point

Consider those you work with.

- Is there a Team Worker among them?
- How does this person(s) manifest the role's strengths and allowable weaknesses?

Completer–Finisher (Figure 6.9)

The author has a friend who is the ultimate Completer–Finisher. Both are interested in model railways. The friend built a 7 mm to the foot (O gauge) model of the London, Midland and Scottish Railway (LMS) locomotive out of brass. Finished in lined red livery it was complete to the (apparently) last rivet. The rivets were reproduced by carefully punching the brass from the reverse side. The model had pride of place in his house until he discovered that there were too many rivets around the cab. He tried to fix the problem but couldn't and ended up selling his pride and joy. Only he knew that it was slightly incorrect (it is doubtful if anybody else would have known) but once it was wrong, it had to go.

The Completer–Finisher worries about what might go wrong. They are never at ease until they have personally checked every detail and made sure that everything has been done and nothing has been overlooked. It is not that they are overtly or irritatingly fussy – their obsession is an expression of anxiety. They make excellent proof readers as they are good at checking details and ensuring that all the spellings and good are correct.

Figure 6.9 Completer–Finisher
Traits: anxious, introvert.

The Completer–Finisher is not an assertive member of the team, but s/he maintain a permanent sense of urgency that they communicate to others to galvanise them into activity. They have self-control and strength of character, and are impatient of and intolerant towards the more casual members of the team. They often find Plants infuriating.

If the Completer–Finisher has one major preoccupation, it is order; they are a compulsive meeter of deadlines and fulfiller of schedules. If they are not careful they can be morale-lowering worriers with a depressing effect on the rest of the team, and they can too easily lose sight of the overall objective by getting bogged down in small details. Nevertheless their relentless follow-through is an important asset.

Strengths of the Completer–Finisher

Attention to detail, meets deadlines.

Allowable weaknesses

Worries and can become overanxious and bogged down in detail.

Think/discussion point

Consider those you work with.

- Is there a Completer–Finisher among them?
- How does this person(s) manifest the role's strengths and allowable weaknesses?

Specialist (Figure 6.10)

The Specialist was a role that was added to the theory at a later stage. It will be noted that the original eight roles do not have any specialist skills attached to them. Any of them could come from any part of the organisation. Work by the author in 1992 (further information on the web site for this text) suggested that certain professions and jobs attracted particular team roles as discussed later in this chapter.

There are times, however, when the team needs specialist input – often for technical, financial or statistical reasons. The Specialist makes a valuable input at these times, as while his or her focus is narrow, it is very detailed and knowledgeable. Then the problem may arise that the Specialist is unable to see the larger picture.

Strengths of the Specialist

Single-minded, knowledgeable in his or her own field.

Allowable weaknesses

Can contribute on only a narrow front.

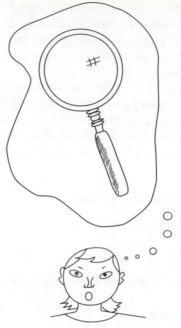

Figure 6.10 Specialist
Traits: Intelligent, introvert, stable.

___

Think/discussion point

Consider those you work with.

- Is there a Specialist among them?
- How does this person(s) manifest the role's strengths and allowable weaknesses?

The balanced team

The team role concept has been validated in both academic and organisational trials across the globe. When used in organisations, team role profiling has confirmed the special advantages of a full and balanced team. The absence of one of the roles obviously weakens any team, but equally the presence of too many of one type produces predictable kinds of failure: for instance, with too many Plants, many good ideas are produced but never taken up: a team composed entirely of Plants and Shapers may look brilliant, but will be beaten by a combination that is properly furnished with the less conspicuous and coruscating members who help to compose a full and balanced team. Too many Completer–Finishers and the team may have few ideas and can quickly be bogged down in detail. Too many Team Workers and the conflict that is actually necessary to maintain momentum may be missing.

- Based on what you have read above, what do you think your natural primary and secondary team roles are?
- Are there any roles that you are not equipped for?

An extra role?

Is it scientifically permissible to ask whether the Solar System contains a 10th planet that is so far from the sun that it is difficult to detect? Some astronomers believe there may be. In the same vein is the question of whether there is a 10th team role type.

The author noted while working with a large number of teams that when things became difficult, humour often helped to lighten the situation. This is particularly noticeable in military situations where the humour might be very black indeed and yet serves a vital psychological process by lightening the tension.

It may be that the Joker (Figure 6.11) is a necessary team role type. Like all team roles the strength of lightening tension will carry with it acceptable weaknesses, possibly involving inappropriate timing. This is an area that merits further research.

Figure 6.11 Joker

- Does your team have a Joker?
- If so, how do they assist team performance?

Team size

Most teams do not consist of 9 (or 10) individuals. Larger teams often split to form *sub-teams*. Smaller teams, if properly constructed, pose no problem as individuals tend to exhibit a primary team role plus one or more secondary roles that they can display if the role is not represented as a primary one within the team. An effective team can operate with three or four people if all the team roles are covered. Indeed a small, well-constructed team is likely to be more effective than a large one that has an imbalance of team roles.

It is important to note that the building of teams by the balancing of team roles does not carry the same importance in every kind of organisational activity. A group whose main function is to oversee a process that does not change much over the years needs less balancing than one operating in areas of rapid changes in the workforce, products, processes, markets, costs or where there is competition and need for quick decisions and actions. In the latter case having all the different team skills available in a balanced team becomes of vital importance. This type of situation is frequently found in the modern world.

The Apollo Syndrome

In *Management Teams – Why they Succeed or Fail* (1981), Belbin reported on a phenomenon he referred to as the Apollo Syndrome. He discovered that teams comprised entirely of highly intelligent individuals tended to do worse than other, more representative teams. Such 'Apollo' teams tended to engage in considerable abortive debate and the members were adept at picking out and exploiting the weaknesses of their colleagues. On occasions where the Apollo teams were able to recruit members based on team role concepts, they performed much better. These results suggest that just picking a team on intelligence alone may be counter-productive and that team roles and personality must also be taken into account.

Team-role sacrifice

In some circumstances, an individual will need to forgo using his/her preferred team role and adopt a secondary team role in its place. This may be necessary owing to the lack of a good example of a desired role within the team or because another person is already contributing a team role to a stronger degree. Such a shift from preferred behaviour is known as 'making a team-role sacrifice'.

Testing for team roles

Belbin developed a hand-scored questionnaire for testing for team types. While this was useful for providing insight into team-role preferences it was not possible to produce weighted results that could withstand statistical scrutiny. INTERPLACE® is the computer version of the hand-scored questionnaire and is based on similar questions.

The questions are divided into a series of sections 10 questions per section. For each section, the individual must allocate 10 points between the questions that best describe their behaviour.

The sections are:

1. What I believe I can contribute to a team
2. If I have a possible shortcoming in team work it could be that . . .
3. When involved in a project with other people I . . .
4. My characteristic approach to group work is that . . .
5. I gain satisfaction in a job because . . .
6. If I am suddenly given a difficult task with limited time and unfamiliar people . . .
7. With reference to the problems I experience when working in groups . . .

Reliability and validity of INTERPLACE®

Reliability and validity are concepts commonly used in evaluating psychometric tests such as INTERPLACE®. *Reliability* is a measure of the internal consistency of a test, while *validity* relates to whether a test measures what it purports to measure, in this case team-role preferences.

Internal consistency is highest where test items are repeated, but this narrows their focus. Rather than repeating questions, or dealing with items that are virtually identical, the INTERPLACE® software seeks to find *clusters* of useful forms of related behaviour. For example, the Shaper cluster refers to an individual who is challenging, competitive, hard-driving, tough and outspoken. However, that does not mean that everyone who is competitive happens to be outspoken.

Most Psychometric tests rely on self-reporting. However, here the behaviour assumed may not correspond with what others observe. The strength of INTERPLACE® lies in its emphasis on validity, for its counselling outputs are designed to take account of a consensus on observed behaviour from a number of observers, usually colleagues. This can be made evident by looking at how far the Observers agree with each other. Formal correlations are, however, difficult to calculate, as Observers are not required to make any fixed number of responses. Genuine responses are more easily obtained, and are more valuable, when forced choices are avoided. Differences in perception between the self and others provide valuable leads for action. There is clearly an issue when the individual believes that they are a Shaper, Plant and Resource Investigator and his or her colleagues believe that they show Monitor–Evaluator and Completer–Finisher behaviours. In such an instance, it may well be that the individual has an unrealistic image of himself or herself.

The author has carried out many hundreds of analyses using INTERPLACE®. Of these analyses approximately 85 per cent of individuals agree with what the analysis reveals, often suggesting that it is uncanny. This is hardly surprising, as they have completed the initial self-perception questionnaire! Of the 15 per cent who disagreed with the analysis, the colleagues of over half said that it was an accurate analysis.

The demands of jobs also have to be taken into account when assessing validity since the many varied forms of behaviour can be seen as effective or ineffective according to the context. Here the fit between the profile of the individual and the profile of the job plays a key consideration.

Is one role better than another?

The author's observation of organisations suggests that many senior managers are either Shapers, Coordinators, Implementers or Resource Investigators. A consideration of the strengths of these team-role types shows that they have the dynamism, motivational skills, discipline or contacts needed for those at the very top. This does not necessarily mean that other team-role types are not found as senior managers but it may be that Team Workers, Plants, Specialists, Monitor–Evaluators and Completer–Finishers may be less comfortable in such roles. No team role is better than any other, as it is only through having a balanced team that effectiveness is developed.

Team roles and recruitment/selection

In the modern constantly changing work environment, where job flexibility, team working and high individual performance are of vital importance, many traditional practices for defining and reviewing jobs have become ineffective.

Whereas previous generations thought in terms of jobs for life, authorities such as Belbin and Handy (1989) have described the current trend towards individuals having a series of jobs and even careers during their working lives.

As Belbin himself has written on the Belbin web site, 'A job is a continuous developing moving thing.'

The limitations of current procedures for setting up and recruiting to jobs are becoming increasingly recognised. The need for a new approach has come about owing to a realisation that the concept of a 'job' or 'post' is undergoing a profound change. The job and its administrative manifestations, the job description and the job specification, with its notion of a fixed work content, are being seen as too rigid for coping with modern circumstances.

Job descriptions and specifications often become obsolete almost as soon as they are written. They can lead to disputes over who does what and rates of pay and discourage initiative.

Using team-role theory as a starting point, Belbin developed the concept of Work Roles and the computerised system WorkSet™, a concept described in *The Coming Shape of Organization* (1996).

What is a BELBIN® Work Role?

Behaviour at work depends on a number of factors. Here three prime roles need to be taken into special account – the professional role, the team role and the Work Role. A Work Role is determined by the specific demands of the job. This can be shown as in Figure 6.12.

The better differentiation and definition of various aspects of the job provides a more effective means of communicating a person's Work Roles. The information is conveyed through colour.

Jobs also need to take account of changing circumstances. Here the jobholder makes an important contribution. Under the Belbin system jobholders are *encouraged to extend the boundaries of the job* in response to pressing needs of both the job and the organisation, to identify activities that contribute nothing of value and to put forward improvements. The complex and delicate nature of communication between manager and jobholder is facilitated by an extension of the core colour sets (Figure 6.13).

What is a BELBIN® WorkSet™?

WorkSet is the name of a computerised performance management system that has been designed to define and continually update Work Roles. It has been developed by Belbin, Barrie Watson and the BELBIN team and has involved extensive pilot trials in the public and private sectors in the UK, Sweden and Australia.

Just as Belbin's pioneering work in developing team-role theory provided a practical non-hierarchical, non-confrontational way of dealing with inter-personal issues, the same philosophy and imagination has been used to fashion a new approach to defining Work Roles.

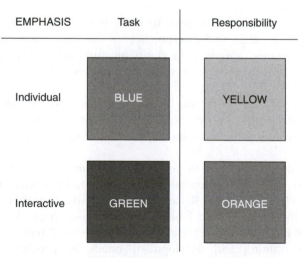

Figure 6.12 Work Roles

CONDITIONS		COLOUR SET		OUTCOME
MANAGER BRIEF TO JOBHOLDER	Comply with instructions and procedures	⇒ BLUE ⇒		Preservation of standards
	Use personal discretion and judgement to achieve an objective	⇒ YELLOW ⇒		Personal empowerment
	Provide help and support to others	⇒ GREEN ⇒		Greater job flexibility
	Joint responsibility and discretion for achieving an objective	⇒ ORANGE ⇒		Promotes team working
JOBHOLDER FEEDBACK TO MANAGER	Takes on additional work as deemed necessary	⇒ GREY ⇒		Adds value to job
	Uses personal initiative	⇒ WHITE ⇒		Innovation and improvements
	Reports where time is being wasted	⇒ PINK ⇒		Raises productivity

Figure 6.13   The BELBIN® Work Roles Colour Sets

How does WorkSet™ differ from traditional practices?

There are four significant differences to be considered:

1. WorkSet™ is designed to *facilitate feedback between managers and jobholders.* The use of meaningful colour removes the ambiguities that beset current practices. Lengthy job descriptions can be replaced by a much shorter, but clearer, jobholder brief.
2. WorkSet™ is a *dynamic system*. To meet the needs of today's workplace where the job needs to be responsive to changing demands, WorkSet™ adopts a dynamic approach to clarifying and continually updating Work Roles. This contrasts with the relatively static nature of the traditional job description.
3. Jobholders play an *active role in shaping their jobs*. Whereas traditional practices place the main emphasis on the manager in defining the job, WorkSet involves jobholders much more in shaping and developing their job.
4. The WorkSet Review leads to performance improvements. Recent research shows that traditional appraisals often fail to raise morale, motivation or performance. The WorkSet Review, however, leads to positive outcomes by involving the manager and jobholder in *two-way discussion*. This process culminates in joint decisions being made on how the job should be realigned and what training and development needs be provided to maximise performance.

Benefits of using Work Roles and WorkSet™

Managers benefit from understanding Work Roles and using WorkSet™ in the following ways:

- The encouragement of *personal initiative* by jobholders – within a clearly defined framework.
- A means of securing *more flexible working practices* along with the reduction of unproductive activities.
- Relief from the chore of writing *detailed job descriptions* and *job specifications*.

For jobholders the system provides:

- The opportunity to influence the *shape of their jobs*
- The possibility of using the existing job as the basis for *personal development*
- A method of ensuring that managers understand their *preferred working styles and aspirations.*

The system provides the whole organisation with:

- A method for implementing human resource strategies, where these focus on empowerment, team working and continuous improvement
- A colour language that improves comprehension, raises interest and improves morale, especially in a multi-cultural workforce
- Continually updated information on personal working styles and on current work practices.

Think/discussion point

- When were your current job specification and job description drawn up?
- When were they last updated?
- How adequately do they reflect what you actually do?

The importance of team and work roles in the recruitment/selection process

The team-role and work-role concepts are not just theoretical niceties. By providing an understanding of individual behaviour within a team they allow a non-prejudicial language to be developed. In addition the ability to test for team-role types provides organisations with a means of filling team gaps.

It is often too easy to recruit those who are like us when what is needed are different team and functional skills. Focusing on the benefits of a balanced team, team-role and work-role concepts allows managers to recruit people with both the functional and the team skills needed to assist the team development process discussed in Chapter 5.

More and more organisations are including INTERPLACE® or similar systems as an integral part of recruitment and selection procedures.

SUMMARY

● Function roles indicate the job that somebody *does*
● Team roles indicate the person's *importance to the team*
● Team roles are a function of *personality*
● Effective teams have a *balance of roles* within them
● Individuals display a *primary* and a number of *secondary* team roles
● Each team role has its *characteristic strengths* and *allowable weaknesses*
● Recruitment and selection should not be restrained by *job descriptions* and *job specifications*.

QUESTIONS

1 How can a knowledge of team role theory assist organisations in building more effective teams?
2 What is an allowable weakness, and how should it be managed?
3 Describe how each of the Belbin team roles behaves in a typical team situation – how can these strengths aid synergy?
4 Why are job descriptions and specifications becoming outmoded in modern organisations?

Recommended further reading

For more information about team and work roles you are advised to refer to the following books by Dr Meredith Belbin:

● *Management Teams – Why they Succeed or Fail* (1981).
● *Team Roles at Work* (1993)
● *The Coming Shape of Organization* (1996)
● *Changing the Way We Work* (1997)
● *Beyond the Team* (2000)
● *Managing without Power* (2001).

There are also software packages for INTERPLACE® and WORKSET® in addition to videos that illustrate the major principles.

Web site

⟨www.belbin.com⟩ is the Belbin Associates web site.

Answers to the team-role pictures

6.2 The **Co-ordinator** would like more than two as s/he has to touch every team member in order to get the best out of them.

6.3 The **Plant** switches on to ideas just like a light bulb.

6.4 The **Shaper** deals with obstacles – if they cannot be jumped s/he will go round them.

6.5 The **Monitor–Evaluator** balances ideas and suggestions.

6.6 The **Implementer** is like the cog of a piece of machinery. Often unseen, if the cog is not there the whole machine can fail.

6.7 The **Resource–Investigator** is a network person. S/he needs to be in communication with others.

6.8 The **Team Worker** is concerned with personal relationships.

6.9 The **Completer–Finisher** is a checklist person.

6.10 The **Specialist** knows a great deal about a narrow field – s/he can provide detailed knowledge.

◼ ☑ **7** The role of the leader

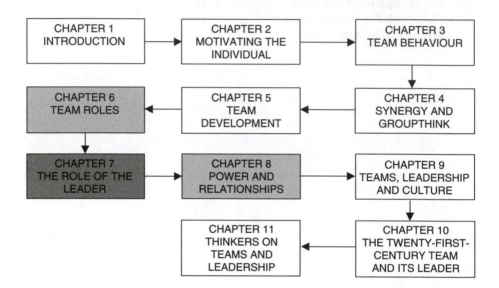

CHAPTER 1 INTRODUCTION	CHAPTER 2 MOTIVATING THE INDIVIDUAL	CHAPTER 3 TEAM BEHAVIOUR
CHAPTER 6 TEAM ROLES	CHAPTER 5 TEAM DEVELOPMENT	CHAPTER 4 SYNERGY AND GROUPTHINK
CHAPTER 7 THE ROLE OF THE LEADER	CHAPTER 8 POWER AND RELATIONSHIPS	CHAPTER 9 TEAMS, LEADERSHIP AND CULTURE
	CHAPTER 11 THINKERS ON TEAMS AND LEADERSHIP	CHAPTER 10 THE TWENTY-FIRST-CENTURY TEAM AND ITS LEADER

Learning outcomes – What is leadership? – The leadership spectrum and the leadership matrix – Traits of leadership – Becoming a leader – Styles of Leadership – the leadership continuum – The Managerial Grid – Linking the Managerial Grid to the Belbin team-role concepts – The work of John Adair – Contingency leadership – Leadership, power and influence – Summary – Questions – Recommended further reading

---

LEARNING OUTCOMES

By the end of this chapter you should understand:

- The differences and similarities between *management* and *leadership*
- Leadership *traits*
- Leadership *styles*
- The *leadership continuum* and the *Managerial Grid*
- Linking *Belbin team* roles to the Managerial Grid
- The *Peter Principle*
- *Contingency* approaches.

What is leadership?

In researching this section the author searched through a large number of volumes on leadership. What appeared to be missing from all of them was a simple definition of what leadership actually is. There seemed to be an assumption that the reader would instinctively know. This may be correct, but the author believes that it is important to set out a definition to act as a starting point.

Cleveland (1997) described leadership as both an art and a science, the latter because there are leadership techniques and skills that can be developed. He also saw leadership as an art that involves vision, risk and overcoming obstacles.

In the context of this book, a leader can be defined as:

'The person, selected or emergent, who moves others in the direction of goals that are clearly fixed as a vision in his or her mind and uses those others to achieve the desired end state.'

Thus leadership can be defined as:

'The movement of others in the direction of goals that are clearly fixed as a vision in the mind of the leader and the use of those others to achieve the end-state desired by the leader.'

Managers and leaders

Management and leadership are often confused. While there are similarities in the roles of managers and leaders, indeed they may often overlap, there are also significant differences.

Warren Bennis (1998), one of the most influential writers on leadership has described some of the major differences between managers and leaders.

Perhaps the key difference between managers and leaders as described by Bennis is that managers look *downwards* towards the bottom line while leaders lift their gaze *upwards* to the horizon.

Other key differences are shown in Figure 7.1.

Another point made by Bennis and one that is easy to remember is that managers *do things right* and leaders do *the right things*. While this is a powerful point, it could be argued that leaders do not always do the right things. It would be difficult to argue that Hitler's actions were the right things to do, but it would be impossible to deny that he was a leader.

The leadership spectrum and the leadership matrix

Experience shows that not all managers exhibit purely managerial qualities as listed above, just as those who are recognised as leaders do not show all of the leadership qualities. Many of those in senior positions exhibit some managerial and some leadership items. What is closer to reality is the idea of a *leadership*

Manager	**Leader**
Administers	Innovates
Maintains	Develops
Copies others	Originates
Controls	Engenders trust
Short-term viewpoint	Long-term viewpoint
Accepts convention	Challenges convention

Figure 7.1 Differences between managers and leaders
Source: Based on the ideas of Warren Bennis.

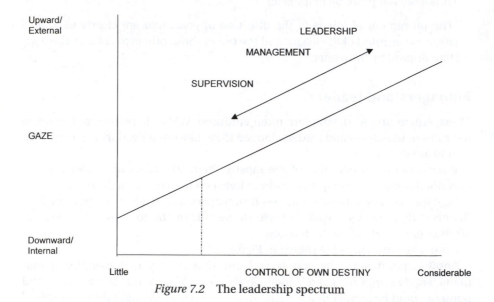

Figure 7.2 The leadership spectrum

spectrum (Figure 7.2) (not to be confused with the leadership styles continuum to be discussed later in this chapter). The spectrum ranges from administration through supervision and management to leadership.

Another means of considering the relationship between management and leadership is to see the concepts in the form of a *matrix* (Figure 7.3).

It should be noted that the matrix is *situational*. Those who aspire to leadership at work may well do so in other aspects of their lives. We shall look at each element of the matrix in turn.

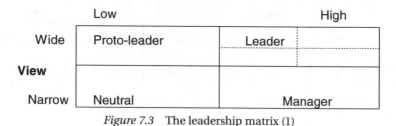

Figure 7.3   The leadership matrix (1)

Neutral

In terms of the work situation the Neutral is the individual who turns up, does his or her job and then goes home again. As stated above, this individual may have leadership abilities and desires but chooses to fulfil them in non-work situations, youth, church, hobby and political activities being good examples.

Such individuals should not be ignored as it may be possible for the organisation to tap into any leadership skills they possess. It is not unusual for managers to be amazed when they find that an unassuming member of their staff has been honoured for activities outside the workplace. They should not be amazed, as they should regard finding out about staff as a priority. Much useful experience and skills are lost to organisations because they do not know about the leadership abilities of staff members.

Manager

The Manager was covered earlier in this chapter. Managers have narrower vision than true leaders, but share the commitment to the goals.

Proto-leader

The Proto-leader has a breadth of vision but has not yet developed the goal commitment of the true leader. If he or she does so, then they will be better placed to fulfil their leadership potential.

Leader

Once an individual has moved into the leadership box their success will depend on a further set of factors as another matrix operates within that box, as indicated by the dotted lines in Figure 7.3 (Figure 7.4).

The second part of the leadership matrix concentrates on *communication skills and tenacity* – i.e. how resilient the individual is and how good his or her communication skills are. We shall again examine each element in turn.

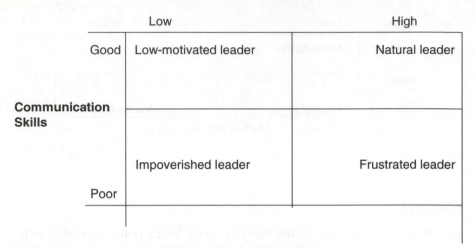

Figure 7.4 The leadership matrix (2)

Impoverished leader

The impoverished leader may possess the vision and commitment but has such poor communication skills and tenacity as to be incapable of generating the necessary drive in others. Their goals, however laudable are likely to remain unfulfilled, as the message never gets across to those who need to assist in meeting them.

Low-motivated leader

The low-motivated leader has the communication skills to put the message across, but lacks the resilience needed for the long haul. Again it is unlikely that she will be able to have the goals met although others, influenced by the strength of the message, may step in to take over the leadership role.

Frustrated leader

It is a lack of communication skills that let the frustrated leader down, as they are unable to put the message across. They become frustrated by this in the same way as a child does when he or she is unable to articulate their feelings. Despite his obvious oratory skills there are reports that Adolph Hitler sometimes became so frustrated that others did not follow his ideas to the letter that he became hysterical and appeared to eat the carpet.

Communication skills are the key to effective leadership – without them there can be no followers and one cannot be a leader without followers. Leadership may be lonely but it can never be solitary.

Natural leader

The natural leader not only has breadth of vision and clear goals but also backs these up with high tenacity and resilience coupled with excellent communication skills. Such an individual, given the right circumstances, is often the natural choice for the leadership role.

Traits of leadership

Authorities on leadership have been divided as to whether leadership is a naturally occurring trait or something that can be learned and is therefore available to the vast majority of individuals.

The idea of a *genetic leadership trait* that is displayed by a minority of individuals has been used to legitimise the idea of a ruling elite – traditional-type leaders – as will be discussed later in this chapter. It is more likely, however, that if there is a 'leadership gene' it is present in the vast majority of the population. As leadership and group dynamics are an integral part of primate behaviour the likelihood of such a gene is quite strong. Like all genes, however, its potency will be influenced by other genes and the external environment. It does not require much human ingenuity to move from the idea of a ruling elite, biologically programmed for dominance, to the concepts of eugenics and race put forward by Hitler.

The truth (if there is a universal truth about leadership) is probably somewhere in between the two extremes.

Even if somebody has all the requirements of a natural leader, as discussed earlier, they still need the right *experiences* and *education* and to be in a situation where they can exercise their leadership role.

What are the leadership traits?

As part of an exercise with large numbers of managers and supervisors, the author asked two questions:

1. Can you name a great leader from either history or the present day?
2. What are the traits you look for in a leader?

The results of this exercise, carried out a number of times over a period of years were very interesting.

The names in Table 7.1 were quoted again and again.

What makes a great leader?

As to what makes a great leader, the following were the most frequent responses:

- Intelligence
- Good communicator
- Honest

Table 7.1 Great leaders

Political	Chairman Mao, Stalin, Hitler, Churchill, J. F. Kennedy, Abraham Lincoln, Ghandi, Margaret Thatcher, Queen Elizabeth I, De Gaulle, Martin Luther King, Nelson Mandela, Desmond Tutu
Religious	Christ, Mohammed, Buddha, Moses
Commercial	Richard Branson, Alex Ferguson (manager of the Manchester United Football team from 1996), Henry Ford, Bill Gates
Military	Nelson, Wellington, Napoleon, Genghis Khan, Norman Schwartzkopf (CinC of the Allied forces in the Gulf Conflict of the early 1990s), Eisenhower, Montgomery (British Field Marshall in the Second World War), Francis Drake, Ulysses S. Grant (US General in the Civil War and later President)

- Charismatic
- Believable
- Vision
- Self-confidence
- Tenacious
- Ruthless
- Enthusiastic
- Energetic
- Brave
- Empathy.

It is actually quite difficult to link the great leaders with these traits with any statistical degree of confidence. A number of the names listed certainly did not possess honesty and integrity, Hitler and Mao being examples.

A closer look at what makes a good leader brings one back to the leadership matrix discussed earlier. All of the leaders named earlier demonstrated the following traits:

- Wide vision
- Commitment to goals
- Tenacity
- Good communications
- Empathy.

Handy (1976) also noted that great leaders tended to be either above or – interestingly – below average height (Napoleon was quite short), be in good health and come from the upper socio-economic levels of their particular society. There are, of course, exceptions. Roosevelt was crippled by polio and many revolutionary leaders have risen from lower socio-economic groups.

The concept that there might be a *leadership elite* has of course been used to perpetuate rule by certain sectors of society. Even today, as shown below, this concept has not entirely disappeared as traditional-type leaders are still found in the upper echelons of church, government and commerce.

Intelligence

Very high intelligence does not seem to be a pre-requisite for a leader although average intelligence is. More than pure intelligence, it appears that 'cunning' (in a non-prejudicial sense) is of more use to a leader. Leaders need to be manipulative and devious at times, concepts that can be combined in the idea of cunning.

Empathy

There has been a long-running debate concerning the importance of a leader being able to carry out the tasks s/he asks of subordinates. In organisations where leaders have come up through the ranks they are usually familiar with the tasks and routines carried out in their department. Where leaders have come in from outside there has been the criticism that they are unaware of what the job entails, and can lose the respect of subordinates.

The contention in this book is that leaders do not have to be able to carry out the tasks they ask of their subordinates, but they must possess *empathy*. The leader needs to understand the task, and what it entails. A leader who adopts a 'please tell me how you go about doing this as I want to understand what you do' approach is one that leads to mutual respect.

Becoming a leader

Individuals reach leadership positions using a variety of methods that link to their use of power and influence (to be covered in Chapter 8). The means by which a leadership position can be obtained are:

- Traditional
- Appointed
- Situational
- Charismatic
- Created
- Ceremonial.

None of the above is exclusive. Leaders may be chosen in a traditional manner but still be the best person for the role and possess charisma.

Traditional

Traditional-type leaders become leaders because of their background. They are typical of either the concept of a ruling elite or the hereditary principle. Royal families and political dynasties such as that of the Kennedys in the USA are examples of traditional means of becoming a leader. The concept has considerable disadvantages but also some advantages. There is no guarantee that just because a person's father or mother was a good leader that they will be, but at least their upbringing is likely to have imbued the person with what is involved in leadership. On a smaller scale, many family businesses are passed from generation to generation. It can be assumed that those taking the reins from the previous generation of leaders have had an education in what is involved in running the business.

Interestingly, even in *meritocracies*, where leadership is supposed to be open to all, it is often those from the original ruling elites (provided they have not been removed by execution or exile) who often rise to senior positions. This may well be because they have been brought up to behave like leaders and thus understand how to win general support. The converse is also often the case where a respected leader is succeeded by a son or daughter who does not understand the mood of the people and very quickly undoes years of work.

For generations, the appointment of military leaders in many cultures was based on the traditional method. Officers came from a particular section of society and it was difficult for ordinary soldiers or sailors to break into their ranks. It was only with the introduction of large-scale conscription during the First World War that the officer caste became open to a larger section of the population. The German army solved the problem of royalty wishing to be military leaders in a very effective manner that will be covered under ceremonial leadership later in this section.

Think/discussion point

- Have you had experience of a traditional leader in any section of your life?
- How effective was the individual?

Appointed

In meritocracies, a social state of affairs, that is aspired to in most modern societies, leaders are appointed on the basis of *past achievements* and *behaviour*.

While this is very democratic, it does not necessarily mean that the person will be a good leader. Barrie Pitt (1962) writing about the events of 1918 and the defeat of the German army, has noted that there were those who were superb battalion commanders but failed when promoted to command a regiment and those who showed flair with regiments but could not command an army. Perhaps we all have a level beyond which progress becomes counter-productive. Appointments are based on past evidence and future potential, and that potential is not always realised.

This concept is known as 'promotion to the level of incompetence', and has been studied by L. J. Peter and R. Hill and named the Peter Principle.

The Peter Principle

No matter how efficient an individual has been in a role, this is no guarantee that s/he will be as effective in a higher role. Past performance may be indicative of ability, but it is no guarantor of it. The Peter Principle of Promotion to the Level of Incompetence says that the only way to know that a person is in a position beyond that for which they are equipped is to put them in it. It is then necessary to live with the consequences.

Trust and competence

One of the important components of leadership is that followers need to recognise that the appointed leader is in fact a true leader. If s/he does not display leadership qualities then it is likely that s/he will be sidelined and another individual will assume a *de facto* leadership role.

It is often said that one does not have to like one's leader but it is necessary to trust them. It is very difficult to trust somebody when there are concerns about their competence. An appointed leader who cannot perform in a leadership role may well damage team morale dramatically.

Think/discussion point

- Do you know of situations where somebody was appointed above his or her competence level?
- How did their lack of competence manifest itself?
- What was the effect on their subordinates?

Situational

In Sir J. M. Barrie's classic story (later made into a motion picture), *The Admirable Crichton*, a British aristocrat, his family and their butler, Crichton, become marooned on a desert island. Only Crichton has the necessary survival skills and thus becomes the leader, completely overturning the social conventions of the time. Eventually he achieves almost regal status. As soon as rescue, in the form of a British warship appears, the officer in charge of the landing party, on finding that there is an aristocrat involved, defers to him and not Crichton. Crichton's reign as leader lasted just as long as the situation did.

Situational leaders may appear at just the right moment and then fade away into obscurity. Natural disasters often throw up situational leaders. Winston Churchill has been considered by some as a situational leader. It is correct to say that he was just the person Britain needed in 1940, but he also possessed charisma and was a member of the traditional elite, having been born at Blenheim Palace, the ancestral home of the Marlborough family.

Charismatic

Many, if not the majority of the leaders quoted earlier possess or possessed *charisma*. Charisma can be defined as the ability to inspire followers with devotion and enthusiasm. It is a quality that is easier to spot than to define objectively. Hitler had it, Kennedy had it and Christ had it. Charisma is the reason that such leaders have such devoted followers.

Whether charisma can be taught is a matter of debate. There are, however, aspects of charisma that we can all develop, including:

- Listening skills
- Communicating
- Thinking before acting

- Seeing the other person's point of view
- Analysing situations to see what the concerns of others are
- Appearance (see the work of Morris later in this chapter).

Charisma can exist without some of the above but, for example, once a charismatic leader ceases to listen then he or she begins to lose some of their charisma. *Charisma is in the mind of the follower.*

Michael Burleigh in his 2001 Samuel Johnson Prize for Non-fiction text, *The Third Reich – A New History* comments on how Hitler's charisma as perceived by the majority of the German people began to fade not so much because of the defeats in Russia and North Africa in 1943, but because he seldom left his headquarters and became remote from them. Charisma appears to be something that needs constant topping-up, this being another point made by Morris and covered in the section on his 10 Golden Rules for Leaders.

The problem of decline for charismatic leaders

Charismatic leaders grow old and may become out of tune with their followers. Unfortunately success as a leader can also breed arrogance. It is rare to find a charismatic leader who knows when it is time to step down especially as few of them actually train up a successor. The defeat of Margaret Thatcher in a leadership contest within her own party in 1992 showed how precarious the position of a leader can become if they are perceived as being unwilling to listen. Winston Churchill, for all his charisma, oratory and energy was voted out of office in 1945 by a war-weary British electorate. Unusually for such a leadership type Churchill retained the leadership of his own party and served a second term as Prime Minister between 1951 and 55, after which he retired but remained a revered figure until his death aged 90 in 1965.

Those leaders who rely primarily on charisma need to surround themselves with subordinates who will stand up to them – no easy task. It is almost as if such a leader is a surfer riding a wave. As long as the wave is fully formed they are propelled along majestically but eventually the wave breaks and they are cast up on the shore. It is remarkable to consider how many charismatic leaders have been removed by violent means, including assassination. They are either deeply loved or hated, but there is rarely an ambivalence towards them.

Think/discussion point

- How would you define charisma?
- Who would you choose if asked to name three charismatic leaders?

Created

The power of the media is now so great that it appears that it can create leaders. This can occur in a variety of sectors. While older generations might quote politicians and military types as leaders, younger people have their own leadership icons. Many of these icons have been the product of intense media hype. Is it the song and the voice that makes one person a pop star and another a nonentity, or is it the media hype around the former?

The US elections of 2001 were surrounded by intense media attempts to promote Gore and Bush as potential leaders of the free world. Given the uncertainty of the final result and the attendant court battles there were many who believed that George W. Bush was a leader only in so far as the media said he was. On 11 of September 2001, the day of the terrorist attacks on the World Trade Center and the Pentagon the author was actually in Washington DC. He watched, with US colleagues, the President's broadcast to the nation. There is no doubt that whatever had been perceived prior to those dreadful events, George W. Bush most certainly gave an impression of controlled anger and that he both looked and spoke like a true leader. Perhaps this was an example of a situational leadership scenario occurring and the free world was fortunate that the man in the White House proved equal to the task.

Ceremonial

The final type of leadership is that described as Ceremonial. A ceremonial leader has no real power but acts as a figurehead for the real power sources. Such a leader may possess influence but is unable to apply any sanction other than his or her resignation. In the UK, the Royal Family now has little real power although pronouncements from senior members carry influence. The chairman/woman or president of many companies may be a well-known figure but the real power is likely to lie with the CEO or managing director.

Barrie Pitt (1962) has noted how the First Word War German army solved the problem of members of the German royal family wishing to have a military role and title. The Germans were happy to let such people have titular command of an army and to undertake ceremonial duties. The real business of fighting, however, was planned by the Chief of Staff, a role held by a senior professional soldier.

The Sword of Damocles

However an individual reaches a leadership position, there is always the 'sword of Damocles' hanging over them. Damocles was a courtier of Dionysius the Elder, who was tyrant of the city of Syracuse in Sicily around 368 BC. According to a legend recounted by the Roman writers Horace and Cicero, Damocles on one occasion commented to his sovereign on the grandeur and happiness of rulers. Dionysius invited his courtier to a luxurious banquet, where Damocles enjoyed the delights of the table until Dionysius directed his gaze to the ceiling above the throne of the King. Damocles saw a sharp sword hanging above him by a single horsehair. Dionysius made Damocles realise that insecurity might threaten even leaders who appeared to be the most fortunate.

Leaders can often become paranoid that others are plotting to take their position. As the saying goes – 'just because you are paranoid does not mean that others are not out to get you!' A truly strong leader has no problem in designating and training a successor. A paranoid leader may refuse to accept the need for succession. However nobody lives forever and succession is important to the well being of every organisation, government and family.

Dionysus could also have shown Damocles that there may well be somebody trying to sever the thread holding the sword. Leaders need to know who to trust and who is after their role if the leader should suffer a premature demise.

Styles of leadership

An understanding of how individuals become leaders is only part of the leadership picture. Much effort has been devoted into considering the appropriateness of *leadership styles*.

The discussion of style will be started by considering work from the anthropologist Desmond Morris. Morris (1969) studied on the leadership role in primates (see Chapter 1). He developed 10 Golden Rules for the leader of any primate group – baboons, gorillas, chimpanzees or humans. These rules can be used to form the foundation for basic effective leadership within the work situation.

Morris' 10 golden rules for leaders

1 **Leaders must display the trappings and body language associated with leadership**

To be a leader, one must first look like a leader. This can range from flamboyant dress to very simple dress where this is appropriate. Idi Amin (the Ugandan dictator) wore a military uniform full of gold braid and medals. Ghandi (and to a degree Hitler) wore very plain dress showing that they 'were at one with their followers'. Many leaders position themselves on a dais or throne, thus elevating themselves above their followers.

F. D. Roosevelt, the US President before and for most of the Second World War, was crippled by polio but took pains to ensure that few ordinary Americans saw him being helped by his aides. Hopefully in these more enlightened times such subterfuge would not be necessary.

The manner in which people dress can say a great deal about the way they wish to be perceived. People can dress up in order to impress (the very rich and powerful may also dress down so as to be inconspicuous). When attending a job interview it is the visual impression created in the first 20 seconds that can mean the difference between success or failure. Leaders should look smart (according to the norms prevailing in the situation) and should never appear flustered. Many of the so called 'perks' of leadership – such as parking spaces, office fittings and even job titles – are more important for the image of the holder they convey than their practical use.

In the 1980s the leader of the UK Labour Party was Michael Foot – a man of brilliant intellect. Unfortunately he was eccentric (for a public figure) in his dress (often wearing a well-worn duffel coat) and appeared clumsy. He was never able to win a general election as, among other things, he did not look like a potential leader.

The leader of a group of gorillas, the alpha male, develops a silver back on achieving the leadership. This provides an immediate visual clue of who is the leader to other members of the group and to outsiders.

2 In moments of internal rivalry towards the leader, the leader must threaten rivals aggressively

Violence should never be part of the workplace although leaders of other primate groups may have to contend with physical attacks by rivals. In human work society, the rivalry is more subtle, but can be just as damaging as a physical attack.

Leaders who pretend that they know everything are more open to efforts to undermine them than those leaders who seek expert advice. A rival can make much capital out of a leader who has managed to become undermined.

While leaders of human groups should refrain from actual physical threats, the tone of voice and gestures used to put down rivals are a throwback to our primate ancestors. A scowl or glance can convey disapproval not only to the rival but also to the rival's followers and others. If a rival has made a move in public, then the put-down may also need to be in public.

The best advice to a leader is to admit that one does know something before a rival demonstrates that you don't know. In the animal world, although there are constant battles between rivals, they seldom result in injury. There are complex body language gestures and pheromones (chemicals released by the body that are detected by smell) to show submission. It is rare, however, for a deposed leader to carry on as a member of the group – just as it is in human groups.

3 In moments of external physical challenge the leader (or the leader's delegate(s) must be able to overcome the opponent(s)

Human leaders should never resort to physical violence. Unfortunately, wars are still with us. The last British monarch to lead troops into battle was George I in the early 1700s, but even before then it was not considered fitting for the leader of a country to always risk their life on the battlefield. In medieval times the ruler appointed a champion to fight on his or her behalf. In modern times the leader's delegates are the generals and admirals in charge of the country's armed forces. Physical prowess is not a require-ment of a leader, but the ability to obtain delegates who can meet force with force is.

4 Leaders must be able to outwit subordinates

The need for cunning and manipulative skills has been mentioned earlier in this chapter. It is possible to be devious, but in a benign manner. Leaders cannot always be up-front about situations. During the Second World War British cryptologists at Bletchley Park broke the German Enigma code. This provided the Royal Navy with an indication of the operational tactics of German submarines. Coded intercepts, however, also provided details of a planned bombing raid on the City of Coventry. Churchill, as the Prime Minister and war leader had a very difficult decision to make. If he ordered extra anti-aircraft guns and fighter aircraft to the Coventry area it might be possible to break up the raid. Such actions would, however, raise suspicions in the German minds that the British had been forewarned, perhaps by having broken the German code. The codes would be changed and the Battle of the Atlantic made even harder. Churchill took the view that protecting the convoys that were carrying vital foodstuffs and war materials from submarines was more important than saving Coventry, hard as that decision might seem. Coventry was bombed but the codes were not changed.

The example above involved outwitting an external rival. Leaders need to be able to do the same with internal rivals. It is acceptable for the leader to use a delegate to deal with a physical challenge, but unacceptable to use one for a challenge that is intellectual. Followers will accept weakness physically but not intellectually.

5 Leaders must repress quarrels within the group

Teams and groups should devote their resources and energies to fulfilling their objectives; internal squabbling detracts from the tasks in hand. Internal dissent also gives a strong message to the outside world that all is not well with the group. This can make the group vulnerable. It is not unusual to note that a football team that is in the headlines one week for internal problems between its manager, players and directors is soundly beaten by previously less successful rivals the next week. Quarrels lower the group's morale, while at the same time raising that of rivals.

The leader has a key role in settling squabbles in such a way as to provide a Win – Win situation (see Chapter 9) so that no group member is too resentful.

Leaders may at times set one subordinate against another so as to deflect any challenges to their position. Hitler was a master of this. It is, however, only a short-term strategy. Once the subordinates realise what is happening they may gang up on the leader to depose them.

6 Immediate subordinates must be rewarded with benefits that befit their high rank

'It's a perk of the job' – a phrase often used to explain those 'extras' that individuals receive as they move up the organisational hierarchy. Parking spaces, company cars and executive toilets are often associated with senior staff. Many perks may well be either or partially in the gift of the leader. One of the ways leaders can satisfy highly placed rivals is by rewarding them for their loyalty. This can backfire. In January 1943 Hitler promoted General Paulus the commander of the besieged German 6th Army at Stalingrad to Field Marshall. Hitler's stated reason for this was not to reward Paulus but that no German Field Marshall had ever surrendered – he expected Paulus to commit suicide. Paulus did not oblige.

In baboon groups it is only the highest-ranked males that are allowed to mate, thus ensuring that only the genes of high-ranking individuals are passed on to the next generation.

While it may be a sad reflection on human nature, leaders often have to buy loyalty, not usually with cash but with those things that promote the image of their immediate subordinates.

7 **Weaker members of the group must receive protection from undue persecution and harassment**

Those members of the group who are furthest from the leader may paradoxically receive their greatest protection from him or her. They may also blame the leader's immediate subordinates for any persecution even if the leader ordered it. This happened in 1930s Germany where Nazi bullying was ascribed to those below Hitler, and that if only Hitler knew about it he would stop the persecution. This was far from the truth.

It is natural for groups to protect their weaker members, but for the leader there is the added bonus that it shows a caring side. There is the further advantage that individuals who feel secure at work are likely to be more motivated, and motivating people is one of the prime tasks of any leader.

8 **The leader should make the final decisions regarding the social activities of the group**

Of all the Morris rules for leaders this is perhaps the least applicable on the personal level to modern society. Work and social activities are now widely separated, but it was not always so. Employers used to play a large role in the social activities of the workforce, with workplace social clubs and outings a common feature in the UK.

On the organisational level, progress towards equality for women and the removal of race discrimination, should be driven by the leader setting an example. If the leader acts in a proper manner then subordinates will follow suit. If the leader allows harassment and is resistant to social change, it will hardly be surprising if subordinates adopt the same position.

9 **Extreme subordinates need reassurance from the leader from time to time**

Tom Peters (1987) coined the term MBWA (Management By Wandering About). Effective leaders make sure that they are seen by all under their leadership and not just their immediate subordinates. British royalty have perfected the walkabout as an integral part of any visit. Politicians also ensure that they are widely seen in their constituencies, especially when an election is in the offing – people have become cynical as they realise that this is the only time they might meet their local MP. Effective leaders make a point of regular visits to subordinates: if they are seen too infrequently, a visit may imply some form of trouble brewing or be seen as a checking up.

The advantage to the leader of regular visits around the group is that it strengthens the bonds of loyalty and provides first-hand information about what individuals are thinking.

10 **The leader must take the initiative in repelling external threats**

Whenever there is an external threat to the group then it is the leader who must take the initiative. If he or she fails to do so they are likely to be deposed in favour of a leader who will offer protection. External threats can promote immense group cohesion. Unscrupulous leaders have manufactured such threats in order to increase their power. In the early 1980s the author spent some time in the then Soviet Union. He was amazed to find that people genuinely believed that Britain and America would attack the USSR if they could. Creating such an external threat allowed the Soviet leadership to adopt a hard line with their people.

- To what degree can you see Morris' rules reflected in your own work situation?
- In your experience, do effective leaders follow these rules?

While Morris was principally looking at primate groups other than humans, there are steps that leaders of human groups can take to make themselves more effective. They can:

- Dress appropriately and use appropriate body language
- Keep rivals in check
- Be knowledgeable about what is going on
- Act to suppress arguments that may be counter-productive
- Reward loyalty
- Motivate the group
- Set an example
- Be seen and heard by all subordinates
- Listen to all subordinates.

The leadership styles continuum

Consider the following two scenarios:

1. Fire breaks out in the group's workplace.
2. The group are planning their work schedule for the next month.

Should the leader of the group adopt the same leadership style for both scenarios?

In the case of the fire, the leader will be expected to give clear and authoritative instructions. The second scenario allows for discussion and debate. It is not a good idea to initiate a debate in an emergency situation such as a fire.

Leadership styles can range from the authoritarian, almost military style of giving orders and expecting them to be obeyed, through to debate and discussion. No one style is correct. The style should be *contingent on the situation*. The sign of a good leader is that they are able to adopt the most appropriate style for the particular situation at hand.

Hastings and Jenkins (1983) have reported the experiences of the captain of one of the Royal Navy warships involved in the 1982 Falkland Islands conflict between Britain and Argentina. Trained in the latest ideas of management and leadership the captain had always been concerned to listen to the views of others and act accordingly. However once the bombs began dropping on his ship this was an inappropriate way to lead. There were only a few seconds in which to take action and his crew wanted instructions, not discussion. Discussion could be carried out after the action when what had happened was analysed, but during the action it was clear decision-making from the leader that was needed.

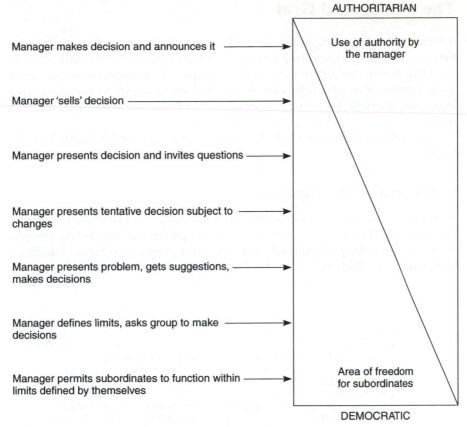

AUTHORITARIAN

Manager makes decision and announces it ——————▶ Use of authority by the manager

Manager 'sells' decision ————————————————▶

Manager presents decision and invites questions ———▶

Manager presents tentative decision subject to ————▶ changes

Manager presents problem, gets suggestions, ————▶ makes decisions

Manager defines limits, asks group to make ————▶ decisions

Manager permits subordinates to function within ———▶ Area of freedom limits defined by themselves for subordinates

DEMOCRATIC

Figure 7.5   The leadership continuum
Source: Cartwright *et al.* (1993), with permission

Tannenbaum and Schmidt (1958), Vroom (1980) and Blanchard (2000) are among those who produced models of leadership styles. In all these models there is a progression along a continuum from an autocratic style to a participative one (Figure 7.5).

One means of describing the continuum is that it stretches from the leader *Telling* subordinates what to do (highly autocratic and authoritarian, i.e. 'we will do this') through *Selling* the leader's idea (still autocratic, but with some sensitivity towards subordinates, i.e. 'we will do this because . . .') to *Joining together* (much more democratic, i.e. 'this is what I think we should do, what do you think?') and then *Delegating* (very democratic, i.e. 'this is the problem, come up with a solution').

There can be a problem with being too democratic in that it might be seen as the leader abdicating his or her responsibility. As will be seen in Chapter 8, even if the leader delegates responsibility the accountability still remains with them. A leader who abdicates accountability also abdicates leadership.

The Managerial Grid

A simple way of characterising leadership behaviour is to consider the balance between the leader's concern for *people* and their concern for the *task*. Work in the USA during the 1950s showed that groups led by supervisors who were 'people-oriented' tended to be more productive than those where the supervisors were 'task-oriented'. Based on this work, Robert Blake and Jane Mouton (1964) produced a grid of leadership styles (Figure 7.6).

It can be seen from Figure 7.6 that there are five main styles available to the leader.

Impoverished management

Little concern about the task and little concern about people. Here is a leader who has given up. Perhaps they are near retirement, perhaps morale is low, perhaps they have domestic problems; whatever the cause, they are no longer fulfilling a leadership role. Their attitude will transmit itself to their subordinates and not

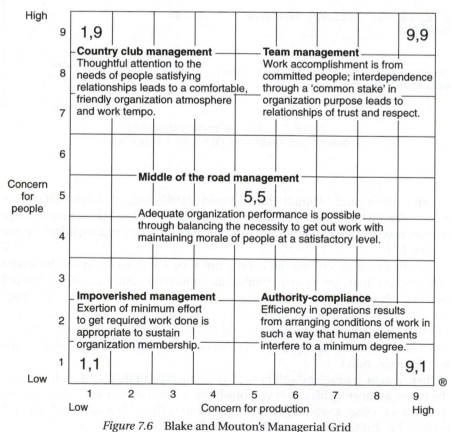

Figure 7.6 Blake and Mouton's Managerial Grid
(as adapted by Cartwright *et al.* In Charge-Managing People, Oxford, Blackwell, 1993)

only will the task of the organisation suffer but so will the web of relationships within the affected group.

Task management (Authority/Compliance)

The leader who concerns him or herself solely with the task is neglecting an important leadership function: the *relationships between people*. In times of crises it may be in order to be completely task-centred, but that cannot last for too long. People need to know that they matter as individuals and that their needs are being considered.

Country club management

The opposite of task management. The country club style is very comfortable and relationships are good. People enjoy coming to work for the social aspects but the jobs are not being given enough emphasis. Country club style puts the *group* and not the customer first, and in the long term can be as dissatisfying as task management.

Management team

A high emphasis on people coupled with a high emphasis on task was found to produce the best result. The concern for people and an emphasis on quality leads to a team approach to tasks and increased efficiency and productivity. This is the ideal position, and the one the supervisor/first line manager should aim for.

Middle of the road management

The usual state of affairs for many leaders. The leader at work has an *average concern for people and an average concern for the task*. It is likely that most supervisors and managers oscillate between (7.3) and (3.7) – sometimes people predominate, sometimes the task:

A truly competent functional leader is operating as a (9.9) leader of a management team, but even if that is beyond some people they can still ensure that they achieve a suitable balance between their concern for people and their concern for the task.

Think/discussion point

- Can you recognise different styles of leadership in operation at your place of work?
- Are they appropriate to the situation?
- What is the result when an inappropriate style is deployed?

The US airline, United is one company that has made considerable use of the Managerial Grid in order to move pilots away from too great an emphasis on operating in isolation. Tasks are actually undertaken more effectively in the 9.9 situation – i.e. when the task and the people involved are taken into account.

Linking the Managerial Grid to the Belbin team-role concepts

The Managerial Grid styles can be linked to the Belbin team roles as shown below. The author first made the linkages as part of a dissertation on the team role preferences of professional groups in 1992.

Blake and Mouton, as discussed earlier, saw major problems in all but the 9.9 and the 5.5. situations. They considered that the 9.9 'Team management' situation, with its high concern for the task, matched with care about people was the ideal and that the compromises in the 5.5 'Middle of the road' could also be successful. 1.1 'Impoverished management' is always likely to be unsatisfactory. 9.1 'Task management' may often occur, and indeed work well during a short-term crisis but the lack of consideration given to the needs of the human resource makes it likely that motivation will drop and with it production. 1.9 'Country club management' is a situation where the task may appear incidental to the lack of conflict and group cohesion and fellowship.

The Belbin team types can be fitted into the positions in the grid shown in Figure 7.7.

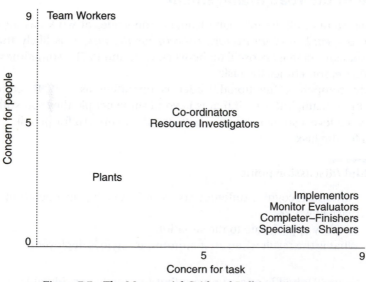

Figure 7.7   The Managerial Grid and Belbin team types

Team Workers slot neatly into the I.9 Country club position with Co-ordinators and Resource Investigators being at 5.5 and equally concerned with people and the task. All of the other types bar the Plant are task-oriented.

The position of Plants came about as a result of long discussions with groups of managers in which the consensus of opinion was that the Plant is more concerned with the idea than the task and that much of their motivation is creativity-rather than organisationally-based. 9.9 Team management occurs when there is a balanced team with all the roles present.

The work of John Adair

Adair (1983), writing about leadership, saw the effective leadership of groups as a balance between the needs of the task and/or organisation, individual needs and the needs of the group or team. Successful leaders were ones who managed to balance these needs so that individuals were motivated, group needs for social cohesion and belonging were met and the task was effectively carried out. Adair's model can be represented diagrammatically as in Figure 7.8.

The size of each circle will vary according to the priorities of the time. Most work time should see the task circle being the largest. If a member of staff has a personal problem – bereavement, domestic issues and illness – then the leader may need to 'enlarge' the individual circle. The office party should see the emphasis on the group needs circle. The Adair model is useful in that it brings into focus the fact that groups and teams have collective needs outside those of the individual members.

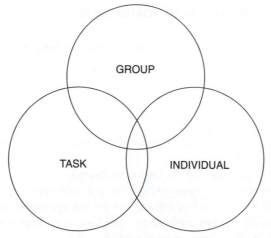

Figure 7.8 The Adair model

It appears that the group role emerges over time. When groups first come together the task role is predominant but as time goes on the group role increases in importance. The individual role remains at more or less the same level.

Contingency leadership

Rather than there being just one correct leadership style, current thinking is that a contingency approach is the correct one. In the contingency approach, as first described by Fiedler (1967), the effective leader is able to vary their style according to the circumstances. This requires the leader avoiding being trapped in a *leadership groove*. There is also the issue of *consistency*. Subordinates need to know where they are with a leader and that decisions are fair. Contingency leadership implies that different subordinates can be treated in different ways. An experienced subordinate may receive censure when they make an error while a new one might be praised for trying, even if they need further training. Leaders must strike the correct balance: the closer the relationships within the group, the more the leader can act flexibly.

The demands of contingency leadership form the bulk of Chapter 10 dealing with twenty-first century leadership. That chapter will also consider the role of the leader as a coach and empowerer rather than as a controlling influence.

Richard Pascale who came to the fore with his 1981 text *The Art of Japanese Management*, written with Anthony Athos, has been one of the management thinkers exploring the links between management and organisational behaviour and the natural world. In *Surfing the Edge of Chaos* (2000) written with Mark Milleman and Linda Gioja, he shows how the evolution of companies mirrors that of the natural world, with the most adaptive having the best chance of survival in turbulent times. As Pascale *et al.* point out, *adaptive organisations require adaptive leaders*.

Leadership, power and influence

How leaders exercise power and influence in order to fulfil their vision forms the subject of Chapter 8 of this book.

SUMMARY

- Leadership can be considered in terms of the *traits* of leadership or the *styles* of leadership adopted
- *Empathy* is an important trait for leaders to develop
- There are differences between *management* and *leadership*
- Leaders reach that position by *differing routes* – e.g. appointed, traditional, etc.
- The *Peter Principle* involves promotion to the level of incompetence
- The *Sword of Damocles* hangs over all leaders

- Leadership styles vary from the very *autocratic* to the very *democratic*
- There is no one right leadership style, contingency approaches require leaders to choose the style *most appropriate for the situation*
- Leaders must balance *task*, *group* and *individual* needs.

QUESTIONS

1 Describe the means by which individuals reach leadership positions. What are the advantages and disadvantages associated with each method?
2 What traits and skills appear to be common to all leaders?
3 Show, using the leadership continuum concept and the Managerial Grid, how different styles of leadership can be used according to differing circumstances.
4 What do you believe makes a good leader?
5 What is the Peter Principle, and can it be avoided?

Recommended further reading

There are a large number of books on leadership. You are recommended to read John Adair, *Effective Leadership* (1983), Warren Bennis, *On Becoming a Leader* (1998), Warren Bennis and Robert Townsend, *Reinventing Leadership* (1995), Richard T., Pascale, Mark Milleman and Linda Gioja, *Surfing the Edge of Chaos* (2000).

■ ⊻ 8 Power and relationships

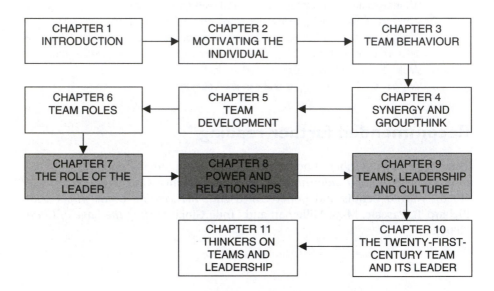

Learning outcomes – Power – Power and influence – Why use power? – Sources of power – Authority – Responsibility and accountability – Delegation and empowerment – Submissiveness, aggression and assertiveness – Power and the team – Conflict – Negotiation skills – Summary – Questions – Recommended further reading

---

LEARNING OUTCOMES

By the end of this chapter you should understand:

- The different *sources of power*, and how they are used
- The main source of *your power*
- The difference between *aggression* and *assertiveness*
- The difference between *responsibility* and *accountability*
- The advantages and disadvantages of *delegation*
- What is meant by *empowerment*
- How *conflict within teams* should be managed
- The importance of *negotiation skills.*

This chapter is concerned primarily with how leaders (and other team members) use power. Power, in simple terms is the resource that 'gets things done' (Cartwright, 2002a).

Power

It is also necessary to define what is meant by the term 'power'. Power, as defined in the everyday world, is the resource that drives things. Anything that 'gets something done' possesses this force known as power. As will be shown below, money, information, position within the hierarchy, expertise and personality all contain aspects of power.

The word 'power' is often used in a negative sense as if exercising power is somehow wrong. Without power, nothing would happen. Power itself is neutral – it is what it is used to achieve that can be positive or negative.

Power is also *dynamic* and can never be either absolute or purely one-way (Drummond, 1992). A hermit may possess considerable potential power but unless he or she is in contact with another sentient being, even if it is only a dog or cat, the power cannot be exerted. Power is in fact what drives influence – i.e. power is the resource that allows an individual or organisation to influence another individual or organisation to do something that the power source requires. In any application of power all of the parties are changed in some way through the interaction, hence power can never be one-way or absolute.

The power of any individual within an organisation is usually derived from a number of sources of power, as described below, with perhaps one or two being the dominant power sources for that individual.

Power and influence

Power is a resource while influence is what the resource provides. The degree of influence and its extent is contingent both on the type of power employed and the perceived strength of that power by those upon whom influence is brought to bear. Like power, influence is *dynamic* and acts on all parties. Not only is the party being influenced changed in some way, but so is the person doing the influencing.

At the end of each section on the types of power a consideration is given of the type of *influence* connected with that power.

Influence may be *overt* – i.e. visible – or *covert* – and thus unseen.

Why use power?

Like power, the use of the term 'force' usually invokes negative connotations when considering work/commercial issues. However the negativity comes from the way the word 'force' has become contextualised into making somebody do something that they would not wish to do. In physics the word 'force' means something rather different.

Newton's First Law of Motion states that: 'a body will remain at rest or continue in a straight line at a uniform velocity unless it is acted upon by an external force.' In physics, force is that which changes direction or velocity. Without a force in operation, nothing happens.

The motivational impetus that may be given to a sales team to market a new product is, in Newtonian terms, a force, and one that will be, hopefully, beneficial to all concerned. The strength of a force is defined as its *power*.

Force, is, like power, neutral – the positive and negative aspects depend on the *use* to which it is put. In organisational terms those forces that act so as to benefit the organisation and its individual members can be termed **impelling forces** – i.e they move things forward. Those forces that act against the organisation and its members are **frictional forces** – they slow the organisation down. Sometimes this may be necessary as organisations can grow too quickly, often running out of cash in the process.

Sources of power

Physical power

In most organisations, the use of physical power is not a necessity. There are, however, certain times when the possession of such power ('I am bigger than you are') by the leader or his or her delegate as described in Morris' 10 Golden Rules (Chapter 7) ('My dad's bigger than your dad') may be an advantage. Law enforcement, the military and certain sports are places where physical power may be useful. Unfortunately this source of power is becoming needed more and more in hospitals and local government front offices as violence and threats against staff members increases. In such circumstance there is often the case of the client relying on physical power and the employee using personality and negotiating skills.

Within non-human animal groups that have male leaders, physical power is very important. In those groups where the leader is female – e.g. elephant groups – physical power is less important, being replaced by expertise. Human work groups tend to put a greater emphasis on expertise over physical prowess but body language and dress are still important facets of leadership.

Physical power is exerted through the *overt* use or threat of force.

Making an impression

It is not unusual to hear somebody saying, 'he/she looks the part'. In Chapter 7 the importance of appearance for leaders was introduced. Just presenting an *image* that exudes authority can lead others to perceive that a person has more power than is actually the case, hence the importance some executives place on power dressing.

Linked to physical power is the phenomenon of *body language*. Humans are highly visual animals (as are all primates) and as such we gain over 80 per cent of our information about the world through what we see. If a person is saying one thing but their body language indicates an opposite view ('that's OK', said through clenched teeth) then the body language cue is more representative of what the person feels than what they actually say. It is difficult for individuals to hide their true feelings, as body language is often instinctive.

Physical power is a function of personality and confidence as well as physique. Physical power is not exerted because A is stronger than B but by the fact that B *believes* that A is physically the stronger.

Personality power

Personality power is another name for charisma. Charisma as a component of leadership was discussed in Chapter 7. It has been the principal source of power for many well-known leaders, including Richard Branson, Jesus Christ, Mohamed, Gandhi and Hitler. Many others have it to a lesser extent and the ability to use one's personality for the good of the organisation and also oneself is a most useful trait. While everybody has a personality, the possession of charisma to any great extent may be the preserve of just a few. Charisma cannot be taught, but those who have it can be sensitised into using it for good. It is not difficult to find charismatic leaders at both ends of the good and evil spectrum.

Those who possess charisma should reflect very carefully on how they use it. Of all the sources of power charisma can project the most influence. Other forms of power produce the force necessary to move forward, but personality power/charisma is a 'hearts and minds' form of power. As such, it alters not just the behaviour of the person to whom it is applied, but also impacts upon their philosophy of life.

Personality power uses *persuasion* as its overt means of gaining compliance with the wishes of the leader. The covert use of this form of power is very subtle. It relies on the aura that the charismatic leader has around himself or herself. Such a leader may not always realise that they are influencing their followers. Followers of such leaders tend to imitate the leader's philosophy and even dress sense. The icons for many young people tend to be from the worlds of sport and entertainment and may not realise that they are in a leadership role. They need to be careful that they set a positive example to those who see them as their leader.

Charles Handy (1976), whose work is included as recommended reading at the end of the chapter, uses the term 'magnetism' to describe the way personal power *attracts followers*.

Expert power

Technological advances carry with them the possibility of individuals using expert power. In monetary terms, the earnings that can be made by those who understand modern information and communication technology (ICT) systems give testimony to this. Expert knowledge can confer considerable power on an individual, especially if s/he is working with those who have considerably less expertise in the particular field. One of the problems with expertise as a source of power is that it only requires one wrong call for credibility to fall quite rapidly. Expertise is also much more than just knowing the jargon – an expert who cannot make good on his or her words is eventually exposed as a charlatan.

Expert power is a very old form of power. As human ingenuity has produced new technologies – the wheel, the use of metals, pottery, sailing ships, steam engines, the internal combustion engine and computers – technicians who understand these technologies have been needed.

Leaders relying on expert power need to ensure that they remain up to date with the technology. In the 1970s and 1980s those who could operate a computer wielded considerable expert power. However as more and more computers came into use, the power of these experts declined as non-computer department staff found that they could operate a computer without the need for a high level of technical assistance.

Those using expert power often display the Belbin Specialist team role (see Chapter 6). Their contribution is often on a narrow technical front. They tend to be quite up-front and proud of their expertise and their influence can be described as *procedural*.

Resource power

Resource power can often be exercised by those quite low down in the organisation if they have control of a resource that is urgently needed. Resource power is similar in many ways to expert power, in fact it can be argued that expert power is just a special type of resource power. The resource in that case would be expertise and knowledge. Much negotiation and bargaining at all levels of domestic, business and governmental levels revolves around resource power: 'If you give me this (which I want), I will give you what you want.' The aim is to try to avoid a situation where there is a win/lose, lose/win, or lose/lose situation and create one that is win/win so nobody has to give away too much without receiving an adequate resource reward in return. Negotiation is a topic covered later in this chapter.

The resources that can be used as a form of power include anything that somebody else might need. They may be physical, financial, forms of information or even emotional support. There is nothing wrong with using a resource on a *quid pro quo* basis, but no leader or subordinate should ever resort to using the resources they control as a blackmail weapon.

While it may not make good business sense for individuals and groups within an organisation playing political (with a small 'p') games with resources, it is, in fact, almost a natural reaction.

Users of resource power gain influence through *exchange*.

Position power

If people believe that somebody has the authority to act in a certain way (see later in this chapter), they will assume that he or she also has had the necessary power conferred on them. How often do we question a person in a uniform that appears commensurate with the surroundings? The importance of such assumptions was highlighted after the terrible events of 11 September 2001 in the USA. Prior to the attacks, how many people would have questioned the authority of somebody in a pilot's uniform in an airport? Hindsight gives us 20/20 vision but the answer is probably very few indeed. Much position power is conferred on people by their *job titles* or even *job grade*.

As discussed in Chapter 7, there is a common perception that somebody who has reached a certain position must possess the necessary skills and expertise in order to have been promoted – the 'Peter Principle' of promotion to the level of incompetence. Position does not always indicate competence, but it often signifies power. Job descriptions often detail the degree of power conferred in a particular job title.

Position power is difficult to question. Rules and procedures often have the power attached to the position clearly stated. There is no point in saying, 'you can't do that' especially if what is really meant is, 'you are not competent to do that.' If somebody has been given the authority, to be defined later in this chapter as 'the use of legitimate power' then they can do it.

Influence is gained through position in the hierarchy.

Relationship power

The old saying 'it's not what you know but who you know' is as true today as it ever was.

The importance of *networking* is stressed in nearly every business and self-development book. It is a fact that those close to the people who hold power are often seen as having a portion of that power themselves. Ask yourself a question: Who is the second most powerful person in your organisation? Often it is not the deputy CEO or deputy chair but the personal assistant or even secretary to the CEO or chair. The person who controls access to the person with power often wields considerable power themselves. Gatekeepers have always been powerful figures.

Just being related to somebody with power may confer a degree of influence that is unwarranted. It is presumed by others that the relative will have extra influence or access to the power figure. Those born into leadership dynasties may find that they need not necessarily acquire the right skills to progress – their name may do it for them. Not a democratic approach but one that is still in evidence today.

Relationship power is often irrational but it can be a very potent force and its influence is often covert but keenly felt.

Think /discussion point

- What is your main source of power at work?
- What is your main source of power at home?
- What is the main source of power used by your boss?

Authority

Authority is the outward manifestation of power. It is a sign to others that the person or organisation is sanctioned to act in a particular manner. Quite rightly authority is normally given together with limitations on its use. These may be simple rules as at school or as complex as a country's constitution.

Authority can be defined as the use of *legitimate power*.

In the military, authority is often easy to spot, as the badges of rank often signify increasing levels of authority. Thus Commanders can issue orders to Lieutenants but not to Captains. There are often occasions, however, when expertise (see earlier) is held by a lower-ranking individual and it is a wise senior who realises that 'with respect sir, I would reconsider that action' actually means 'if you do that you will be acting very unwisely – Sir!' It is often the case that the more junior person has expertise power, while the senior may rely on position power.

Think/discussion point

- How much authority do you have at work?
- What is the source of that authority?

Responsibility and accountability

Responsibility

Responsibility is the obligation on the individual or team actually to carry out a task. This is something that can be delegated down to them (see delegation later in this chapter). Those carrying out the task may have had no input into the initial decision-making process at all. In order to carry out tasks, the individual or team may also need to be given the authority and power required.

Accountability

Accountability is the obligation to ensure that certain tasks are carried out. The accountable person does not have to carry out the task but they will be held to account for it. Delegation does not carry accountability with it, only responsibility, authority and power. Accountability still rests with the delagator who then makes the delegate responsible. A degree of accountability can be passed to somebody else if it is part of the *empowerment process* to be discussed later.

Think/discussion point

- List those things you are accountable for at work, and those for which you have responsibility.
- In the case of the former, who is responsible for them, and in the case of the latter who retains accountability?

Delegation and empowerment

Delegation is the handing down the responsibility for action, together with the necessary resources and authority to somebody else, usually low down in the organisation. Under delegation, the delegator still remains accountable (see earlier) for the task and its manner of implementation. Accountability cannot be delegated. Empowerment is delegation plus the encouragement of considerable initiative and a degree of accountability.

Developing people through delegation

Leaders tend to have two main reasons why they delegate tasks:

1. They do not have the skills nor the time to do the task themselves
2. They wish to develop the delegate.

Both of these are valid reasons for delegation although, in terms of the Blake and Mouton Managerial Grid (see Chapter 7) the former is a task-oriented approach while the latter is a team management process, as it is designed to benefit the delegate. The delegate may also gain new skills, experiences and insight if the reason for delegation is to save the leader's time, but staff development is incidental to the more practical aspects of delegation in this instance.

Leaders cannot delegate a task without providing the *resources* for the completion of the task. These resources include:

- Training where necessary
- Time
- Finance
- Raw materials
- Authority.

The leader also needs to ensure that success criteria are in place and that these are fully understood by the delegate. Criteria should be in C-SMART format, as discussed in Chapter 1. Delegates need to be able to *measure their success*.

Reluctance to delegate

Not all leaders are willing to delegate. Delegation can be seen as a threat if the leader is not comfortable with his or her abilities and performance. While it is acceptable to refuse to delegate to somebody who the leader feels cannot cope with the task, the question of why has that person not been developed must be asked.

It is not unusual for leaders to be distrustful of their deputies and for deputies to believe that they can do a better job than the leader. The ideal situation is one where the leader uses his or her position to develop their deputy, thus building mutual trust and respect.

Empowerment

Delegation gives responsibility to the delegate but leaves the delegator with the accountability. Modern thinking on developing people centres on the concept of *empowerment*.

Murrell and Meredith (2000) have defined empowerment in terms of the *enabling* of someone to assume greater responsibility and authority through training, trust and emotional support – it is also appropriate to add both financial and physical resources.

Bill Ginnodo, editor of *The Power of Empowerment* (1997), has described empowerment as a mechanism whereby employees and managers work together to solve problems traditionally reserved to higher levels of the organisation.

The difference between empowerment and delegation is that the former has decision-making and accountability components that are lacking from the latter. The author (2002a) has described an historical trend that has been moving from delegation + control to empowerment + facilitation – approaches that require the use of very different managerial/leadership mindsets. Leaders often say things such as 'at the end of the day the buck stops with me', indicating that they retain accountability. Empowerment means the sharing of accountability or even task accountability being devolved downwards, with accountability for the development of the team being the main focus of the leader. Nevertheless the leader will still retain a measure of accountability for the team's actions.

Ken Blanchard, John P. Carlos and Alan Randolph, writing in 1999 under the title *The 3 Keys to Empowerment*, considered that the essence of empowerment lay in the knowledge, experience and motivational power that is already in people but is being severely underutilised.

The author's (2002a) definition of empowerment is:

'The process of releasing the full potential of employees in order for them to take on greater responsibility and authority in the decision-making process and providing the resources for this process to occur.'

Think/discussion point

- If you are the leader in your job – what are you doing to empower your team?
- If you are not the leader in your job – what is your leader doing to empower you?

Submissiveness, aggression and assertiveness

In order to use power it is often necessary to be forceful. There is a difference, however, between *assertiveness* and *aggression*. A submissive leader is unlikely to survive for long and an aggressive one will make enemies.

In any human relationship, the moment there is any potential or actual conflict (and leadership may involve people being asked to do things that they would rather not) the people involved can adopt one of three states:

- Submissiveness
- Aggressiveness
- Assertiveness.

Unfortunately most human beings tend to adopt one of the first two. Submission avoids the conflict for the time being but can breed resentment and leaves nothing resolved, while aggression may make somebody feel good for a short time but it can lead to violence. Both submission, because it can breed festering resentment, and aggression, because adrenaline is released stimulating heart rate and increasing blood pressure, are actually physically bad for the body. An aggressive leader is likely to have a red face and display facial grimacing.

Submissiveness involves giving in and aggression involves forcing somebody else to give in. Neither of these is a tactic that will lead to a long-term resolution of issues. Aggressive leaders may well discover that they receive increasingly aggressive responses to their own aggression.

Aggressive behaviour is when somebody violates the rights and beliefs of the other person while standing up for their own rights and beliefs. Aggressive behaviour is far from calm and tends to make quite rigid statements on what the other party *must* do. Submissive behaviour is when a person allows somebody else to violate their rights and is not something that leaders should display. A team will expect their leader to stand up for not only his or her individual rights but also those of the team.

Assertive behaviour

The best approach for a leader to adopt is to be *assertive*. Assertive behaviour is when a person stands up for their rights and beliefs without violating the rights and beliefs of the other person.

A leader displaying assertive behaviour:

- Stands up for his or her own views but demonstrates that the views of the *other party* are understood
- Seeks *solutions* not blame
- Enhances the assertive party but does not *diminish* the other
- The assertive party wins and at worst the other party *doesn't lose*
- Is *succinct* and to the point
- Asks *open questions*
- Is *calm and reasoned*.

Good leaders should also respect assertive behaviour from those whom they lead.

Whatever source of power is used, it is important to remember that aggression and coercion never produce more than the minimum effort needed to avoid problems.

Think/discussion point

- Considering your own situation, analyse a recent situation where you have been:
  - Submissive
  - Aggressive
  - Assertive
- How did your behaviour help or hinder matters?

Power and the team

Chapter 4 included a discussion on synergy. Synergy is also a feature of the way in which teams project power. The power of a well-constructed team may be well in excess of what might be expected when considering the individual members.

Force multiplier

The concept of a force multiplier (a term introduced in Chapter 2 to explain the concept of a motivational multiplier) comes from the military. A force multiplier is an asset that allows a vast increase in power projection. It may be offensive in nature or supportive. An aircraft carrier is an example of an offensive force multiplier, while refuelling aircraft are supportive force multipliers. The strike power both in terms of amount of firepower and the range over which it can be projected is increased many times over by the addition of an aircraft carrier to a naval formation. The ability to refuel aircraft without them having to land means that more force can be exerted over a greater distance. The strength of the carrier task force as used by the US Navy is that it employs the aircraft carrier and refuelling aircraft operating from it as potent force multipliers.

A well-constructed team can be a *force multiplier for an organisation*, allowing it to extend the scope of its operations considerably. The more a team is aware of its goals and understands the philosophy of the leader, the easier it is for the leader to use the team as a force multiplier.

Think/discussion point

- Is your team a force multiplier?
- If not, why not?

Socialisation

Chapter 2 of this book introduced the concepts of motivation while Chapter 5 was concerned with team development. This section builds on those ideas with a consideration of how team membership can alter individual behaviour through the power of the team.

The three stages of individual adaptation

Individuals joining a team change the team, and are themselves changed by their membership. This process was considered in Chapter 5 in the section on task force Re-forming.

The psychological process a new team member goes through is a four-stage one consisting of:

- Compliance
- Adaptation
- Identification
- Internalisation.

Those familiar with the coping cycle of Adams, Hayes and Hopson (1976) will recognise that these are the stages that humans go through in any change scenario.

Compliance

When an individual joins a team for the first time they have little knowledge of how the group behaves. They will tend to comply with the rules, norms and working practices of the group so as not to draw untoward attention to themselves. The group, in turn needs to school the newcomer into its modes of operating. The newcomer often needs to serve what is akin to a term of *apprenticeship* before they are fully accepted into the group.

In most work group situations the members of the group make every effort to ensure that the newcomer is made welcome. There may be times, however, when established members of the group feel threatened by a newcomer. The concerns may manifest themselves in actions that will belittle the newcomer or make them fail at a task.

In some groups, especially those where there is a strong tradition and hierarchy, for example military formations, newcomers may have to undergo a process known as *mortification*.

Mortification

Handy (1976) describes research in the 1950s that chronicled the process of mortification new cadets to the US Coast Guard Academy had to undergo. Similar examples can be found from military training schools across the globe, although more enlightened regimes are now being put in place.

Cadets were presented with traditions and regulations derived from the experiences of older cadets. These traditions and rules were not those written down as part of the offical constitution of the Academy. Cadets could and were punished quite harshly for any breaches of the student body-derived norms. A similar situation is known to have occurred in the 'Gun Room' of British Battleships in the early twentieth century. (The Gun Room was the name given to the midshipmen's mess.) Punishments known as 'evolutions' were given out for minor infractions of a set of norms. Some of these evolutions were highly dangerous, and could result in serious injury or even death.

It might be expected that those in authority would stamp out such practices. However they had once been cadets and thus subject to mortification and saw it as part of the apprenticeship stage. What may have started as a ritual became a means of integrating people into the group. Those who were not damaged too severely (either mentally or physically) by the process came to see it as a rite of passage and were then willing to inflict it upon others. Unfortunately mortification still occurs in some work situations and school playgrounds. It can do immense harm. Newcomers comply with mortification because it is the gateway to full group membership.

Adaptation

As the individual spends more and more time with the group so their behaviour begins to adapt to that expected by other group members. The behaviour of other members will also have to be adapted to take the newcomer into account.

The newcomer is now well into his or her apprenticeship and will be beginning to take on board the norms of the group rather than merely complying with them. The individual still tends to perceive themselves as a newcomer at this stage.

As behaviour becomes closer and closer to that of the group, the group members may begin to co-opt the individual into their own projects. This brings the individual in closer contact with other group members, leading to *identification*.

Identification

By the identification stage the individual perceives themselves a fully-fledged member of the group. Their apprenticeship is over. They belong. The importance of belonging as a motivator was highlighted in Chapter 2.

Internalisation

When we internalise something it becomes part of us. Internalising group norms means that they are no longer just complied with – they are lived. The dangers of groupthink were covered in some depth in Chapter 4. Those who have internalised group norms may be prone to groupthink as they are less likely to question what they are doing in the name of the group. Monitor–Evaluators (see Chapter 6) have an important role to play, as they will question internalised norms, however unpopular that may make them with other members of the group.

Internalisation is self-motivating. Things are being done for the group rather than the organisation. This can be a threat to the organisation: it is often sensible not to let groups become too secure – new blood will facilitate group members questioning their internalised norms.

Think/discussion point

Thinking about your team:

● Where are you in respect of compliance, adaptation, identification and internalisation?

Conflict

While conflict is rarely pleasant, it is a fact of corporate and personal life. Morris' 10 Golden Rules for Leaders (Chapter 7) stressed the need for leaders to settle squabbles between subordinates.

Conflict can be negative or positive, internal or external.

Potter-Efron (2000) has described how three principles apply to conflict:

1. *Too much* conflict destroys morale
2. *Unresolved* conflict saps confidence
3. Low morale and diminished confidence *diminish confidence.*

Potter-Efron also makes the valuable point that conflict is a natural state of affairs and something that can never be eliminated from the human condition, but it can be *managed.*

Just as there are phenomena known as 'road rage' and 'air rage', Potter-Efron believes that 'work rage' is becoming a major issue and that organisations need to take steps to manage disruptive conflicts.

Negative conflict

Any conflict that results in team members becoming demoralised or resentful is negative. Conflict that uses up time that could be allocated to meeting goals is also negative.

Positive conflict

Positive conflict, while it may be uncomfortable at the time, acts to spur people on and define problems. Unless, however those involved in positive conflict act *assertively* and not aggressively it can soon become negative.

Internal and external conflict

Internal conflict is that which occurs between team members. The leader should have the power to ensure that if there is conflict, it is positive. There is nothing worse than a team that is suffering from internal divisions.

Where the team is in conflict with an *external* agency then the leader should be the one who represents the team's views. The team should meet to discuss the issues and then the leader or his/her delegate should represent the team in negotiations.

Think/discussion point

- How have you handled recent positive and negative conflicts at work?

Negotiation skills

Negotiation is a means of *solving problems without coercion.*

Most negotiations are carried out in a ritual manner. There will always be a maximum amount that each party can concede and a minimum amount that they can accept. Provided that the minimum that A will accept is less than the maximum that B can concede then agreement is possible.

As Fisher *et al.* (1991) have shown, far too often people begin negotiations from a fixed, unyielding position. Unless both parties are prepared to move, then negotiation may be fruitless. This explains why, in the bargaining ritual, both sides ask for more than they expect or offer less than they can. Anybody who has visited those parts of the world where haggling is a normal part of business will recognise the ritual.

Behaviour in negotiations

Negotiations can be stressful. The types of response from either side include being:

- Angry
- Resolute
- Disappointed
- Self-satisfied.

Each of these factors makes it very easy to turn a bad situation into a worse one. Anger and the feelings associated with it is an emotional state, driven by the hormonal (endocrine) system in the body. The major hormone in the anger response is the 'fight or flight' hormone, adrenaline, secreted from the adrenal glands above the kidneys. It is adrenaline which prepares the body for action by transferring blood from the digestive system to the muscles (hence the red face often associated with anger), which makes the hair stand on end (in many mammals this makes them look bigger and more threatening) and in general tenses up the body and quickens heart rate.

The hormonal system works using chemical levels in the body while the nervous system is more akin to an electric current (although it works on a chemical differential). Imagine a standard incandescent light bulb – it emits both light and heat. Press the light switch and the light is emitted immediately but the heat takes slightly longer to build up. After an hour if the switch is moved to off then the light is immediately extinguished but the heat remains for some time (as anybody who has burnt his or her fingers removing a light bulb that has just been switched off can testify). The light is analogous to the human nervous system, the heat to the hormone system.

Once a hormonal response has been triggered it will take time to subside and thus anger responses may continue even when the cause for the anger has been removed.

To deal effectively with anger requires considerable interpersonal skills. If the parties are face to face, it may be beneficial to retire to a quiet area and sit down. People who are standing are much more likely to invade each others' personal space and thus appear threatening. Even if one of the parties raises his or her voice, responding in the same way will only make matters worse. If somebody is shouted at, then their adrenaline levels will rise even further and they will take much longer to recover. The whole idea should be to calm the person down and this is best achieved by letting them have their say.

There are four states to any human transactions (Figure 8.1).

The ideal state is WIN–WIN, where both sides are satisfied.

Result for A	Result for B
WIN	WIN
WIN	LOSE
LOSE	WIN
LOSE	LOSE

Figure 8.1   States of conflict resolution

A situation where the organisation A WINS but B LOSES is to be avoided. A's victory is likely to be short-lived as B may well be resentful and looking for a way of gaining revenge. There may be some short-term satisfaction to be gained from 'getting one over on somebody' – it may be one of those destructive 'games that people play', as described by Berne, (1965), but in the end all that is actually achieved is resentment.

LOSE–LOSE is an all too common situation. By refusing to compromise both parties end up unsatisfied. Unfortunately perhaps for many, LOSE–LOSE is the next best option to WIN–WIN. The whole of the nuclear defence strategy in the Cold War was based on a concept of MAD – Mutually Assured Destruction. If the other side launched their missiles at us, in the few minutes we had left we would launch ours at them. We might be dead but at least they would be dead too – a classic (and sad) LOSE–LOSE scenario!

Think/discussion point

- Can you think of a situation where you have preferred LOSE–LOSE to somebody else winning and you losing?

SUMMARY

- Power is what *gets things done*
- Power is *neutral* – it is neither good nor bad
- People have a variety of *power sources* that they can use
- Authority is the use of *legitimate power*
- Responsibility can be *delegated*
- Accountability *cannot be delegated*
- Of the three ways of responding to conflict (submissiveness, aggression and assertiveness), *assertiveness* is likely to be most effective
- New team members go through a *socialisation process*
- Conflict can be either *negative* or *positive*
- In negotiations, a win–win situation should be the goal.

Questions

1 Describe the various sources of power. How do they differ?
2 Using examples, show the difference between accountability and responsibility. Why cannot leaders delegate full accountability?
3 How does assertiveness differ from aggression, and why is it usually more effective?
4 What are the advantages of empowering other team members?
5 'If I cannot have win–win, I'd prefer lose–lose.' Discuss this statement and show why win–lose or lose–win is the least acceptable outcome

Recommended further reading

Among the large number of texts dealing with power and conflict, the following are recommended to support this chapter:

Belbin R. Meredith, *Managing Without Power* (2001), Helga Drummond, *Power – Creating it, Using it* (1992), Charles Handy, *Understanding Organisations* (1976), Ronald E. Potter-Efron, *Work Rage* (2000, originally published as *Working Anger*, 1998).

■ ☑ 9 Teams, leadership and culture

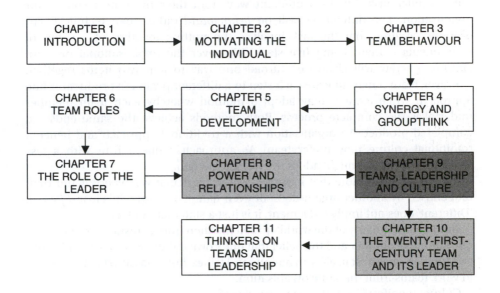

Learning outcomes – What is culture? – How culture is developed – Transmission of culture – Organisational culture – Culture clashes both within and between teams – Cultural change – National culture – Cross-cultural teams – Summary – Questions – Recommended further reading

---

LEARNING OUTCOMES

By the end of this chapter you should understand:

- What *culture is*
- How culture *develops and is transmitted*
- The different types of *organisational cultures*, and their significance for teams and leaders
- The implications of *national and ethnic cultures* for teams and leaders.

What is culture?

Although the word 'culture' is often used to mean different things, in national, group/team, organisation and business situations the simple definition of culture is:

'The way things are done around here.'

From this, it can be discerned that there may well be different ways of doing the same thing. A team of people in one organisation may be just as effective carrying out a similar task, but in a different way from their rivals in a competitor organisation. The differences will be *behavioural* rather than technical. For example, assume that the task involves the putting together of a series of components – there being five steps. Whatever the organisational or team culture, a screw will always be turned one way to join two items together. However, team A may allocate each step to a different person (a production-line approach) while team B may adopt a method whereby each team member undertakes the complete process. Both methods achieve the same ends – a completed product. An organisation with a traditional approach and hence a traditional culture may prefer team A's approach, while a firm with a less traditional approach might adopt the team B method.

It is important to note that in many cases a particular way is not better than that chosen by another organisation or even national group – it is just *different*. 'Different' does not imply judgement, it is just a statement of fact.

Unfortunately many of the world's problems stem from a misunderstanding by one culture of another and the belief that one's own culture is best. Not only does this problem manifest itself with nations and tribes, but it has also been observed in work teams from the same organisation.

Culture manifests itself through a system of:

- Values
- Attitudes
- Beliefs.

Members of a cultural group sharing a common values system, will have similar broad beliefs and display certain behaviour patterns that reflect their attitudes.

Think/discussion point

You are responsible for setting up appointments for people to see your boss. Somebody offers you a large bribe to put them in to see him ahead of others who have been waiting for some time. Do you:

(a) Refuse?
(b) Take the bribe and move somebody else down the queue?

There are cultures where (b) would be the perfectly normal response. If you are outraged at this it is because you have a particular set of values that says, 'First come, first served'. Others may have different values.

Culture is something that develops over long periods of time and is transmitted from one generation to the next. In the context of national cultures this is done from parents to children and through the education system. *Organisational culture* is transmitted from longer-serving staff to new employees via corporate events, publications and interaction with long-serving colleagues. The early stages of the socialisation process covered in Chapter 8 are concerned not only with the acquisition of skills but also the induction into the culture of the team. In Chapter 5 the Forming and Norming stages of team development were introduced. Performing begins to occur when the team members have developed a common culture.

How culture is developed

The individuals who make up a team come to the team with their own motivations (as discussed in Chapter 2) and their own culture. The culture they bring with them will have been developing since their birth.

The organisation to which the team belongs will also possess a culture that has been developing since the organisation was founded. The younger the organisation, the more its culture will reflect that of its founder(s).

A third cultural influence (one not always mentioned in texts on teams and leadership) is the culture of the *customer*. If the customer for the team's activities is an internal one, then the team and the customer will have similar cultures. If the customer is outside the organisation, then the team will need to ensure that its output to the customer is compatible with the culture of the customer.

Think/discussion point

- To take a simple example. The team is in Germany and the customer is in the UK. What language should the team use in speaking to the customer, English or German?

Language is an important aspect of culture so the answer should be English. The team should, unless there is a very compelling reason not to, use the language of the customer. It may be acceptable to use a third common language – this is often English. English is, for example, the common business language used in India, a country with a large number of cultures and languages. For aircraft safety reasons, for another example, there is a common language, English, used for air traffic control. One cannot expect air traffic controllers and pilots to be such polyglots that they can give instructions in all of the world's languages.

Figure 9.1 shows the influences on the culture of the team.

Note that the arrows are double-ended; the culture of the organisation is *influenced* by individuals at the same time as they are *being influenced* by the culture of the organisation.

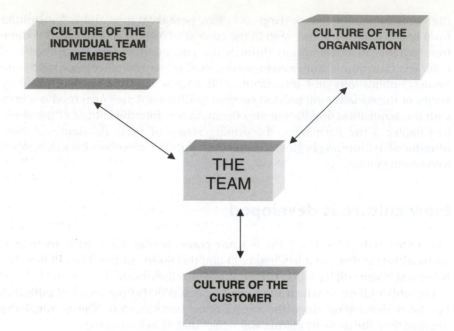

Figure 9.1 Influences on the culture of the team

Transmission of culture

Whatever type of culture – organisational, national, youth, team or popular culture-there needs to be a *means of transmission*. Culture evolves in a similar manner to species evolution. The pattern for the young of a species is carried as genes attached to the chromosomes found in each cell. In asexual reproduction each new organism is formed by a straightforward division of the cells of the parent and is thus a copy of that parent. This form of reproduction is used by many single-cell organisms (and also in the cloning techniques that so excited scientists at the end of the twentieth century), but does not allow for any differences others than those caused by accidental mutation. In sexual reproduction the new individual receives half of its genetic code from one parent and half from another. This combination of genes means that the new individual will be genetically unique (except in the case of identical twins, triplets or in rare cases even more identical siblings) and while it may have many of the characteristics of its parents, it will not be a 100 per cent copy. Sexual re-production encourages genetic variation and is the main method of re-production for most living organisms. Animals that produce multiple young do so by having a number of eggs fertilised simultaneously, as in the case of non-identical human multiple births. Over millions of years the subtle changes to each generation may produce a completely new species. Darwin's concept of the 'Survival of the fittest' was that those changes which confer a *competitive advantage* on a species (this may be connected with speed, vision and types of food eaten) are likely to be perpetuated over successive generations, while those individuals possessing disadvantageous characteristics will be less successful and will eventually die out.

It is possible to suggest that similar systems are involved in organisation and team evolution. When organisations merge, it can be akin to a form of sexual reproduction. Cultural genetic material from the merging organisations is combined to form a new organisation. If one of the merging organisations is much bigger and stronger then the new organisation it may be more in its image, but if the two organisations are of equal strength, then the new organisation will hopefully have the best from each of them as part of its 'organisational genes'. The human genome project is currently working on plotting the position and function of human genes on the chromosomes and concepts from genetics may provide useful information on how organisations evolve, merge and grow. When new members join the team they bring with them their 'cultural' genetic material to be placed in the pool of the team's cultural genes. If the new member is dominant then his or her material might 'punch above its weight'. A new leader will bring very strong genetic material to the team. A person joining the team in a subordinate position will find that the team's genetic material dominates the individuals. To some degree or another both the individual and the team evolve due to the combination of genetic cultural material.

Organisational culture

Teams function within organisations. The organisational culture is the major influencing factor on the culture of the team. A team that has developed a culture that is radically different to that of its parent organisation will find effectiveness difficult to achieve.

Just as McGregor (see Chapter 2) described the two opposite assumptions about people and work – Theory X and Theory Y – so Schein postulated two types of organisation differentiated by their culture.

The first, which was entitled Organisation A, had a culture that believed that:

- Ideas are generated by *individuals* throughout the organisation
- People accept *responsibility* for their actions
- Truth is arrived at by *conflict* within the group
- Such conflict is not destructive because the group operates as a family and has *control mechanisms* in place to prevent conflict from getting out of hand.

Organisation B, on the other hand, possessed a culture that believed that:

- Truth tends to come from the older, wiser and more *senior* members of the organisation
- People are capable of *loyalty* and *discipline*
- Organisational relations are both *horizontal* and *vertical*
- Individuals have their own organisational '*personal space*'
- The organisation is responsible for the *well being* of individual members of staff.

Organisation A has a culture that promotes *openness*, not only in thought and words but even in layout. Open plan offices are far more likely to be found in Organisation A cultures. The organisation may appear chaotic to an outsider as there is often argument and informality.

Organisation B is likely to have separate offices and work spaces and considerable formality. The *hierarchy* will be obvious, as will the formality.

Of these two cultures it is not possible to say that one is better than the other. The effectiveness of either of them will be *contingent on the situation.*

Think/discussion point

- Do you work in an organisation A or organisation B culture?
- How is the culture of your organisation manifested?

Effective team working is best suited to organisation A cultures as an effective team can be hindered rather than assisted by formality and a strict hierarchy.

It is possible to write whole books about organisational culture, as has indeed been done. Charles Handy (1976, 1978) has produced a simple to understand but highly effective descriptive method for illustrating organisational cultures. He has identified four types of organisational cultures, each with its own distinctive behaviours.

Role culture

The role culture that Handy represented as a Greek temple, a highly stable structure, represents the typical bureaucratic organisation. Handy equates Apollo, the god of order and rules to this organisational culture (Figure 9.2).

Such organisations often have a plethora of rules and regulations with departmental boundaries clearly defined. They are often slow to change, seeing in stability their means of survival. The role culture places great emphasis on

Figure 9.2   Role culture

stating what a person's *job title* is rather than what the person actually does. In this respect, role cultures tend to neglect the personality aspects of team membership – the team roles that formed the subject of Chapter 6. There tend to be barriers to interdepartmental communication across the pillars of the temple with most communication being up and down individual pillars. Such a structure is typical of many large organisations and has often been identified with the traditional public sector/governmental organisations. In recent times many organisations have been trying to move away from the inflexibility that such a structure can create.

Teams in a role culture

Teams in role cultures have a tendency to be *hierarchical* – reflecting the culture of the organisation. The chair or convenorship is a fixed position held by the most senior member of the team. Ideas may well be elicited in order of 'rank', with senior staff being asked first. The most effective leaders of such teams often use reverse order of seniority in order to avoid the problem of juniors agreeing to ideas because somebody senior made the initial suggestion (see groupthink in Chapter 4).

In addition to the hierarchical nature of such teams they may also be composed of members from the same department. Even the most staid of organisations have begun to see the effectiveness of multi-functional teams but these often cause a conflict of loyalties for their members. Those working in role cultures need a loyalty both to the organisation and to their department or section. Departmental pressures in a role culture can be brought onto the team member to act in what are perceived as the best interests of the department. Most of the time departmental interests will coincide with those of the organisation, but not always. The team may make suggestions that are beneficial to the whole organisation but not so beneficial to a particular department. In the wonderfully comic *Yes Minister* and *Yes Prime Minister* (1981–3 and 1986–7) books and television series Jonathan Lynn and Anthony Jay provide an insight into cabinet government as they believe it was practiced in the UK during the 1980s. The fact that the Prime Minister of the time, Margaret Thatcher, is reputed to have found the material most entertaining points to the fact that there must have been some truth in what they wrote. In the fictional cabinet, Ministers are torn between loyalty to country, party and department. The conflict of loyalties led to decisions being taken that benefited the department but were detrimental to the country. It would have been sensible (especially in resource terms) to abolish the Department of Administrative Affairs (the department of the fictional minister). It did not happen, as the minister and his civil service officials ensured that the department would survive even if it cost the taxpayer money.

Club/power culture

The god Zeus is ascribed by Handy to the spider's web of the Club/Power culture. Zeus was the supreme god in Ancient Greek religion. Power rests in the *centre*, often with a single individual with a strong personality. It is not unusual for that person to be the founder of the organisation. The more charismatic the leader, the more power they exert. Power flows outwards from the centre. This is a culture that suits the entrepreneur who can keep an eye on operations. Club/Power cultures can respond very quickly but only in the direction personally favoured by those at the centre. The UK-based Virgin Group with Richard Branson in the centre became a byword for entrepreneurship in the 1990s with operations that included an airline, rail operations, music, personal finance and publishing – all interests of Sir Richard (Figure 9.3).

Teams in a Club/Power culture are often provided with considerable latitude and authority to act. The power source at the centre of such an organisation is often the team's sponsor so that the team needs to be well aware of his or her agenda, philosophy and culture. The Club/Power culture is one of *facilitation* within the boundaries set by the centre. There is also another component, that of the philosophy of the leader of the organisation.

During 2001 the author was researching entrepreneurship both in terms of individual entrepreneurs and entrepreneurial organisations (Cartwright, 2002b, 2002c). One area that was of considerable interest was the need for sections of the organisation to be routine rather than entrepreneurial. While the Club/Power culture can respond quickly (it only requires the leader to make a decision), the Role culture is much better at handling routine tasks. The most successful entrepreneurs and entrepreneurial organisations were found to be those that included teams with a Role culture managing routine tasks and procedures. There were tensions. Those with a love and aptitude of routine (Implementers and Completer–Finishers – see Chapter 6) found problems in dealing with sudden changes of corporate direction. Nevertheless they provided a stabilising influence on the Club/Power culture.

The above illustrates the important fact that organisations are not homogeneous in culture but contain a *balance of teams* operating to different organisational cultural norms to the benefit of the organisation as an entity.

Figure 9.3   Club/Power Culture

The Club/Power culture is often found in newly formed teams with a strong leader. The emergence of a very strong leader at an early stage can give rise to problems among the remaining team members. This can precipitate the Storming stage of team development discussed in Chapter 5. It cannot be stressed too highly that leaders need to understand followers just as much as the followers need to be cognisant of, and accept, the leader's philosophy.

Just as Role culture teams can be frustrated by the flexibility of a Club/Power culture organisation, Club/Power culture teams can become impatient with the methodical approach of a Role culture parent organisation.

Leadership in a Club/Power culture team is either held by the overall leader of the organisation or by a delegate that s/he appoints directly.

Task culture

In the 1980s and 1990s many larger organisations began to adopt a Task culture approach as they moved away from the Role culture discussed earlier. The Task culture has been ascribed by Handy to Athena, the goddess of craftsmen. Power in a Task culture lies in *expertise* and *creativity* rather than in job titles.

Task cultures can be represented as a matrix. While in a Role culture team position may be ascribed to reflect the individual's position within the wider organisation, position in a Task culture is based on expertise. The leadership role may rotate between members with different individuals taking on leadership tasks that relate to the activities of the moment. Task cultures actively break down departmental barriers and provide a means for the effective deployment of multi-functional teams (Figure 9.4).

In a Task culture team the leadership role need not be fixed but can rotate among team members according to expertise. A lack of any formal hierarchy characterises teams with this culture. Job titles and seniority can be 'checked in at the door' – Task culture teams are meritocracies.

Existential culture

Existential culture is represented in Handy's work by the god Dionysus, the god of wine and song. Handy (1978) points out that the Role, Power/Club and Task

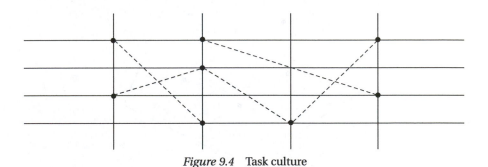

Figure 9.4 Task culture

cultures all have one thing in common: the individual is there to serve the organisation (it might be argued that this does not apply to individual or the small group at the centre of a Power/Club culture). In the Existential culture, the *organisation exists to serve the needs of those in it*. Partnerships of doctors, architects and lawyers are examples of an Existential culture. Such organisations suit professionals who may well appoint a manager to oversee the day-to-day running of the organisation but the professionals themselves operate on the basis that they are all equal. Many of the new companies that were founded in the late 1990s in order exploit the opportunities offered by the Internet had Existential cultures. Often a group of young men and women came together with an idea: Netscape, the Internet browser company, is an example. In the case of Netscape the young founders brought in an experienced older manager, Jim Barksdale (Price, 2000) to 'supervise' the young management team. The lack of rules and procedures in an Existential team may actually make it difficult for those outside the team to communicate with it.

Only small groups of individuals with similar backgrounds and seniority can form a true Existential team. If such a team begins to grow or brings in new members with different seniority, a hierarchy often begins to develop (Figure 9.5).

There are interesting interreactions that can occur when two different team cultures interact in either a competitor situation or a customer–supplier relationship (even in an internal customer–supplier situation).

It is not difficult to imagine the frustration those in a Role culture team might experience if they need to work with an Existential team; the former's rules might well be totally alien to the latter.

Think/discussion point

- Do you work in a Role, Task, Club/Power, Task or Existential culture?
- How is your organisation's culture manifested in terms of the Handy Scheme of cultures?

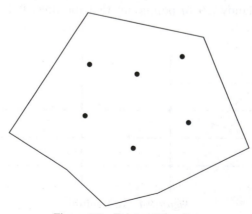

Figure 9.5   Existential culture

Culture clashes both within and between teams

It is perfectly possible for there to be different cultures operating in different teams within the same organisation. The accounting team may be a role culture team while the marketing team may operate in a more task-focused manner and include members from a number of departments. Nevertheless, especially within the same organisation it is important that the cultures 'get on with each other' and this requires a knowledge of organisational culture from team members. Those working within another cultural form within an organisation may have difficulty dealing with the bureaucracy of a Role culture, while those in a Role culture may tear their hair out at the lack of procedures in a part of the organisation with an Existentialist format. However, at least if they understand each other they can make allowances for differences in behaviour. A different culture is not a worse culture. Like many of the areas of organisational behaviour, the culture adopted by the team should be *contingent on the circumstances*.

It may well be that huge organisations actually have divisions or controlled subsidiaries that operate to different cultural norms, especially if they are located in a different geographic region – an issue that is dealt with later in this chapter.

To paraphrase the poet John Donne, 'no organisation is an island entire of itself.' There are no such things as closed systems in reality (a closed system is a scientific construct that assumes no interaction with any external variables). Every organisation has to deal with those outwith its own boundaries – suppliers, customers, government and competitors. While the organisation may be able to control the cultural behaviour within itself to a degree, that of outside organisations may be completely outwith its control.

Again, knowledge and a willingness to work together to overcome any cultural differences for mutual benefit is required. It is a truism throughout humanity that however different we are, our similarities are normally much greater, and this is also true of organisations. A willingness by all concerned to bend a little works wonders. Cultural clashes, like the allowable weaknesses introduced in Chapter 6 when discussing team roles, are something that should be *managed* rather than removed.

There are, however, certain situations where cultures cannot co-exist, although they are rarely encountered. Earlier in this chapter the fact that culture is manifested through values, attitudes and beliefs was introduced. If a team had a value system that encouraged dishonesty, there might be no way in which another team could accept that cultural norm.

Cultural change

There is a *generational* aspect to culture. It is rare for the culture of one generation to be accepted by the next. Part of growing up appears to be challenging the cultural norms of the previous generation. Parents cannot understand 'where their children are coming from' and children seem to reject (at least temporarily) their parents' value system.

This being the case, cultural change is also often generational. It is easy for the senior management to announce that they wish the culture to change, much less easy to achieve it in anything other than the long term. Values, attitudes and beliefs – whether they are personal, national or organisational – are deeply held – indeed wars are often fought over them and people may be willing to lay down their lives for them, so they can be changed only gradually, hence the concept of generational change. Team culture may be slow to change until a new generation of team members joins. Teams move through generations far quicker than the natural time experienced by an organisation.

Think/discussion point

- Is the 2002 Manchester United football team the same as the 1982 team?
- Quite clearly there are no players from 1982 in the 2002 team. The manager and even the kit has changed. The only commonality is the name and the Old Trafford stadium. Nevertheless it is still Manchester United, but a generational advanced Manchester United.

Cultural change is uncomfortable. Older members of the team will see their belief system being questioned. Provided that there is the necessary emotional support provided, they can hopefully, follow the change model introduced in Chapter 8 – they need to *adapt* and *internalise* if they wish to remain a team member. The more deeply held a belief is, the harder it is to change. Newcomers to teams need to have patience. Existential and Task cultures are much quicker to adopt cultural changes than a Role culture. Club/Power cultures can also change quickly, but only if the source of their power changes first.

National culture

As the world, especially the world of business, becomes smaller through improved communications, so, paradoxically, does the importance of understanding cultural diversity become more important. As stated earlier, cultural change is generational and responds at a much slower rate than technological change. Thus, while communications between different cultural groups are much quicker and much easier, the differences between those groups still remain. Only perhaps in the field of popular culture such as music and fashion is there more rapid *global convergence*.

It stands to reason, therefore, that as organisations undertake their operations on an increasingly global basis, the need for cultural understanding becomes greater and greater. As will be shown in Chapter 10, ICT (Information and Communication Technology) allows for the formation of *dispersed teams*. If the team are all in one place it is likely that the members will share similar values, attitudes and beliefs. If the team is spread over the globe, this assumption cannot be made.

Fons Trompenaars (1993) set out to explore the cultural diversity aspects of business, and one can only recommend his work to the reader in the highest terms. This section seeks to summarise Trompenaars work as it applies to teams and leadership as a taster for those who wish to examine his findings in more detail.

Trompenaars considered cultural diversity in terms of a series of differing attitudes held by various national groups. It should be noted that such attitudes are always just a tendency – not all Britons will react in one way to a particular set of circumstances and all Brazilians another, but his research did show a series of *national tendencies*.

Building on Trompenaars' work, certain *cultural attributes* can be shown as being critical to an understanding of team and leadership behaviour:

- Attitudes to time
- Universal v. particular
- Individualism v. collectivism
- Specific v. diffuse
- Achievement v. ascription
- Attitudes to age
- Attitudes to gender.

Attitude to time

It might be thought that time is a universal constant, as an hour is an hour is an hour whether it be in London, New York or Shanghai. In looking at the cultural effect of time, however, it is not the absolute nature of time that is important but the *attitudes* towards it.

Eastern cultures often have a reverence for ancestors and historical precedent. People from the USA, according to Trompenaars' research, were less interested in the past and much more in the future. Even the *importance of time* is an issue. In many Western cultures, punctuality is a very desirable virtue. In other cultures, punctuality is perhaps of less importance. This can immediately lead to a cultural clash. A dispersed team may need to rely on the punctuality of its members in accessing video-conferencing facilities. Team members must be confident that other members will deliver on time.

A team working across cultures must adopt a culture that all the members are comfortable with. When it is necessary for delivery dates to be met, the team leader should adopt a sympathetic method of insistence, with the reasons being clearly stated, including the implications for the work of other members of the team, and not just a blanket insistence demanded.

Universal v. particular

In some cultures, a set of rules or laws is *universally applied* (or so perceived wisdom tells us, despite the fact that there is sometimes one law for the rich and one for the poor, as the old saying goes). In others, rules and norms may be applied *contingent upon the circumstances*. Trompenaars points out that relationships such as friendship may confer special rights and obligations in a particular-oriented culture while those rights will be less acceptable in a universal one. In a universal culture, your friend has much less right to expect you to cover up for them than in a culture where particularism is the accepted norm.

Within a team the same rules need to apply to all unless all the members agree to change them. It is possible for there to be flexibility: if a team member has a domestic crisis it would be permissible for the other members to provide some flexibility for that person. The important point is that in a universal culture such flexibility is temporary and applies only to the particular set of circumstances.

As Trompenaars points out in his excellent tips for doing business with different cultures, in a universalist culture there will be *one way of doing things* while in the particularist there may be a *number of alternatives*.

Individualism v. collectivism

Of considerable importance to working in teams is whether individuals regard themselves as a member of the group first and an individual second or vice versa. Perhaps not surprisingly, the USA and the UK appear to tend towards *individualism-oriented* culture whereas the Japanese came out, together with countries such as Nepal and East Germany under the communist regime, as tending to show a more *collectivist* approach.

In conducting business, it is important to realise that it may be the group as opposed to a key individual who need to be satisfied in a collectivist-oriented culture and that the building of collective relationships will be of great importance.

Individuals from an individualist culture are making more of a sacrifice when working in a team. Despite the fact that we all know that we need other people, the cultural difference is one of emphasis. Anecdotally it is said that the personal stereo originated in Japan as a means of listening to music without disturbing anybody else – collectivist. In the West, it is said that it is a means of listening to music without being disturbed by others – an individualist viewpoint.

Specific v. diffuse

In many cultures, there is expected to be a personal relationship between those involved, whereas in others, the relationship is more organisation-to-organisation. In some cultures work and home are closely related, in others, people are not expected to bring domestic issues into their work place. This begs the question of how one is supposed to leave a problem at home – it is the belief that the two should not mix and not the actual reality that is important here. Trompenaars quotes China as a very diffuse culture, using the example of how many respondents would refuse to help their boss paint his house. In China 72 per cent would help, whereas in the much more specific culture of the UK only 8 per cent would agree to give up their own time this way (the US figure was 11 per cent). Similarly, in China, 89 per cent of employees believed that the organisation had a responsibility to help house its employees, compared to 55 per cent of Japanese but only 18 per cent of those in the UK and 15 per cent of US respondents. (There has been a change here in the UK since during the late nineteenth and early twentieth centuries organisations often provided housing for staff.) In terms of team behaviour it may well be that an individual would be prepared to help the team leader paint his or her house. Team relationships can be very strong. The whole organisation may be specific, but within the team diffuse relations can develop. Team members may socialise with each other outside work but not with others from the same organisation.

Team relationships can become so close that the team may forget that it exists to further organisational objectives (Task-centred, as described in Chapter 7) and become more of a Country club interested in its own agenda at the expense of the organisation's.

An organisation in a specific culture may appear, to those also adopting that culture, to be much more focused on its objectives, whereas in a diffuse culture time may be spent talking about non-organisational-related issues – precisely what can happen in a team. Leaders should ensure that the team has time for social intercourse in addition to the task in hand, as it is such intercourse that binds the team together and aids the development of synergy.

Achievement v. ascription

An achievement-oriented culture ascribes status dependent on what people have *done*, whereas ascription is about *position*, *connections* and even *birth*. The USA is an excellent example of an achievement-oriented culture. Americans pride themselves on the belief that with hard work and education anybody can rise to the top, as the careers of many early emigrants and their immediate descendants has shown. Achievement cultures ask what somebody studied and what they know and can do, whereas ascription ones may be more concerned with where the studies occurred. To that extent, even the USA, with its Ivy League of Universities (for example Harvard and Yale) is not a wholly achievement culture, and neither is the UK.

Titles and qualifications are much more important in ascription-oriented cultures and great offence can be caused by omitting them or quoting them incorrectly.

Teams based on ascription tend to be very hierarchical, with senior positions being given to individuals based on time served rather than expertise. Achievement teams adopt a more Task culture structure, where achievement is used to denote position.

Attitudes to age and gender

Different cultures have very different attitudes to age and gender. Age is revered in many Eastern cultures whereas it may be difficult for an over-40 to find employment in the West.

Similarly the position of women differs from one culture to another. Sending a young man or woman to negotiate on behalf of the organisation may be good practice in certain cultures but frowned on in others, especially if they are ones that appear to ascribe a lower social status to women or revere age.

Gender should have no part in team construction. Organisations that discriminate against people on the grounds of age, gender or even race do themselves a grave disservice as well as breaking the law of many developed jurisdictions. It is amazing how much talent can be lost to the organisation through discrimination. Sex and race discrimination is illegal in the UK and to these are added age in the USA.

Think/discussion point

- What are your personal cultural norms in respect of
  - Attitudes to time
  - Universal v. particular
  - Individualism v. collectivism
  - Specific v. diffuse
  - Achievement v. ascription
  - Attitudes to age
  - Attitudes to gender?

Cross-cultural teams

As will be shown in Chapter 10, modern technology has made the formation of cross-cultural teams much easier. Even where the team operates in the same building, migration and the global expansion of organisation means that the team may well contain a mixture of cultures.

Any team needs to be analysed from three viewpoints:

- The *skills* mix
- The *team role* mix
- The *cultural* mix.

The key to effective team working lies in the individual members understanding and respecting the attributes of their colleagues and then using them to the best advantage. It is also important that the team operates in a manner that does not conflict overtly with the cultural norms of the parent organisation.

Fortunately the resources needed to find out about the cultural norms of other people and regions are fairly easy to acquire. Trompenaars' work is presented in a very understandable form, as is that of Richard D. Lewis. Lewis' *When Cultures Collide* (1996) is one of a new type of book that provides information culture by culture and country by country.

Lewis makes the point that in the modern commercial world, where business people tend to dress in a similar pattern, it is what is *said and done* that give out cultural clues. He has also introduced the concept of *Culture Shock* – a phenomenon that occurs when an individual comes into contact with a culture that has very different values attitudes and beliefs.

Lewis concedes that stereotyping can be dangerous. Every new team member or person that the team has contact with should be considered as an individual first and a member of a particular culture second. Even within a small country there may be a number of cultures in operation. In the UK there are cultures that have their origins in the Celtic tradition, that of the Anglo-Saxons and the Norman French. In addition there are those with a West Indian or African or Asian background who also have distinct cultures. Such cultural diversity is a wonderful opportunity, as it can provide the team with different viewpoints on the same issue and may therefore encourage more options to be explored.

It is not enough to understand the business aspects of culture when the team is dealing with those from a different culture. The team also needs to be informed about humour, dress, religion, language and food. Part of the *induction* process for a new team member should be an introduction to the culture of the team. It is also important, however, to ensure that the team is *inducted* into the culture of the new member.

SUMMARY

- Culture can be *defined* as 'the way we do things around here'
- Culture is *manifested* through a set of values, attitudes and beliefs
- Culture is *transmitted* via education
- Cultural change tends to be *generational*
- There are four main *organisational cultures* – Role, Club/Power, Task and Existential
- Teams need to consider the *national/ethnic cultural norms* of those they deal with.

QUESTIONS

1 Describe the four main types of organisational culture, showing the problems that might occur when they interreact
2 Outline the steps you would take in inducting a new member into the team if that individual is from a different culture

Recommended further reading

Extremely useful information on the cultural aspects of business can be found in:

Charles Handy, *Gods of Management* (1978).
Richard D. Lewis, *When Cultures Collide* (1996).
Fons Trompenaars, *Riding the Waves of Culture* (1993).

■ ν **10** The twenty-first-century team and its leader

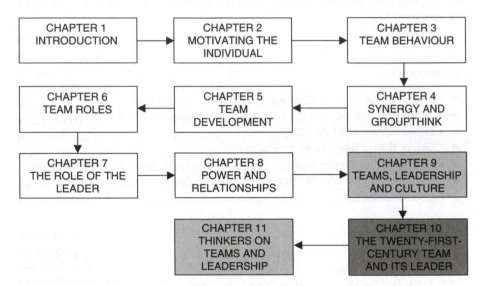

CHAPTER 1 INTRODUCTION	CHAPTER 2 MOTIVATING THE INDIVIDUAL	CHAPTER 3 TEAM BEHAVIOUR
CHAPTER 6 TEAM ROLES	CHAPTER 5 TEAM DEVELOPMENT	CHAPTER 4 SYNERGY AND GROUPTHINK
CHAPTER 7 THE ROLE OF THE LEADER	CHAPTER 8 POWER AND RELATIONSHIPS	CHAPTER 9 TEAMS, LEADERSHIP AND CULTURE
	CHAPTER 11 THINKERS ON TEAMS AND LEADERSHIP	CHAPTER 10 THE TWENTY-FIRST-CENTURY TEAM AND ITS LEADER

Learning outcomes – The development of ICT – Technological synergy – Virtual teams – Organisational boundaries – Managing the virtual team – Developing the virtual/diverse team – Planning in the twenty-first-century team – The 'invisible team' – Flexible leadership – Understanding the culture – Empowerment – How empowered teams behave – Leaders as empowerers – Leaders as change agents – Trust and support – Conclusion – Summary – Questions – Recommended further reading

---

LEARNING OUTCOMES

By the end of this chapter you should understand:

- How *technology* can aid dispersed/virtual teams
- What is meant by *technological synergy*
- The difference between *collocated* and *virtual teams*
- How to *lead* a virtual team
- The *planning process* for meeting team objectives
- What is meant by *empowerment*
- The difference between *blame* and *reward cultures*.

Whether it was 2000 or 2001 when the Millennium was celebrated, for many in all kinds of fields it provided a natural break between what was and what would be. In practice 2000 came and went just like any other New Year without the Year 2000 (Y2K) bug that it was believed might paralyse computer systems.

In geological time, a period of 20 years is miniscule. The advent of wide access to computers and telephones (known collectively as Information and Communication Technology – ICT) from the 1980s onwards has dramatic implications for teams in the twenty-first century.

The development of ICT

The Internet began with the linking together of a series of computers in the US Defense Agency Research Projects Administration (DARPA) to form what became known in 1969 as ARPAnet and was designed to protect military communications in the event of a nuclear attack – a very real fear in the political climate of the time as the Cold War between the West and the Soviet Bloc was at its height. The system used three university hosts in California and one in Utah. Later in the 1970s the US academic community, wishing to free itself from reliance on the military, set up a purely civilian network funded by the National Science Foundation (NSF) which linked an increasing number of US and foreign universities via NSFnet. For the first time academics and researchers could communicate text via a new medium – electronic mail, rapidly contracted to e-mail.

As students who had used e-mail began to take up positions within the private sector, it was not long before large commercial organisations in the USA, beginning with the computer companies such as IBM and Hewlett-Packard, began to talk to each other via e-mail, linking their systems to the NSFnet. In the UK large local authorities, Kent being a good example, also began to put electronic networks in place.

In 1993 Marc Andeesen and his group at the University of Illinois introduced the first web browser software (Mosaic), a software application for the UNIX operating system, but later adapted for Apple Macintosh and Microsoft Windows®. NSFnet gradually became less relevant and the commercial world saw the birth of ISPs (Internet Service Providers) so that by the middle of the 1990s organisations in both the public and private sectors were not only using e-mail but were beginning to design and post web pages. The World Wide Web (WWW) had been born.

The main implications of the Internet have been in communications. Other titles in this series deal with the more commercial aspects of the Internet within business, but internally the Internet and e-mail have revolutionised both internal communications and the critical supplier–organisation interface.

Technological synergy

The power of ICT is less in the attributes of the individual components – computers, telephones, radio transmission and cameras – but in the *synergy* that can be obtained when they are used in conjunction with each other. Computers can manipulate information very quickly while telephone lines can transmit it at the speed of light. The real potential for ICT comes when the *calculating/storage power* of the computer is combined with the *transmission capabilities* of modern telephone/modem systems using satellites and microwaves in addition to wires. ICT provides the potential for dispersed teams to be as effective as those that operate with the members in close proximity to each other.

To give examples of just how rapid change has been – up to 1830 the fastest that a normal person could send a message to somebody else was about 15 mph – the speed of a horse. By 1829, the locomotives of the Liverpool and Manchester Railway could achieve double that, and by 1904 the Great Western Railway locomotive 'City of Truro' had achieved 100 mph. The development of railways produced to a need to communicate for signalling purposes and this led to the development of first the electric telegraph, then the telephone and later wireless (radio) communications. These operated at the speed of light, and thus in a few short years communication speeds had increased from a few miles per hour to many thousands of miles per second.

Think/discussion point

- How has ICT altered the way you work as an individual and as a team member?

Virtual teams

While the speed with which team members could communicate with each other over long distances had been theoretically the speed of light (to all intents and purposes, instantaneous) in practice, the type of effective communication needed for team working became possible only in the 1990s.

The earliest means of instantaneous transmission used the dots and dashes of the Morse Code. While the actual code was transmitted instantaneously the process was slowed down by the speed of the operator's hand on the sending key and the need for the receiver to de-code the message before replying, as the same wire had to be used in both directions. The means of conversation was alternate – i.e. send then receive then send – and it was difficult to interrupt as in a normal conversation. There was also no means of indicating tone and pitch – i.e. the nuances of language. Early e-mail had the same problem, as will be shown below. The development of the telephone and radio in the early part of the twentieth century allowed for proper communication over distance. A traditional 'telephone call' can be thought of as a letter in real time. The development of and the growth in use of the facsimile (fax) machine in the 1980s was in fact just that – a real-time method of sending documents. Written material does not allow for the easy transmission of feelings, although it is a permanent record. The telephone call, on the other hand, does allow for some expression although voices may be distorted. More than one operation involving selling over the telephone has 'smile as you dial' displayed in big letters for the sale staff, because just as eyes can pick up body language clues, our ears can detect the difference in speech patterns of somebody who is smiling or not, as different muscle groups are used and this alters the tone of voice.

E-mail, the latest alternative to the telephone, suffers like the use of the early telegraphs in being a very curt method of communication. There are protocols for expressing emotion, but the use of symbols for a smile cannot have the emotional impact of an actual smile. There has also been an issue as to the number of e-mails people receive. It is so easy to send a copy to all the people on a mailing list but is it really necessary to e-mail the person next to you?

The use of videoconferencing as a device to link sites and team members has grown rapidly in recent years, aided by the availability of PC compatible web cameras using Windows® software and operating through the Internet. However even with the best definition available the body language clues are hard to pick up, as reported by the author in a case study on the use of such technologies (Cartwright, 2002d). The pixel definition of even the most expensive technology is nowhere near as good as the human eye. There always tends to be a minute time lag between people on the system, and this confuses the interpretation of the visual clues.

Where the Internet has proved to be a boon is in the area of *corporate dissemination* and the ability to form *diverse multi-functional and dispersed teams*. Colin Hastings and his colleagues in the UK (1994) have stressed the importance of managing 'the team apart' in their work on Superteams. ICT can help ensure that all members of a team or project group are as informed as soon as possible about developments and that there can be electronic conversations between them.

In their 2000 text, *Virtual Teams*, Lipnack and Stamps (see Chapter 11), quoting Allen (1977), distinguish between *collocated teams* and *virtual teams* by defining the latter as a team where the members are more than a mere 50 feet apart for the majority of the time. They also make the very valuable observation that as distance between members grows so can the number of time zones between members increase.

We tend to think of a team, if not located together as at least sharing the same time. Virtual teams might not only have the distance between them to contend with but also the issues of time. Consider a team that has members in Hong Kong, Denver, New York, London, Edinburgh, Berlin and Bangkok. The team's leader is in London and schedules a team talk (using videoconferencing or e-mail for 12.30 pm (1230) on 3 December – i.e. 2 pm Greenwich Mean Time (if the meeting was in the Summer, the timings would have to be increased by 1 hour).

The times that the team members would have to be at their locations are shown in Figure 10.1.

The team members in Edinburgh and Berlin will be quite happy with this arrangement, but for the members in Denver and New York it is early morning, while for those in Asia it is the evening. Part of the team is at work, part has finished work and the remainder have not yet started work. As things happen at work that will affect the team, some will already know about it and some will not. Virtual teams are teams whose members are dispersed in terms of space, time and organisational boundaries and which coordinate their activities using ICT.

Hong Kong	8.30 pm (2030)
Denver	5.39 am (0530)
New York	7.30 am (0730)
London	12.30 pm (1230)
Edinburgh	12.30 pm (1230)
Berlin	1.30 pm (1330)
Bangkok	7.30 pm (1930)

Figure 10.1 Time zones

Organisational boundaries

In preparing research on globalisation, the author (2002e) examined the ways in which the US aircraft manufacturer, Boeing, had developed the effective use of virtual teams. The world-famous Boeing Aircraft Corporation has been headquartered around Seattle since its founding by Bill Boeing in 1917. Since then it has grown dramatically and by the middle of the 1990s was one of the two largest aircraft manufacturers in the world, the other being the European Airbus Industrie.

By the time the Boeing 777 long-range twin engined passenger aircraft was under consideration in the early 1990s Boeing had an excellent track record of producing jet transports. The Boeing 707s, 727s, 737s, 747s (Jumbo), 757s and 767s were familiar sights on the runways of the world's airports. Boeing believed that the airline industry was ready for a large twin-engined airliner capable of performing on long-haul sectors. The use of two engines cuts the costs of both purchase and operation considerably, but requires a high degree of reliability. The 777 was the first airliner to be built to gain ETOPS (Extended Twin-Engine Operations) clearance by the FAA (Federal Aviation Administration) from its introduction. Previous twin-engined jets always had to fly within 60 minutes of a landing site for two to three years to assess the reliability of the engines before ETOPS was granted. This cut out many over-water routes. A twin-engined airliner offering a range of 5,500 to 7,000 nautical miles and carrying 300 to 400 passengers was likely to be very attractive to the world's airlines especially as it was predicted to be very fuel-efficient.

The way in which the 777 was designed was revolutionary and made considerable use of virtual teams. Previous engineering projects had involved the production of vast numbers of blue prints that needed to be sent to other designers and production facilities. Using computers, however, designers no longer had to take their drawings or models to a colleague on another floor or even another city or continent to see if it was all right. The whole process could now be carried out over a network of computers. This was one of the most

Table 10.1 Manufacture of 777 components

Outboard flaps	Italy
Passenger doors	Japan
In-spar ribs	Japan
Elevators	Australia
Rudder	Australia
Spar assembly tool	Wisconsin (USA)
Prototype's engines	Connecticut (USA)
Nose	Kansas (USA)
Fuel gauges	UK

important and groundbreaking uses of networks in recent times, holding out as it did the prospect of *global co-operation* on design and manufacturing without any of the problems of distance, geography, or time. No longer did designers have to waste precious hours on travelling.

A modern airliner is a highly complex machine requiring a considerable number of carefully engineered components. Manufacturers such as Boeing contract out a great deal of the component manufacturing. This has the advantage that the contractor has to bear the start-up costs, but the disadvantage that Boeing have to make their proprietary information available to an organisation that may be also working with a competitor or may actually become a competitor in the future. Nevertheless it has proved more effective for companies such as Boeing to work this way and involve others in the process.

For the 777 the manufacture of components was spread across the world as shown in Table 10.1.

Modern technology allowed Boeing to link their designers to the contractors and even to the actual machine tools.

One of the problems in designing something as complex as an airliner is that of interference – two components trying to occupy the same space. In the days of two-dimensional drawings this was an all-too-frequent occurrence. Computer aided design (CAD) can produce drawings in three dimensions and thus show the relationship in space between components.

Boeing put together a massive amount of computer power in a system known as CATIA (Computer-graphics Aided Three-dimensional Interactive Application) and EPIC (Electronic Preassembly in the CATIA). EPIC allowed a computer model of the finished aircraft – a virtual airliner – to be produced. CATIA was linked to component manufactures so that the specification of parts designed on the system were immediately available to them and could be fed, if necessary, directly to the machine tools.

Aircraft design is a process rather than an event and there are often many design changes. Before systems such as CATIA these might be posted, faxed or even hand-delivered. With the system used by Boeing, everybody concerned with that component would know of changes as soon as the new design was on the system. The time savings were immense.

As EPIC could spot any interference, it meant that the finished product was much more likely to fit together properly, as it did. The whole process was documented for an excellent book – *21st Century Jet*, by Karl Sabbach, and also for a joint US / UK television series. Sabbach reports how the computer checked for interferences on the 20 components that make up one of the 777's wing flaps. It made 207,601 checks and found 251 cases of interference. These might not have been discovered under the old system until an attempt was made to install the flap on the prototype, any problems then forcing the designers back to their drawing boards.

Each component or major group of components was the responsibility of a DBT (Design Build Team) that could include remote members from the component manufacturers as the Internet and ICT made e-mail and video-conferencing an easy and useful tool. The whole process could now be carried out over a network of computers. This must be one of the most important and groundbreaking uses of networks in recent times, providing global cooperation on design and manufacturing without any of the problems of distance, geography, or time.

Each component of The DBTs also formed a forum not only for discussion but *ownership* of a component. By using the technology to involve team members at remote locations, everybody was bought-in to the project. This is an important motivational point often neglected when sub-contracting. The further away the sub-contractor's staff are, the less likely they are to feel part of the team and to thus own the project. Ownership gives a huge boost to quality.

Boeing is not the only organisation to have developed virtual teams. The associated web site to this text contains case material on other examples of virtual/dispersed teams.

Managing the virtual team

The intensity of light or sound diminishes with distance in an inverse square relationship – i.e. if the distance is doubled the intensity goes down by a factor of 4 (2 squared). The power and control over members of a virtual team also diminishes according to distance.

The leader of a collocated team is able to practice what Tom Peters (1987) has described as MBWA (Management By Wandering About). The leader of a virtual team may be able to wander around in cyberspace but has much less contact with individuals than his or her counterpart in a collocated team. *Effective management of the team* when the members are apart was one of the key criteria for the Superteams described by Hastings *et al.* (1994). The important factors they described for teams that were dispersed were:

● *Trust* – team members had to be able to expect that colleagues would deliver on time and to the agreed specification

- *Control* – deciding what should be held in tight control, for example objectives and finance, and what could be left to the individual to prioritise
- *Motivation* – in a collocated team members can motivate each other by physical contact and body language. This is not as easy to do in a virtual team. The team needs to invent methods of socialising in cyberspace – the use of a dedicated chat room where shop talk is forbidden is one method. Many virtual teams actually come together physically occasionally in order to strengthen the membership bonds
- *Communication* – virtual teams depend on the effectiveness of the communication methods used. If everybody is aware of the difficulties that e-mail and videoconferencing have in giving the subtle verbal and body language cues that we rely on in face-to-face encounters then these can be compensated for. One virtual team that the author worked with had cue cards that were held up during videoconferences. The cards read: LAUGH, RUBBISH, WHAT? and other responses – they were very effective.

Developing the virtual/diverse team

The *team development model* presented in Chapter 5 (Forming, Storming, Norming, Performing, Re-forming, Adjourning) is even more important for teams that are not collocated. The process of Forming the team is best accomplished by bringing the members together if at all possible. While this may be expensive it will be a good investment. Many organisations use a short residential period at the beginning of a project in order to bring the people together, first to brief them but second to allow them to interact socially and begin to bond. Such a meeting is an ideal opportunity to test for the team roles (as described in Chapter 6) of the members.

Storming can be very problematic for a virtual team. In a collocated team it is easy to see if somebody is unhappy and even the degree of feeling, but in a virtual team it is necessary to rely on an individual making their feelings known.

Considerable effort needs to be put into the introduction of a new member to the team – if possible they should be given the opportunity to meet at least one other team member face to face.

Lipnack and Stamps (2000) also stress the importance of keeping *goals and objectives* in clear focus. When people are interacting in physical proximity to each other on a regular basis it is much easier to ensure that they are operating so as to further the team's objectives. It is less easy to do this in a virtual situation. As simple as it may seem, just heading every e-mail with the main objective of the team can assist in keeping minds focused.

Think/discussion point

- If your organisation has virtual/dispersed teams, how does it co-ordinate them and maintain motivation?

Planning in the twenty-first-century team

As Hastings *et al.* (1986) have pointed out, it is necessary to plan for things that the team know are likely to happen but it is also necessary to have contingencies in place for the team to deal with the *unknowns*. There are five states to the knowledge needed for planning:

- Known
- Likely
- Possible
- Unknown
- UNK-Unks.

Known

Much of the known will come from the team members' experience and research. It is known that toy sales increase at Christmas and production and distribution schedules can be planned accordingly. In the UK the majority of people take vacations in the Summer. These factors, known as they are, form the first part of any planning process.

The skills and team roles of the team members can be used to allocate tasks that are known about to the most appropriate members. Known activities can also be used to assist in the development of team members by pairing the inexperienced member with a colleague who is experienced.

Likely

Any team that is carrying out a proper analysis of its environment will know those things that are likely to happen. Manufacturing organisations know the anticipated lifespan of components, and thus know when it is likely that a replacement will be required.

Experience shows that there is a high probability of icy roads in the winter. If the team were working for an organisation responsible for road safety, they would be remiss in not ensuring that their plans took a need to grit the roads at night into consideration.

Possible

As the author pointed out in a companion volume to this book (*Mastering the Business Environment,* 2001) it is possible that London or Edinburgh may suffer a devastating earthquake, but the likelihood is very low. If a team is based in those cities, earthquake contingencies may not be part of the planning process. Were they setting up in California or Japan, such contingencies would need to be taken into account – indeed there may well be a legal requirement to do so before planning permission was granted.

The Hegelist Principle, named after the German Philosopher Georg Wilhelm Friedrich Hegel (1770–1831), in a simplistic form states that if something can be thought about then it must in some ways exist (if it can happen – it will!) – Hegel was concerned about the nature of reality. In the context of this book, whatever may be possible must be considered if the probability of it happening makes it sensible to do so. No team would be criticised justly for failing to build in major earthquake protection into their London buildings, where it is known from historical data that the danger is very slight; that would not be the case in Los Angeles or Tokyo.

A key task of those team members carrying out an analysis of the external environment is to determine what is possible and then what is the probability of it occurring. Such an analysis can only really be carried out with historical data. Just because there is a high probability of something happening does not mean that it will, but the team should have a *contingency plan* in place.

Unknown

In the ideal world there should be no such thing as an unknown, if everything is possible, however remotely, then it should be known. However, managers and planners are human and are caught out by unexpected events. 'Unexpected' is perhaps a better word than unknown. Again it is easy to be wise after an event but part of any environmental scanning should be the encouragement of those involved to undertake some brainstorming based on unexpected but possible factors.

Unk-Unks

Unk-Unks (Unknown, Unknowns) were quoted by Karl Sabbach (1995) as part of his study into the Boeing 777. These are events that are so unlikely that nobody has considered them. Often they are things that somebody should have dealt with but didn't, often through the vagaries of human nature.

Barry Minkin, a US-based best-selling author, consultant and futurologist was one of the people who first realised the potential of linked computers – the forerunner of the Internet – and has spoken about 'two-steppers' in his seminars. Many people can see the one step – say, from the mainframe to smaller computers – but it takes a very imaginative mind to see the next step. H G Wells and Jules Verne were two-steppers. Few organisations possess such people, and even fewer know how to use them to their full potential.

It is worth remembering that something can only be an unk-unk once. Thereafter the problem and its solution should be recorded by the team for future reference. Failure to anticipate an unk-unk is excusable – not learning from it is a corporate sin!

Whenever the team encounters and then solves (or not) an issue or problem for the first time, it should come together later to analyse and learn from what occurred.

The 'invisible team'

The concept of the 'invisible team' was introduced in Chapter 3. The twenty-first-century team is likely to include far more invisible members. Virtual teams are heavily reliant on technology; those who maintain and set up the vide-conferencing or the computer networks become vital invisible members of the team. It is important that they know what and why the team is using their expertise for.

A team that neglects its invisible ancillary members can never be 100 per cent effective. Bring these people on board and they can add to the synergy of the team.

Location and loneliness

One means of cutting costs has been to invest in *home working*. Members of teams in service industries may be able to carry out their routine tasks from their home linked to their office base and customers via a modem. While tasks can be carried out in this manner it is important that the leader of the team does not neglect the *social needs* of the individual team member. Working from home might seem idyllic but it can be very lonely. Team members who feel cut off from their colleagues rarely perform to the maximum level.

Flexible leadership

The twenty-first-century leader will be working with teams composed of members with a greater knowledge of the world than has been the case in the past. Leadership in the fast-moving world of the twenty-first century requires new skills, and – above all – flexibility. Black, Morrison and Gregerson (1999) believe that the key competencies for the modern leader operating in a global environment are:

- Inquisitiveness
- Perspective
- Character
- Savvy.

Note the lack of any form of controlling competence. Black *et al.* believe that future leaders need to be aware of the world around them, to seek out opportunities, to be able to fail occasionally as well as succeed (strength of character) and have savvy. Savvy is more than just common sense. It is a political (with a small 'p') *awareness of the processes at play* in both the internal and external environments.

These competences can be developed. Analytical skills are not genetic but learned through understanding how to seek out, sift and process information. The leader does not have to carry out the full acquisition and processing of information (this can be carried out by subordinates) but s/he needs a wide perspective – or 'helicopter view,' as it has been called – to see how the information gathered fits in to the corporate picture and how it can assist the furtherance of corporate goals.

Understanding the culture

Whether they are collocated or virtual teams, the teams in the twenty-first century will be far more culturally diverse than those in the twentieth. No society is homogeneous to any large degree. Population movements mean that there are representatives of nearly every culture, race and national origin in all of the major regions of the world. Leaders and team members have to adapt to new cultural ideas and ways of working being brought into the team.

Virtual teams will almost all be multi-cultural. This provides a wonderful development opportunity for such teams to use the best aspects of their constituent cultures to increase their synergy. Teams that wish to be effective will not need legislation to assure membership to groups who might not have been members of teams in earlier times. The 'glass ceiling', that invisible barrier that prevented many able women from rising to the top of their career path, is being dismantled increasingly quickly. No team can afford to reject a member purely on gender.

Empowerment

Empowerment is one of the Millennium buzz words. It was referred to in Chapter 9. Teams in the twenty-first century will be both *empowered* and act as *empowerers* for their members.

Empowerment is part of a triangle, with the three sides being:

- Empowerment
- Education
- Organisational commitment.

On its own each of the above is meaningless. If the organisation is not fully committed to empowerment then the whole exercise is likely to be just rhetoric and have no substance, a state of affairs that leads to frustration. Equally, if those whom the organisation seeks to empower lack the knowledge and skills to make effective decisions then empowerment cannot work.

Empowerment depends upon:

- A committed *organisation*
- Committed *team members*
- Clear *goals* and team *norms*
- *Facilitating* leaders and managers
- A culture of *enterprise* rather than blame
- *Trust* between all parties.

A committed organisation

There is no one right way to manage nor is there only one way to structure an organisation. There are a series of leadership styles that managers can adopt contingent upon the situation.

Tom Peters has gone on to write a large number of books on the subject of excellence, quality and getting the most out of people (see Chapter 8). In the book that brought his name to the fore, *In Search of Excellence* (1982), he and Bob Waterman introduced a series of *attributes for excellent companies*, three of which are particularly appropriate in a consideration of empowerment.

Productivity through people

It is *people who get things done*. Behind every useful machine is a human being programming or operating it. Organisations that do not look after their people may be successful in the short term but will end up losing good employees to organisations that have a more people-oriented attitude. Organisations that commit resources to developing balanced teams are showing a commitment to their people. It seems to be the case that it is much easier to let down the organisation than it is one's fellow team members. They are flesh and blood and one can form a relationship with them. Organisations can seem impersonal. Empowered people are an asset because they are able to be more effective and are usually better motivated. The more control a person has over a task, the more efficiently they are likely to carry it out. Empowerment assists people in developing pride in their work, giving them a vested interest that goes far beyond wage remuneration to ensure quality.

Autonomy and entrepreneurship

Peters and Waterman demonstrated that those organisations that provided staff with a degree of autonomy within corporate guidelines appeared more successful than those operating strict controls on staff initiative. Teams, like individuals, need *autonomy* to be effective. Encouraging an entrepreneurial spirit in teams may lead to some failures, but these will usually be far outweighed by the successes. This does not mean that teams should operate without any external controls. There have to be controls but they should be focused on those areas that should be controlled from outside, as discussed below.

Simultaneous loose/tight properties

Whatever happens within a team should be in accordance with the goals and norms of the parent organisation. Effective organisations define the boundaries on autonomy very clearly. The author has called this 'the tennis court principle' – when the ball is in, everything is OK, but if it crosses the line, the point is lost. The organisation should concern itself with balls that are out not ones that are in! Culture, quality standards, financial controls should be tight. Initiative and decision-making can then be subject to empowerment within the guidelines. Once the rules are clearly known, staff can then be empowered to act, knowing that they have the support of the organisation.

Without the commitment of the organisation, empowerment cannot happen. As will be shown below, leaders have to buy-in to the empowerment principle and team members need confidence and security to accept being empowered. Ultimately empowerment depends on *mutual trust.*

Committed team members

Given that recognition and achievement have been shown to be important motivators (see Chapter 2) it might be expected that all team members would welcome empowerment. However empowerment can cause concern and distrust. Empowering people is a relatively new concept with many organisations only just beginning to move away from strict controls, so it is not surprising that employees might be suspicious. Team members used to the leader making all the decisions or for the team to be told what to do by an external manager, need time to adjust to empowerment.

Empowerment is more than just an administrative and skills process, it is also a 'hearts and minds' process. Team members cannot be forced to be empowered, nor will just telling them that they are empowered be enough. Empowerment is very much a *state of mind and an attitude*. To assist the process of buying-in to empowerment the organisation needs to ensure that the final four items in this section are given careful attention. Once team members feel secure with the commitment of the organisation to empowerment as a shared idea, and not a way of imposing on staff, they are likely to be much more amenable to its concepts.

Clear goals and team norms

It is impossible for the team members to make effective decisions unless they are very clear about the *context* within which those decisions will be implemented by the organisation. If empowerment is to be effective, the organisation must ensure that the team understands the goals of the organisation and the norms to which it operates. The team must ensure that its norms, derived in the process covered in Chapter 5, are in line with those of the organisation.

An understanding of what the organisation is seeking to achieve is an important motivational factor and provides the framework around which empowerment can occur. It is difficult for team members to feel secure with empowerment if they are unsure of where the boundaries of their own and of the team's overall authority actually are.

Facilitating leaders and managers

The threat that the empowerment of team members can present first to the leader of the team but also to the external manager/leader is considerable. While team members may often perceive that their leader and their leader's leader are secure, the truth is that many in senior positions worry about their own abilities. It should be a task of every leader to assist and coach his or her subordinates. Unfortunately too many neglect this area of team responsibility.

The leader as a coach is a very important part of empowerment. Logan and King, in *The Coaching Revolution* (2001) have addressed this issue. Like many coaches in sport, the leader may see his or her protégés overtake them in ability. This should not be a threat, as most people who succeed never forget who their mentors were.

A culture of enterprise rather than blame

A 'blame culture' can rarely be one that encourages empowerment. In a blame culture people are far too busy covering a certain part of their anatomy (CYA) to wish to make decisions for which they may then be punished. The whole concept of catching people in rather then out (Chapter 2) is to encourage decision-making. Even the most effective team makes mistakes. It is the role of the leader to work in partnership with the responsible persons to find out what went wrong, why it went wrong and how can it be avoided in future. If people feel that mistakes lead to punishment then they will try to cover them up, and the opportunity to find a solution will be lost.

Empowerment is a soft action. Mistakes that occur by going beyond the guidelines are a different matter. Empowerment carries with it rights and responsibilities and one of the major responsibilities is knowing when to say, 'no, that is beyond my authority or remit'. This is not inflexibility provided that the guidelines are sufficiently broad in the first place.

One of the benefits of empowerment is that the team members begin to act as their own *control mechanism*. They are often far harder on themselves than outsiders might be. They can be harsh as they themselves have ownership of the issues.

Trust between all parties

The final requirement is that the team members need to trust each other and there needs to be *mutual* trust and respect to and from the leader. All of the parties need to trust each other. Team members work better if they know that empowerment is good both for the organisation and themselves. Blame cultures should be eliminated and leaders/managers assisted to move from control to facilitation. Trust is never one-way, it always has to be *reciprocated*. Once there is trust, true empowerment can take place and the full potential of the team's members can be employed in fulfilling the organisation's goals.

How empowered teams behave

Those organisations that have moved their teams towards empowerment show certain characteristics that are less evident in those that still retain tight controls on their teams. Spreitzer and Quinn (2001), of the University of Michigan Business School, have described the five major requirements to using empowerment to set free employee potential:

1. Empowering the person who *matters most* – in the first instance this will be the team's sponsor
2. Continuous *vision and challenge*
3. Continuous *support and security*
4. Continuous *openness and trust*
5. Continuous *guidance and control.*

However empowered teams and individuals are, there always has to be some form of control or there is chaos. The key to control in an empowered environment is that it is not fixed. At the beginning of a project control might be tight, but it can then be relaxed as the competence of the team members grows.

The person who matters most according to Spreitzer and Quinn is actually the *person doing the empowering* – the sponsor of the team followed by the team's leader. Spreitzer and Quinn also stress the need for support and trust and the importance of vision. Once team members understand the vision they can see their role in achieving it.

Leaders as empowerers

Many authorities have seen empowerment as more of a leadership than a managerial role. It could be argued that in a business situation the ability to empower is what transforms a manager into a leader. Blanchard, Carlos and Randolph (1999) have stressed the leadership aspects of empowerment. They make the point that too many managers (including many who think that they are leaders) believe that all they have to do to empower people is to give people the authority to make decisions. The process is very much more complex than that. A true leader will provide *differential empowerment* to meet the skills and aptitude of the individual. S/he will also ensure that all the training and resources required for authority to be exercised are in place.

Empowerment alters the way we have traditionally thought of leadership. It is noteworthy that in his work on team roles, Meredith Belbin does not have a team role dedicated to the leader. He talks about Co-ordinators and Shapers but recognises that leadership can move around the team according to the circumstances.

Leaders as change agents

As Oakley and Krug (1991) have stated, leaders of modern teams are expected to act as change agents for the organisation. As such, the leader needs to understand the *fears* that can be generated by change. The more an organisation is in flux, the more dynamic team membership can become. New members may be being constantly drawn into the team as and when their expertise is required.

The leader of such a team must ensure that the new members are inducted into membership and that threats to more established members are dealt with.

Almost by definition leaders have always been *change agents*. The hunting bands of early *homo sapiens* looked to the leader of the band for any changes that might be needed. As Nicholson says in *Managing the Human Animal* (2000), psychologically very little has changed. Team members will continue to expect leaders to be in the forefront of developments.

Trust and support

Leaders of work teams in previous generations played a policing role. The leader of the twenty-first-century team cannot lead by fear – it is not a good motivator for use with teams.

Blame/punishment and reward cultures

The concept of catching people in rather than trying to catch them out is an important one for the leader of a twenty-first-century team. The more educated the team members are, the more the role of the leader needs to be that of a *facilitator* and *coach* rather than the ultimate control. Rob Yeung (2000) states that *trust* is the key to the leadership of today's teams. It is amazing that at the start of the twenty-first century Yeung still has to remind leaders that they should not put down team members in front of the team.

In a blame culture (where people are caught out and punished) team energy that should go towards meeting objectives is diverted into covering up any errors. In a reward culture where team members know that if a mistake is made it can be admitted and used as a learning tool, all of the team's energy can go towards its stated objectives. Unfortunately there are still leaders who try to catch team members out. It may do wonders for their sense of control, but it only diminishes the team's efforts in meeting its objectives.

- At work, are you in a blame or a reward culture. How can you tell?

Conclusion

Chapter 11 of this book examines some of the key figures in the field of teams, group dynamics and leadership.

The aim in preparing this text was to produce a practical overview that would be of benefit to both team leaders and team members.

Human beings, as primates, have always been team/group animals. Much of our group behaviour is instinctive. The team protects and supports us; the leader provides direction. The work of the people in Chapter 11 has been a means by which we can understand why we behave differently when in a team situation. Teams are composed of individuals, but the sheer fact of joining with others alters the individual – that is why this is such an important subject. The twentieth century saw some truly appalling examples of group behaviour and groupthink. Human nature is human nature, but if we have a knowledge of why we do something we can begin to develop strategies to find other ways of behaving.

SUMMARY

- *Empowerment* is the key concept for the twenty-first-century team. Empower-ment not only for the team as a collective entity but also for the *individual team members*.
- The growth in *virtual teams* requires leaders and team members to have a knowledge of other cultures. Dispersed teams are almost by definition multi-cultural ones.
- Virtual teams go through the same development stages as collocated ones. Leaders need to discover ways to assist the Forming, Storming, Norming and other components of the *team development model process* with members who may be widely dispersed.
- Twenty-first-century teams can be constructed with an appreciation of the importance of team roles. This should assist organisations in forming *balanced teams*.
- The *invisible team* that supports the twenty-first-century team must never be forgotten. It is worth thinking about the fact that if the team does not com-municate its objectives to the members of the invisible team they in turn will not know where to direct their energies.
- Leaders of twenty-frist-century teams have a role that places more emphasis on empowering and coaching team members than on controlling them. Twenty-first-century leaders should go around *catching people in* rather than catching them out.
- Leaders are *change agents*.
- *Blame cultures* divert effort from team objectives.

QUESTIONS

1 How can technology aid the formation of virtual teams?
2 Describe the types of situation that teams should plan for – how can a knowledge of team roles help in the planning process?
3 What is empowerment, and how can it be achieved?
4 Distinguish between a blame and a reward culture – why is the latter more effective in the work situation?

Recommended further reading

The following titles provide an insight into team development in the twenty-first-century:

Stewart J. Black, Alan J. Morrison and Hal B. Gregerson, *Global Explorers – The Next Generation of Leaders* (1999).

Colin Hastings *et al.*, *Superteams* (1994)

Jessica Lipnack and Jeffrey Stamps, *Virtual Teams* (2000)

Michael J. Marquardt and Nancy O. Berger, *Global Leaders for the twenty-first century* (2000)

Ed Oakley and Doug Krug, *Enlightened Leadership* (1991)

Gretchen M. Spreitzer and Robert E. Quinn, *A Company of Leaders* (2001).

■ M ■ ■ Thinkers on teams and leadership

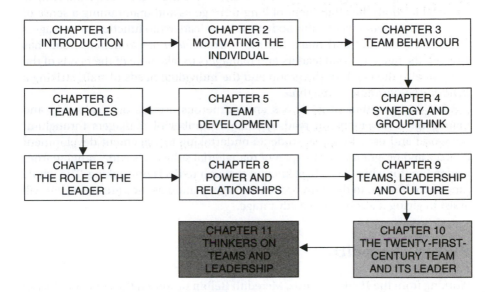

CHAPTER 1 INTRODUCTION	CHAPTER 2 MOTIVATING THE INDIVIDUAL	CHAPTER 3 TEAM BEHAVIOUR
CHAPTER 6 TEAM ROLES	CHAPTER 5 TEAM DEVELOPMENT	CHAPTER 4 SYNERGY AND GROUPTHINK
CHAPTER 7 THE ROLE OF THE LEADER	CHAPTER 8 POWER AND RELATIONSHIPS	CHAPTER 9 TEAMS, LEADERSHIP AND CULTURE
CHAPTER 11 THINKERS ON TEAMS AND LEADERSHIP		CHAPTER 10 THE TWENTY-FIRST-CENTURY TEAM AND ITS LEADER

John Adair – Meredith Belbin – Warren Bennis – Ken Blanchard – Stephen R. Covey – Charles Handy – Kurt Lewin – Richard Lewis – Jessica Lipnack and Jeffrey Stamps – Desmond Morris – Nigel Nicholson – Richard Pascale – Tom Peters – Harvey Robbins – Noel M. Tichy – Fons Trompenaars

The thinkers in the chapter are those who have influenced the author. They have been chosen because they have challenged the way we think about teams and leadership.

There are of course many others. The Bibliography at the end of this book lists those sources that have been consulted. There is also further information on the associated web-site.

Adair, John

Appointed as the world's first Professor of Leadership Studies at Surrey University in 1978, Professor Adair has been named as one of 40 people worldwide who have contributed most to the development of management thought and practices – a considerable accolade indeed. Much of his early thinking was influenced by his army career.

He has also operated as a consultant for a wide range of UK and international companies, including Shell, Honeywell, Mercedes and Unilever. Working with Imperial Chemical Industries (ICI) for nearly 10 years, he assisted the company to develop the 'manager–leader' concept, which supported ICI in becoming the first British company to make £1 billion pounds profit in 1986 and has formed the basis for much of the development of the leadership concepts that appear in his books.

The key Adair message is that no organisation or enterprise can function adequately without *good leadership*. Although management techniques such as team building and empowerment have changed the manager's role, leadership is still vital for both the attainment of long-term goals and maintaining a sense of purpose throughout day-to-day activities. A key leadership function of managers is to lead their staff and make the move from *planning to action*. Adair has stressed the need for good leaders and managers to take note of the needs of the task but also the needs of the group and the individual needs of staff, striking a *dynamic balance* among the three.

Adair is the author of 26 books and numerous articles on leadership and management development, read by a large number of managers throughout the world and used by many students undertaking management development courses and programmes. His span of managerial subjects is wide, ranging from leadership (for which he is best known) through to decision-making. The whole range is of interest to the entrepreneurial organisation as they are areas that will assist in giving it a competitive advantage.

Belbin, Meredith

Working from the 1980s onwards, Meredith Belbin proposed the concept of *team roles* and used it to study successful and unsuccessful teams. His work was first used in the UK but has since spread throughout the world and is used in team building and as a recruitment aid by many organisations. The eight (later nine) team roles that Belbin proposed need to be present in a team to ensure the necessary *balance and synergy* for effective performance. Thus diversity in team membership is to be welcomed. Individuals can be tested for their preferred roles using a questionnaire and Belbin Associates' INTERPLACE® software. Belbin's later work has linked team role theory to organisational design. There are regular INTERPLACE® users' conferences and a newsletter indicating how the software is used in the field by organisations that have adopted it.

One of the most important aspects of Belbin's work as regards teams and leadership is that it provides a language for describing diverse members of a team that is neither prejudicial, insulting, nor threatening to the individual.

The author has used the Belbin team roles and the associated software package INTERPLACE® with a large number of teams around the world. He has found that the concept has been very useful in opening out the discussion of how individuals behave in a team. Once people understand how their colleagues' minds work, team harmony and thus Performing (Chapter 5) is greatly assisted.

Belbin has also examined the way organisations are *structured*, in *The Coming*

Shape of Organisation (1996), the way work is allocated, in *Changing the Way We Work* (1997) and *Beyond the Team* (2000) and also the evolution of power, in *Managing Without Power* (2001).

Included on the web site for this book is some original research work by the author undertaken using the concept of team roles.

Bennis, Warren

A global authority on leadership, Bennis is a Professor of Business Administration at the University of Southern California (USC) and the founding chairman of USC's Leadership Institute. He has written 18 books including: *On Becoming a Leader* (1998, translated into 19 languages), *Why Leaders Can't Lead* (1990), and *The Unreality Industry* (1987), co-authored with Ian Mitroff.

Bennis was successor to Douglas McGregor (see Chapter 2) as chairman of the organisation studies department at the Massachusetts Institute of Technology (MIT). He also taught at Harvard and Boston Universities. Later, he was Provost and Executive Vice President of the State University of New York-Buffalo and President of the University of Cincinnati.

He has published over 900 articles and two of his books have earned the coveted McKinsey Award for the Best Book on Management. He has served in an advisory capacity to US presidents and been a consultant to many corporations and agencies including the United Nations.

Awarded 11 honorary degrees, Bennis has also received numerous awards including the Distinguished Service Award of the American Board of Professional Psychologists and the Perry L. Rohrer Consulting Practice Award of the American Psychological Association. Any book by Bennis is challenging. *Reinventing Leadership* (1995), written with Robert Townsend (of *Up the Organisation* (1970) and *Further Up the Organisation* (1981) fame) looks at how leadership needs to change to meet modern challenges.

Blanchard, Ken

Ken Blanchard, of *Leadership and the One Minute Manager* (2000) fame, believes that the greatest leaders are *situational leaders*, who diagnose each employee's competence and commitment for a task, and then communicate with that person in a style that elicits desired results. He also teaches that those closest to the customer belong at the top of the organisational pyramid and that leaders should serve those who provide customer support.

He personally demonstrates what he writes about leaders 'walking their talk' and aligning personal and organisational goals. At The Ken Blanchard Companies, he's known as 'The Chief Spiritual Officer' and everyone calls him 'Ken'.

He believes that successful *leaders must develop other leaders* by sharing their teachable points of view and compelling stories based on their own experience.

Covey, Stephen R.

The US writer Stephen R. Covey has become known for his work on the *habits of effective people.* He believes that lives should be organised around natural forces rather than trying to manage limited time.

His original work on the *7 Habits of Highly Effective People* (1989) has been developed to consider families and leadership on a principle-cantered basis.

While individuals might not agree with all of Covey's ideas, they are challenging and challenge is precisely what the entrepreneurial individual thrives on.

There are also Covey Leadership Centres around the world dedicated to passing on his ideas and many of his books are also available on audio tapes.

Handy, Charles

For many years, a professor at the London Business School, Charles Handy is now an independent writer and broadcaster, describing himself as a social philosopher. His work with Shell and at the Sloan School of Management at MIT, where he gained an MBA, fired his fascination with organisations and how they work.

Handy's main concern is the implication for *society,* and for *individuals,* of the dramatic changes that technology and economics are bringing to the workplace and to all our lives. His book, *The Empty Raincoat* (1994), is a sequel to his earlier best-selling *The Age of Unreason* (1989), where he first explored these changes, and was named by both *Fortune* and *Business Week* as one of the 10 best business books of the year. In total, his books, which include the popular *Gods of Management* (1992) as well as the standard textbook *Understanding Organisations* (1976) have now sold over a million copies around the world. In both of the latter books, Handy expounded his model of *corporate cultures* and how they interact, adding considerably to the body of knowledge on the subject of managing diversity, in these cases diversity within and between organisations. *The Empty Raincoat* was awarded the JSK Accord Prize for the Best Business Book of the Year in 1994. *Beyond Certainty* (1995a) is a collection of his articles and essays, and *Waiting for the Mountain to Move* (1995b) is a collection of his radio 'Thoughts' over 10 years. In his book *The Hungry Spirit* (1997) he airs doubts about some of the consequences of free-market capitalism and questions whether material success can ever provide the true meaning of life.

Lewin, Kurt

Kurt Lewin is recognised as the founder of modern social psychology. Born in 1890, he completed his requirements for a PhD in 1914, emigrating to the USA in 1933.

Lewin is well known for his work on *group dynamics,* as well as *t-groups,* and his commitment to applying psychology to the problems of society led to the development of the MIT Research Center for Group Dynamics. Lewin developed the *force field* approach to the understanding and implementation of change: for change to take place, the total situation has to be taken into account. If isolated facts are used, a misrepresented picture could develop.

Lewin authored over 80 articles and eight books on a wide range of issues in psychology.

In group dynamics, Lewin developed six major programme areas:

1. *Group productivity*: why are groups so ineffective in getting things done?
2. *Communication*: how influence is spread throughout a group.
3. *Social perception*: how a person's group affected the way they perceived social events.
4. *Intergroup* relations.
5. *Group membership*: how individuals adjust to these conditions.
6. *Training leaders*: improving the functioning of groups.

Group life was to be viewed, according to Lewin, in its totality, not on an individual basis.

Lewin and his colleagues established three major research areas:

1. The conditions which improve the *effectiveness of community leaders* who are attempting to better intergroup relations,
2. The effect of the conditions under which *contact* between persons from different groups takes place.
3. The influences which are most effective in producing in *minority-group members* an increased sense of belongingness, and improved personal adjustment, and better relations with individuals of other groups.

Lewin's work on group dynamics has been utilised in such areas as educational facilities, industrial settings and communities. Great improvements were made in all these areas of interest throughout the twentieth century.

Lewis, Richard

Richard D. Lewis is an authority on the management of *cultural diversity*, thus making his work of especial interest to those working in virtual teams. He is the founder of the magazine *Cross Culture* and in addition to speaking over 12 languages he has worked with a large number of major multi-national organisations. Lewis makes the point that *mutual understanding and sensitivity* lie at the heart of managing across cultures. In both *When Cultures Collide* (1996) and *Cross-Cultural Communications – A Visual Approach* (1999), Lewis stresses the importance of ensuring that the communications process is as robust as possible. The same words and phrases can mean different things in different cultures but (although there are differences) non-verbal, visual communications can often convey true meanings better than verbal ones. *Cross-Cultural Communications* also contains visual materials from Lewis' seminars and this makes the book very useful for trainers.

Lewis provides useful ideas on the *classifying of cultures* and the *traits and tendencies* of members of particular cultures. He also provides very practical advice on behaviour for managers dealing with inter-cultural issues and the management of diversity.

Having developed a model for cultural analysis, Lewis has produced two PC-based packages, the first being the Cross-Cultural Assessor, which is a tool for cross-cultural analysis applicable to both individuals and across an organisation; the second, Gulliver, provides both cross-cultural training and a database to set up 'what-if' scenarios.

Lipnak, Jessica and Stamps, Jeffrey

Lipnack and Stamps are founders and principals of The Networking Institute, Inc., a consulting company that helps organisations work together better across boundaries of all kinds. They are acknowledged as the world's leading experts in *networked organisations* and *virtual teams*. They have spoken in the USA, Canada, Europe, and Japan, appeared on many radio shows, written numerous articles for major publications, and are often quoted in the press. They also have conducted in-house workshops that have launched networks of all kinds within companies, non-profit organisations, major religious denominations and educational institutions. *Virtual Teams: Working Across Space, Time, and Organizations* (2000) was their fifth book on this topic.

In 1993, they served as consultants to Vice President Al Gore's National Performance Review. They designed and facilitated the three-day conference in Washington's Mellon Auditorium that launched NetResults, the cross-agency network that links thousands of federal employees swapping ideas about how to reinvent government.

Howard Rheingold's *Virtual Community* (2000) cites them as among the pioneers in electronic communication. Lipnack and Stamps first went online in 1979 on one of the earliest computer conferencing systems, Roxanne Hiltz and Murray Turoff's Electronic Information Exchange System (EIES). Five years later, Lipnack and Stamps were among the faculty for the first online executive education program at the WBSI School of Management and Strategic Studies in La Jolla, California. From 1983–6, they served as principal consultants to the Presbyterian Church USA's computer conferencing network, PresbyNet.

In March 1996, at a ceremony at the John F. Kennedy Library, Lipnack and Stamps were awarded the 21st-Century Leadership Award by the First Community Bank of Boston. The award states:

'As leading edge thinkers, your book *The Age of the Network* [1994], is helping organizations to move into the twenty-first century of information. You have challenged us to create 'Islands of Trust' and teams that are defined by speed, agility, shared purpose and vision. The web of interconnected relationships called Networks bridge the self and the group, the daily and the eternal, the mundane and the sacred. Visionaries and creators, authors and socially responsible business owners, First Community Bank is pleased to recognize you and The Networking Institute, Inc.'

Morris, Desmond

Born in 1928, Desmond Morris has become famous for bringing anthropology into the public eye. In 1948 following his first exhibition (he is an accomplished artist), he enrolled on a zoology course at Birmingham University. By 1956 he had gained a PhD and moved to London to become Head of the Granada TV and Film Unit at the Zoological Society of London, making films and television programmes on animal behaviour and other zoological topics.

After acting as host for Granada TV's weekly 'Zootime' programme for three years (a programme that many of the author's generation rushed home from school to watch), he left the TV and Film Unit to become the Zoological Society's Curator of Mammals. During the eight years he held this post he continued to present television programmes both for Granada and the BBC, scripting and hosting a total of approximately 500 'Zootime' programmes for Granada and 100 'Life in the Animal World' programmes for BBC 2. In addition, he took part in many BBC radio programmes on natural history subjects and became a regular reviewer of animal books for the *Times Literary Supplement*.

In 1966 he published *Men and Apes*, with Ramona Morris as co-author. During this period he established an informal research unit at the London Zoo comprising PhD students undertaking doctoral work in animal behaviour and other visiting scientists.

The Naked Ape (1967), a zoologist's study of the human animal, was the first of a number of books he produced on the subject of human behaviour, a book that was published in a large number of countries.

Resigning his curatorship at London Zoo he became the executive director of the Institute of Contemporary Arts in London.

The success of *The Naked Ape* led to the publication *of The Human Zoo* (1969). Morris' work reached a general audience, introducing the concepts of our primate ancestry to the general public. Morris was probably the originator of the concept of 'people watching'. He still continues to paint and write about behaviour; one of his latest projects was baby watching – linking infant behaviour to that of our relatives in the animal kingdom.

The importance of Morris to a study of teams and leadership aside from the 10 Golden Rules for Leaders covered in Chapter 7 is that he approached human behaviour from a study of animals: to Morris we were just a naked ape.

Nicholson, Nigel

Nigel Nicholson is a psychologist who has linked managerial concepts to those from evolutionary psychology. His work has won critical acclaim from managerial specialists and psychologists alike. Exploring the psychology of human groups and clans he has been able to provide useful insights into the *workings of human groups* and the *leadership function. Managing the Human Animal* (2000) is easy to read and yet highly informative and takes managerial studies into behavioural psychology in a masterful manner.

Pascale, Richard

Richard Pascale was one of the management authorities who analysed the difference between Japanese management and the management styles of the West, in particular the USA.

The Art of Japanese Management written with Anthony Athos (1981) stressed the leadership differences between the two approaches. Using the giant ITT telecommunications company in the USA, Pascale and Athos were able to show how dependent it was on the personality and character of its long-term CEO and how the organisation began to fragment upon the CEO's retirement.

Pascale's later work has been involved with the way organisations and their leaders adapt to a fast-changing environment. In *Surfing the Edge of Chaos* (2000) Pascale and his co-workers describe how complex adaptive systems exhibit the capacity of *self-organisation and emergent complexity*. Such adaptive systems move toward the edge of chaos when provoked by a complex task. Novelty emerges in the space between rigidity and randomness. They state that it is impossible to direct a living system, only disturb it. Managers cannot assume that a particular input will produce a particular output. 'Experimentation, rapid learning and seizing the momentum of success is the better approach.' While leaders provide the vision and establish the context, solutions to ongoing challenges are generated by the people closest to the action.

Richard T. Pascale served for 20 years as a member of the faculty of Stanford University's Graduate School of Business and is also an associate fellow of Templeton College, Oxford University.

Peters, Tom

From the publication of *In Search of Excellence*, written with Bob Waterman (1982), Tom Peters has become one of the best-known names in the fields of management, change and quality. His message has been delivered on a global basis and has reached a huge audience, initially of senior but more recently including junior staff.

Three quotes express the importance Tom Peters has had on modern organisational thinking:

'In no small part, what American corporations have become is what Peters has encouraged them to be.' (*The New Yorker*)

'Peters is ... the father of the post-modern corporation.' (*Los Angeles Times*)

'We live in a Tom Peters world.' (*Fortune Magazine*)

Tom Peters describes himself as a prince of disorder, champion of bold failures, maestro of zest, professional loudmouth, corporate cheerleader and a lover of markets. *Fortune Magazine* has also referred to him as the 'Ur-guru' (guru of gurus) of management and compares him to Ralph Waldo Emerson, Henry David Thoreau and Walt Whitman. *The Economist* has titled him as the Über-guru (over-guru). His unconventional views led *Business Week* to describe him as business' best friend and worst nightmare – best friend because of the challenges he throws out which if taken up can lead to success, and worst nightmare because his ideas have challenged conventional thinking – always an uncomfortable thing to do.

Tom followed up on the success of *In Search of Excellence* with many more best-selling books including: '*A Passion for Excellence* (1985, with Nancy Austin), *Thriving on Chaos* (1987),' *Liberation Management* (1992 – acclaimed as the 'Management Book of the Decade' for the 1990s), *The Circle of Innovation: You Can't Shrink Your Way to Greatness* (1998).

Tom Peters also presents about 100 major seminars globally each year, and organisations pay considerable sums for their staff to attend them. He has also authored hundreds of articles for various newspapers and popular and academic journals, including *Business Week*, *The Economist*, the *Financial Times*, *The Wall Street Journal*, *The New York Times*, Inc., *Fast Company*, *The Washington Monthly*, *California Management Review*, *The Academy of Management Review*, *Forbes*, and *The Harvard Business Review*.

Tom Peter's philosophy for the re-invention of business and organisations is about *change*, giving power to people and encouraging entrepreneurship. He recognises that we are in a changing, sometimes chaotic world and sees that as an *opportunity* not a threat for organisations with the courage to move forward. The research for *In Search of Excellence* was under the auspices of the McKinsey Organisation and was a review of excellent companies in the USA and how America could re-establish its position in world trade. From those early ideas and the attributes contained within them (see Chapter 6 for this) has developed the Peters philosophy, a philosophy very much concerned with entrepreneurship.

Robbins, Harvey

Harvey Robbins, President of Robbins & Robbins located in Minnetonka, Minnesota, has been a practising business psychologist since 1974.

Robbins has provided international consulting services to numerous corporations and federal and state agencies including the US ATF, American Express, AT&T, Allied Signal, FMC, General Dynamics, Honeywell, 3M, IRS, International Multifoods, Johnson & Johnson, Southern Company, Target Stores, Toro, US West, Winnebago, Upsher-Smith Laboratories, the US Secret Service, and the US Customs. He has also presented papers at many national and international conferences.

Prior to 1982, Robbins worked as a personnel research psychologist for the psychological services branch of the intergovernmental personnel programs division of the US Civil Service Commission (CIA), manager of personnel development and research for Burlington Northern, Inc. and corporate manager of organization development for Honeywell.

Robbins, a native of New York City, received his doctorate in clinical psychology from Texas A&M. He is the author of: *Why Teams Don't Work* (2000), co-authored with newspaper business columnist Michael Finley. This book challenges many of the traditional views of team formation especially the concept that teams will nearly always be more effective than individuals.

Tichy, Noel M.

Noel M. Tichy is a Professor of Organizational Behaviour and Human Resource Management at the University of Michigan Business School, where he is the director of the Global Leadership Program and an authority on business growth.

Between 1985 and 1987, Tichy was responsible for management education at General Electric (see Elton Mayo's work in Chapter 2) where he directed its worldwide management development programs. Prior to joining the Michigan Faculty he served for nine years on the Columbia University Business School Faculty.

Tichy is the author of numerous books and articles. He co-authored *The Leadership Engine: How Winning Companies Build Leaders at Every Level* with Eli Cohen (1997), named one of the top 10 business books of the year by *Business Week*. He is also the co-author with Stratford Sherman of *Control Your Destiny or Someone Else Will: How Jack Welch is Making General Electric the World's Most Competitive Company* (1995) and the author of both *Corporate Global Citizenship* (1997) and *Strategic Change Management* (1983) in addition to a number of texts on leadership and human resource management.

Tichy has served on the editorial boards of the *Academy of Management Review, Organisational Dynamics, Journal of Business Research,* and *Journal of Business Strategy*. He is past chairman of the Academy of Management's Organisation and Management Theory Division and is a member of the Board of Governors of the American Society for Training and Development. He was the 1987 recipient of the New Perspectives on Executive Leadership Award by Johnson Smith & Knisely for the most outstanding contribution to the field, as captured in *The Transformational Leader* (1987) written with Mary Anne Devanna. He received the 1993 Best Practice Award from the American Society for Training and Development and the 1994 Sales and Marketing Executives International Educator of the Year Award. Tichy is the founder and editor in chief of the *Human Resource Management Journal*.

Noel Tichy has been widely consulted by a variety of organisations. He is a senior partner in Action Learning Associates. His clients have included: Ameritech, AT&T, Mercedes-Benz, BellSouth, CIBA-GEIGY, Chase Manhattan Bank, Citibank, Exxon, General Electric, General Motors, Honeywell, Hitachi, Imperial Chemical Inc., IBM, NEC, Northern Telecom, Nomura Securities and 3M.

Trompenaars, Fons

Working originally in the Netherlands for Royal Dutch Shell, Fons Trompenaars has been one of the most influential writers on the management of *cultural diversity*. Shell as a global organisation has considerable experience in managing diversity and Trompenaars set out to put these experiences into a conceptual framework that could be transferred to other organisations. It is hard to find work on cultural diversity within the work situation that does not cite Trompenaars.

His initial work, *Riding the Waves of Culture – Understanding Cultural Diversity in Business* (1993), was bought in large quantities by organisations operating virtual teams, for example British Airways. The book not only provides a contextual framework but also concrete examples of the differing cultural norms that managers are likely to encounter, and strategies for dealing with them in a sensitive and effective manner.

Trompenaars considered seven cultural attributes:

- Attitude to time
- Universal v. particular
- Individualism v. collectivism
- Emotional v. neutral
- Specific v. diffuse
- Achievement v. ascription
- Attitudes to the environment.

Trompenaars is recommended reading for all those dealing with cultural diversity and virtual teams, blending as he does practical advice within a useful conceptual framework.

■ ⊠ Bibliography

Adair, J. (1983)   *Effective Leadership*, Gower.
Adair, J. (1985)   *Effective Teambuilding*, Gower.
Adair, J. (1996)   *Effective Motivation*, Pan.
Adams, J. L., Hayes J. and Hopson, B. (1976)   *Transitions – Understanding and Managing Personal Change*, Robertson.
Allen, T. (1977)   *Managing the Flow of Technology: Transfer and the Dissemination of Technological Information within the R & D Organization*, MIT Press.
Ardrey, R. (1967)   *The Territorial Imperative*, Collins.
Argyris, C. (1960)   *Understanding Organisational Behaviour*, Tavistock Institute.
Asch, S. E. (1951)   'Effects of group Pressure Upon the Modification and Distortion of Judgements', in H. S. Guetzkow, *Leadership and Men*, Carnegie Press.
Bavelas, A. (1948)   'A Mathematical Model for Group Structures', *Applied Anthropology*, 7, 16–30.
Bavelas, A. (1950)   'Communication Patterns in Task-Oriented Groups', *Journal of the Acoustical Society of America*, 22, 725–30.
Bedian, A. G. (1993)   *Management*, Harcourt Brace Jovanovich.
Belbin, R. M. (1981)   *Management Teams – Why they Succeed or Fail*, Heinemann.
Belbin, R. M. (1993)   *Team Roles at Work*, Butterworth Heinemann.
Belbin, R. M. (1996)   *The Coming Shape of Organization*, Butterworth Heinemann.
Belbin, R. M. (1997)   *Changing the Way We Work*, Butterworth Heinemann.
Belbin, R. M. (2000)   *Beyond the Team*, Butterworth Heinemann.
Belbin, R. M. (2001)   *Managing Without Power*, Butterworth Heinemann.
Bennis, W. (1990)   *Why Leaders Can't Lead*, Josey Bass.
Bennis, W. (1998)   *On Becoming a Leader*, Arrow.
Bennis, W. and Mitroff, I. (1987)   *The Unreality Industry*, Birch Lane Press.
Bennis, W. and Townsend, R. (1995)   *Reinventing Leadership*, William Morrow & Co.
Berne, E. (1964)   *Games People Play*, André Deutsch.
Bernstein, B. (1961)   'Social Structure, Language and Learning', *Educational Research*, 3.
Black, J., Stewart, S., Morrison, A. J. and Gregerson, H. B. (1999)   *Global Explorers – The Next Generation of Leaders*, Routledge.
Blake, R. and Mouton, J. (1964)   *The Managerial Grid*, Gulf.
Blanchard, K. (1989)   *The 7 Habits of Highly Effective People*, Simon & Schuster.
Blanchard, K. (2000)   *Leadership and the One Minute Manager*, HarperCollins.
Blanchard, K., Carlos, J. P. and Randolph, A. (1999)   *The 3 Keys to Empowerment*, Berrett-Koehler.
Burleigh, M. (2001)   *The Third Reich – A New History*, Palgrave Macmillan.
Cartwright, R. (1992)   *An Investigation and Analysis of the Correlation between Team Roles and Professional/Occupational Group*, University of Kent, MA (Mgt), dissertation.
Cartwright, R. (2000)   *Mastering Customer Relations*, Palgrave.
Cartwright, R. (2001)   *Mastering the Business Environment*, Palgrave.
Cartwright, R. (2002a)   *Empowerment*, Capstone.
Cartwright, R. (2002b)   *The Entrepreneurial Individual*, Capstone.
Cartwright, R. (2002c)   *Creating the Entrepreneurial Organisation*, Capstone.
Cartwright, R. (2002d)   *Communication*, Capstone.
Cartwright, R. (2002e)   *Going Global*, Capstone.
Cartwright, R., Collings, M., Green, G. and Candy, A. (1993)   *In Charge – Managing People*, Blackwell.
Cattell, R. (1951)   'New Concepts for Measuring Group Syntality', *Human Relations*, 4.

Cleveland, H. (1997)   *Leadership and the Information Revolution*, World Academy of Art and Science.

Cole, G. (2000)   *Management – Theory and Practice*, 5th edn, Continuum International Publishing Group.

Davie, M. (1987)   *Titanic – The Full Story of a Tragedy*, Grafton.

Davies, C. (1997)   *Divided by a Common Language*, Mayflower Press.

Dawkins, R. (1976)   *The Selfish Gene*, Oxford University Press.

Deutsch, M. (1949)   'An Experimental Study of the Effect of Co-operation and Competition upon Group Process', *Human Relations*, 2.

Drummond, H. (1992)   *Power – Creating it, Using it*, Kogan Page.

Fayol, H. (1916)   *General and Industrial Administration*, trans by C. Storrs (1949), Pitman.

Fiedler, F. (1967)   *A Theory of Leadership Effectiveness*, McGraw-Hill.

Fisher, R., Ury, W. and Patton, B. (1991)   *Getting to Yes – Negotiating Agreement without Giving In*, Penguin.

Ginnodo, W. (1997)   *The Power of Empowerment*, Pride Publications.

Handy, C. (1976)   *Understanding Organisations*, Penguin.

Handy, C. (1978)   *Gods of Management*, Souvenir.

Handy, C. (1989)   *The Age of Unreason*, Business Books.

Handy, C. (1994)   *The Empty Raincoat*, Arrow.

Handy, C. (1995a)   *Beyond Certainty*, Hutchinson.

Handy, C. (1995b)   *Waiting for the Mountain to Move*, Jossey-Bass Wiley.

Handy, C. (1997)   *The Hungry Spirit*, Hutchinson.

Harris, T. A. (1973)   *I'm OK, You're OK*, Pan.

Hart, P. (ed.) (1997)   *Beyond Groupthink*, University of Michigan Press.

Hastings, C., Bixby, P. and Chaudry-Lawton, R. (1986)   *Superteams – A Blueprint for Organisational Success*, Gower.

Hastings, C., Bixby, P. and Chaudhry-Lawton, R. (1994)   *Superteams*, HarperCollins.

Hastings, M. and Jenkins, S. (1983)   *The Battle for the Falklands*, Michael Joseph.

Herzberg, F. (1966)   *Work and the Nature of Man*, World Publishing.

HMG (1998)   *Public Interest Disclosures Act of 1998*, HMSO.

Homans, G. (1950)   *The Human Group*, Harcourt Brace.

Huczynski, A. and Buchanan, D. (1991)   *Organizational Behaviour*, Prentice-Hall.

Irving, C. (1993)   *Wide Body – The Making of the Boeing 747*, Hodder & Stoughton.

Janis, I. (1968)   *Victims of Groupthink – A Psychological Study of Foreign Policy Decisions and Fiascos*, Houghton-Mifflin.

Janis, I. (1982)   *Groupthink*, Houghton-Mifflin.

Jay, A. (1975)   *Corporation Man*, Penguin.

Johnson, D. W. and Johnson, F. P. (1987)   *Joining Together – Group Theory and Group Skills*, Prentice-Hall.

Lawrence, D. and Lorsch, D. (1967)   *Organisation and Environment*, Harvard University Press.

Levinson, H. (1972)   'An Effort Towards Understanding Man at Work', *European Business*, Spring.

Lewis, R. D. (1996)   *When Cultures Collide*, Nicholas Brealey.

Lewis, R. D. (1999)   *Cross-Cultural Communication*, Transcreen Press.

Likert, R. (1961)   *New Patterns of Management*, McGraw-Hill.

Lipnack, J. and Stamps, J. (1994)   *The Age of the Network*, Oliver Wight Publications.

Lipnack, J. and Stamps, J. (2000)   *Virtual Teams: Working Across Space, Time, and Organizations*, Wiley.

Logan, D. and King, J. (2001)   *The Coaching Revolution*, Adams Media.

Lynn, J. and Jay, A. (1981–3)   *Yes Minister*, BBC Books.

Lynn, J. and Jay, A. (1986–7)   *Yes Prime Minister*, BBC Books.

Maddox, R. B. (1986)   *Teambuilding – An Exercise in Leadership*, Kogan Page.

Magerison, C. J. and McCann, D. J. (1985)   *How to Lead a Winning Team*, University Press.

Marquardt, M. J. and Berger, N. O. (2000)   *Global Leaders for the twenty-first century*, State University of New York Press.

Maslow, A. (1970)   *Motivation and Personality*, Harper & Row.

McClelland, D. C. (1960)   *The Achieving Society*, Van Nostrand.

McGregor, D. (1960)   *The Human Side of Enterprise*, McGraw-Hill.
Mintzberg, H. (1983)   *Structure in Fives*, Prentice-Hall.
Morris, D. (1967)   *The Naked Ape*, Jonathan Cape.
Morris, D. (1969)   *The Human Zoo*, Jonathan Cape.
Murrell, K. L. and Meredith, M. (2000)   *Empowering Employees*, McGraw-Hill.
Nicolson, N. (2000)   *Managing the Human Animal*, Crown.
Oakley, E. and Krug, D. (1991)   *Enlightened Leadership*, Key to Renewal Inc.
Ouchi, W. G. (1981)   *Theory Z*, Addison-Wesley.
Pascale, R. T. and Athos, A. G. (1981)   *The Art of Japanese Management*, Simon & Schuster.
Pascale, R. T., Milleman, M. and Gioja, L. (2000)   *Surfing the Edge of Chaos*, Texere.
Peter, L. J. and Hill, R. (1969)   *The Peter Principle*, William Morrow & Co.
Peters, T. (1987)   *Thriving on Chaos*, Alfred A. Knopf.
Peters, T. (1992)   *Liberation Management*, Palgrave Macmillan.
Peters, T. (1998)   *The Circle of Innovation*, Hodder & Stoughton.
Peters, T. and Austin, N. (1985)   *A Passion for Excellence*, HarperCollins.
Peters, T. and Waterman, R. (1982)   *In Search of Excellence*, Harper & Row.
Pettinger, R. (2001)   *Mastering Management Skills*, Palgrave Macmillan.
Pitt, B. (1962)   1918 – *The Last Act*, Cassell.
Potter-Efron, R. (2000)   *Work Rage* (originally published as *Working Anger*, 1998), Barnes & Noble.
Price, C. (2000)   *The Internet Entrepreneurs*, Financial Times Publishing.
Pugh, D. (ed.) (1971)   *Organisational Theory – Selected Readings*, Penguin.
Rheingold, H. (2000)   *Virtual Community*, MIT Press.
Robbins, H. and Finley, M. (2000)   *Why Teams Don't Work*, Texere.
Roethlisberger, F. J. and Dickson, W. J. (1964)   *Management and the Worker*, John Wiley.
Sabbach, K. (1995)   *Twenty-first century Jet – the Making of the Boeing 777*, Macmillan.
Schein, E. H. (1980)   *Organizational Psychology*, Prentice-Hall.
Schein, E. H. (1984)   *Coming to a New Awareness of Organisational Culture*, Sloan Management Review.
Shaw, M. (1976)   *Group Dynamics*, McGraw-Hill.
Sherif, M. (1936)   *The Social Psychology of Group Norms*, Harper & Row.
Sherif, M. and Sherif, C. (1956)   *An Outline of Social Psychology*, McGraw-Hill.
Smith, M. (1945)   'Social Situation, Social Behaviour and Social Group', *Psychological Review*, 52.
Spreitzer, G. M. and Quinn, R. E. (2001)   *A Company of Leaders*, Jossey-Bass.
Stewart, S. (1986)   *Air Disasters*, Ian Allan.
Stott, W. J. H. (1958)   *Human Groups*, Penguin.
Tannenbaum, R. and Schmidt, W. (1958)   'How to Choose a Leadership Pattern', *Harvard Business Review*, March–April.
Taylor, F. W. (1911)   *Principles of Scientific Management*, Harper.
Tichy, N. (1983)   *Strategic Change Management*, Wiley.
Tichy, N. (1997)   *Corporate Global Citizenship*, Jossey-Bass.
Tichy, N. and Cohen, E. (1997)   *The Leadership Engine*, HarperCollins.
Tichy, N. and Devanna, M. A. (1987)   *The Transformational Leader*, Wiley.
Tichy, N. and Sherman, S. (1995)   *Control Your Destiny or Somebody Else Will*, HarperCollins.
Townsend, R. (1970)   *Up the Organisation*, Michael Joseph.
Townsend, R. (1981)   *Further Up the Organisation*, Michael Joseph.
Trompenaars, F. (1993)   *Riding the Waves of Culture: Understanding Cultural Diversity in Business*, Economist Books.
Trudgill, P. (1975)   *Accent, Dialect and the School*, Arnold.
Urwick, L. (1947)   *The Elements of Administration*, Pitman.
Vroom, V. H. (1964)   *Work and Motivation*, Wiley.
Vroom, V. H. and Deci, E. L. (eds.) (1980)   *Management and Motivation*, Penguin.
Yablonsky, L. (1962)   *The Violent Gang*, Macmillan.
Yeung, R. (2000)   *Leading Teams*, How To Books.

Web site

Further information about Meredith Belbin and the team role and work role concepts can be found at: www.belbin.com.
The web site for this book also contains links to other useful sites.

■ Ⅴ Index